THE THIRD REICH

THE THIRD REICH

Politics and Propaganda

Second Edition

David Welch

London and New York

First published 1993
by Routledge
2 Park Square, Milton Park, Abingdon, Oxon, OX14 4RN

Simultaneously published in the USA and Canada
by Routledge
270 Madison Ave, New York NY 10016
First published in paperback 1995
Second edition first published 2002

Transferred to Digital Printing 2006

Routledge is an imprint of the Taylor & Francis Group

© 1993, 1995, 2002 David Welch

Typeset in Palatino by
Keystroke, Jacaranda Lodge, Wolverhampton

British Library Cataloguing in Publication Data
A catalogue record for this book is available
from the British Library

Library of Congress Cataloging in Publication Data
A catalog record for this book has been requested

ISBN 0–415–27507–5 (Hbk)
ISBN 0–415–27508–3 (Pbk)

Publisher's Note
The publisher has gone to great lengths to ensure the
quality of this reprint but points out that some
imperfections in the original may be apparent

Printed and bound by CPI Antony Rowe, Eastbourne

CONTENTS

CONTENTS

LIST OF ILLUSTRATIONS

LIST OF ILLUSTRATIONS

ACKNOWLEDGEMENTS

Over the years I have incurred debts to many individuals in the preparation of this work. I have benefited from discussions with several colleagues, who were generous with their time and encouragement. Among these are Jeremy Noakes, Volker Berghahn, Richard Evans and John Hiden. I would like in particular to thank Ian Kershaw who read and made valuable comments on the manuscript. I would also like to thank Andrew Wheatcroft of Routledge for his support. I am indebted to the secretarial staff at Rutherford College, University of Kent for their unstinting assistance in helping me produce the Document Section.

Finally, I would like to thank my wife Anne who was excessively patient and understanding during the researching and writing of this book. Without her loving support this book could not have been written. It is to our children, Chris and Lizzie, that I would like to dedicate this work, not least for the manner in which, in their own ways, they have tolerated their father's preoccupation with history and even developed a resigned sense of humour.

GLOSSARY AND LIST OF ABBREVIATIONS

Alltagsgeschichte	'History of everyday life'
BA	Bundesarchiv, Koblenz
BDC	Berlin Document Centre
Blut und Boden	Blood and soil
BdM	Bund deutscher Mädel (League of German Girls), female branch of the Hitler Youth, for girls over fourteen years of age
DAF	Deutsche Arbeitsfront (German Labour Front)
DDD	German Wireless Service
DFW	Deutsches Frauenwerk (German Women's Enterprise), the Nazi-led federation of women's groups from 1934–1945
Deutsche Wochenschauen	German (Nazi) newsreels
Dienstverpflichtung	Civil conscription
DNVP	Deutschnationale Volkspartei (German National People's Party)
Filmprüfstelle	Film Censorship Office
Führerbefehl	Command from Hitler
Führergewalt	Führer power
Führerprinzip	The leadership principle
Gau	Region, the major territorial division of the national NSDAP organisation
Gauleiter	Regional Party Leader
Gesellschaft	Society
Glaube und Schönheit	Faith and Beauty
Gleichschaltung	'Co-ordination', the obligatory assimilation within the Nazi State of all political, economic and cultural activities
Herrenvolk	Master race
Historikerstreit	Historians' dispute
Hitlerbewegung	Hitler movement

GLOSSARY AND LIST OF ABBREVIATIONS

HJ	Hitlerjugend (Hitler Youth), the Nazi Party's youth organisation
IfZ	Institut für Zeitgeschichte (Institute for Contemporary History). Munich
Jugendfilmstunden	Youth Film Hours
Jugendwert	A special distinction mark for a film considered 'valuable for youth'
Kampfzeit	Time of struggle (before the NSDAP gained power in 1933)
KdF	Kraft durch Freude (Strength through Joy)
Kleinbürgertum	Petit-bourgeoisie
KPD	Kommunistische Partei Deutschlands (German Communist Party)
Kreis	District, territorial unit of the NSDAP into which Gaus were divided
Kristallnacht	'Crystal Night' or 'Night of Broken Glass', of 9–10 November 1938 when synagogues and Jewish property were vandalised
Lebensraum	Living space
Mittelstand	Lower middle class
Machtergreifung	Seizure of power (in 1933)
Neuordnung	The New Order
NSBO	Nationalsozialistiche Betriebszellen Organisation (Factory Cell Organisation)
NSDAP	Nationalsozialistische Deutsche Arbeiterpartei (National Socialist German Workers' Party), the Nazi Party
NSF	Nationalsozialistische Frauenschaft (Nazi Women's Group), the monopoly Party organisation for women founded in 1931
NSLB	Nationalsozialistischer Lehrbund (National Socialist Teachers' League)
NSV	NS-Volkswohlfahrt, the Nazi welfare organisation
OKW	Oberkommando der Wehrmacht (Supreme Command of the Armed Forces)
Prädikate	The distinction marks awarded to films
RAD	Reichsarbeitsdienst (The Reich Labour Service)
Reichsjugendführung	Reich Youth Leadership
Reichsjugendtag	Reich Day of Youth
RKK	Reichskulturkammer (Reich Chamber of Culture)
Reichslichtspielgesetz	Reich Film Law
RMD	Reichsmütterdienst (Reich Mothers' Service), one of the sections into which the DFW's work was divided

GLOSSARY AND LIST OF ABBREVIATIONS

RMVP	Reichsministerium für Volksaufklärung und Propaganda (Reich Ministry for Popular Englightenment and Propaganda)
Reichsnährstand	Reich Food Authority
SA	Sturm Abteilungen (Storm Troopers), paramilitary formation of the NSDAP
Schönheit der Arbeit	Beauty of Labour
SD	Sicherheitsdienst der SS (Secret Police Reports)
Sonderweg	Special path (in German history)
Sopade	Deutschlands-Berichte der Sozialdemokratischen Partei Deutschlands, underground reports from the Social Democratic Party's contacts passed on to the SPD headquarters in exile
SPD	Sozialdemokratische Partei Deutschlands (German Social Democratic Party)
SS	Schutzstaffeln, Nazi elite paramilitary formation, under the leadership of Heinrich Himmler
Tendenzfilme	Films advocating themes and archetypes commonly associated with National Socialism
Untermensch	Sub-human
Vergeltung	Revenge
völkisch	Originally a Germanisation of 'nationalist', it acquired racialist and mystical overtones which an English translation of 'folkish' fails to convey
volksdeutsche	'Ethnic Germans', term used by the Nazis to describe people of German stock living outside the Reich
Volksgemeinschaft	(Community of the People), i.e. a German society purged of 'alien' elements
Volksgenossen	(Nazi) Party comrades
Volksgerichtshof	The People's Court (of law)
Volkssturm	'People's Storm', the armed civilian militia
Wehrerziehungsfilme	Military educational films
Weltanschauung	'View of life', term used to describe the Nazis' all-embracing philosophy of Germany's destiny
Winterhilfe	Winter help
Wirtschaftswunder	Economic miracle
Zeitfilme	Militarist feature films set in a contemporary context

INTRODUCTION

I was prompted to write a book on the relationship between politics, public opinion, and propaganda in the Third Reich by two recent developments in German history. The first was the controversy surrounding the so-called *Historikerstreit* ('historians' dispute') in the late 1980s, which attempted to relativise Nazi crimes against humanity in the light of atrocities perpetrated by Stalin and others; the second, the implications of events in Eastern Europe which created the unexpected possibility of a unified Germany.[1] In their different ways both raise questions about Germany's past and whether or not it is appropriate to talk of 'peculiarities' of German history that led to a 'special path' (*Sonderweg*) of development culminating in the genocidal rule of Adolf Hitler.

Since the end of the Second World War and the division of Germany into two spheres of ideological influence, diverse attempts have been made to explain this allegedly unique German past, ranging from a Marxist–Leninist critique of capitalism in crisis; via the survival and dominance of pre-industrial, neo-feudal traditions and structures in an imperial society that was never truly bourgeois; to the alternative position that actually stresses the bourgeois nature of late nineteenth-century Germany. Historians, then, have been engaged in a long-running (if somewhat artificial) battle that has centred on the questions 'What went wrong?' and 'When did it go wrong?' Although this debate is more concerned with interpreting the imperial period rather than the Third Reich, the shadow of Hitler looms large and has shaped the diversity of interpretations. By introducing the concept of divergence from the pattern of other 'advanced' Western societies, the notion of a *Sonderweg* provides a qualified explanation of why German democracy was so weak and failed to withstand the challenge of fascism.[2] Every country has to some extent its own 'special path'; however, Nazism was largely the product of the peculiarities unique to German history and political culture. Although the origins of Nazism must inform any debate, the aim of this book is not to reappraise Nazism's position in German history and the 'peculiarities' that set Germany apart from other parliamentary democracies. Instead, I am more concerned to explain the

1

popular base of National Socialism and its ability to sustain a consensus (of sorts) over a twelve-year period. In this context increasing attention has, in recent years, been focused on the role played by propaganda as a means of mobilisation and control.

This book was written with these thoughts very much in mind. While most historians would agree on the centrality of Hitler to the phenomenon of Nazism, locating Hitler's precise role within the Third Reich has proved controversial and has become the source of a major and sometimes acrimonious historiographical conflict. This has become known as the 'intentionalist' versus 'functionalist' debate. Briefly this may be summarised as the division of historians into 'intentionalists' like K.D. Bracher and Klaus Hildebrand, who seek to emphasise Hitler's role in forming Nazi policy and the consistency of his ideas and leadership; and the 'structural-functionalists' that include Martin Broszat, Hans Mommsen and Wolfgang Schieder, who see developments during the Third Reich as the outcome of power groupings, largely uncoordinated, shaping policy (the so-called 'dysfunctional' Nazi state). The recent move away from the 'intentionalist' explanation has tended to downgrade the importance of Hitler and stress the 'structural' constraints on policy and the chaotic nature of decision-making. The 'structuralists' do not deny the centrality of the Führer to the phenomenon of Nazism, rather they focus on the structural context of decision making and the role of 'traditional elites' in running the Third Reich and Hitler's inability (or unwillingness) to keep this chaos in check. Thus Hitler, in Hans Mommsen's famous phrase, was in some respects a 'weak dictator'.[3] I do not, however, intend to become embroiled in this debate, which I believe has encased historical inter-pretations of the Third Reich into a methodological straitjacket. Moreover, I am rather impatient with the biographical approach to Nazism. Instead, by looking at the social bases of concepts like 'consent' and 'resistance' to National Socialism, I would hope to offer a synthesis of intention and structure in explaining the Nazi regime. Hitler's intentions were crucial for developments during the Third Reich, but the conditions under which these intentions became reality were not totally controlled by Hitler. The respective roles of propaganda and public opinion exercised an important function in sustaining the Third Reich and need to be examined more closely. By analysing the interaction between State-controlled propaganda and the differentiated reactions of public opinion in a 'closed' society in the wider context of the Nazi regime's problems of mobilisation and control, I hope to arrive at certain conclusions about the nature of Nazi propaganda and its effectiveness – or indeed its limitations.

INTRODUCTION

PROBLEMS AND PERSPECTIVES OF INTERPRETATION

The rise and fall of National Socialism is understandably one of the most closely studied issues in modern European history. Historians have been at great pains to explain why millions of Germans voted for the Nazi Party (NSDAP) in free elections and how such a regime could eventually acquire such an extensive European empire; four decades after the collapse of the Third Reich, fundamental disagreements about interpreting Nazism still exist. Indeed, even in the last few years a number of broad historiographical surveys have appeared which have attempted to come to grips with some of the key interpretational problems.[4] The popular image of German society under Nazi rule is a confusing one, ranging from the adoration of crowds surrounding Hitler and other leading members of the hierarchy, to the bestiality of the concentration camps and fear of the Gestapo. It is a picture which raises questions crucial to our understanding of National Socialism. What, for example, were the respective roles of consent and coercion in sustaining the regime, and what was the nature of that consent? Behind the façade of national unity was there any dissent or even 'resistance', and, if so, was it terror alone that rendered it so ineffective?[5]

In the immediate post-war period, the moral outcry against Nazism prevented serious discussion of these questions. Historians of the victorious powers were eager to seize upon the support for Hitler and to talk of a 'German disease'. In part this was the result of a rather simplistic theory of totalitarianism which dominated the debate of the 1950s. Hannah Arendt and Carl Friedrich in particular did much to establish totalitarianism as the central concept in interpreting National Socialism.[6] Nazi Germany was seen as a 'totalitarian' society in which the population had been 'atomised' and 'mobilised' through a ubiquitous system of terror and sophisticated propaganda techniques. Such an approach was adopted and reshaped in the classic pioneering works of Karl Dietrich Bracher.[7] Other German historians, like Friedrich Meinecke and Gerhard Ritter, responded to accusations of a 'German disease' by arguing that Nazism was the culmination of European, and not specifically German, trends ('the moral crisis of European society'). Reflecting the moral dimension of the 'German question', such a defence saw Nazism as an accidental aberration in an otherwise 'healthy' national development.[8]

In the mid-1960s the crude totalitarian model was being either openly challenged by applying Marxist analyses to fascism or radically re-defined by 'liberal' scholars.[9] In 1966/7, two non-Marxist studies appeared which analysed German society under Nazism in terms of its modernising impact (albeit largely unintended). Two works, by the American historian David Schoenbaum and by the German sociologist Ralf Dahrendorf, arrived at a similar conclusion from different routes: namely, that the Nazis, in their totalitarian control of social life, actually produced a 'social revolution', which brought about the modernisation of German society by destroying traditional values, norms and loyalties.[10] The ironic outcome (according to Schoenbaum and Dahrendorf) of the Nazis' desire for total control was not the *Volksgemeinschaft* (national community) they intended but the basis of a modern *Gesellschaft* (society).

In recent years, German historians in particular have severely criticised the negative implications of totalitarian models that the German people under Nazism had been reduced to an anonymous mass of isolated individuals sublimating their individual political wills in the service of the nation and its leader. By questioning Nazi claims to have created such a 'national community', historians like Martin Broszat have suggested the need to look anew at the concept of 'resistance' to the Nazi regime.[11] In the 1970s, partly as a reaction to such pervasive general theories, and partly as a result of West German teachers' immediate need to explain the experience of everyday life in the Third Reich, German historians discovered the attractiveness of *Alltagsgeschichte* ('history of everyday life') or *Geschichte von unten* ('history from below'). These investigations have provided a mass of detailed empirical studies of the experiences of different social groups at a local or regional level.[12] Although such studies have varied greatly in their quality and have been justly criticised for merely accumulating facts at the expense of clear conceptualisation and critical analysis, nevertheless they provide a wealth of material that the discerning student may use in order to arrive at a deeper understanding of the social impact of Nazism at a micro-level.

The traditional idea, then, of the Nazi regime being simply a monolithic power structure has been almost completely rejected and replaced by a more critical model based on the shapelessness, lack of clear direction, and improvisation of Nazi rule. In this sense, the focus of investigation has shifted away from the 'criminality' or 'banality of evil' associated with the crimes of the regime, to the 'normality of everyday life' which embraces both conformity and dissent.[13]

The problems of analysing Nazism and the changing interpretations have, not surprisingly, had a profound effect on the literature on Nazi propaganda. Although Nazi propaganda has only recently come to receive the attention of historians commensurate with its importance, the degree of consensus about its effectiveness is quite revealing. Historians of widely different political persuasions and approaches have testified to the crucial role it played in mobilising support for the Nazis. Z. A. B. Zeman asserted that the growth of the NSDAP from 'insignificant beginnings' to a truly mass movement 'was due to the skilful exploitation of propaganda techniques'.[14] Even Broszat argued (admittedly in an earlier work) that

the originality of the Party did not consist in its intellectual equipment, but in the manner in which it propagandised and fought for ideas represented by others. It was the dynamics of the Party, its parades, the ceremonial blessing of banners, the marching columns of the SA, the uniforms, the bands, etc., which captured the imagination of the masses.[15]

Similarly, East German historians, although approaching the subject from different ideological perspectives, have stressed the importance of propaganda. In the standard East German text dealing with this period, Wolfgang Ruge noted:

> The fascist party developed a propaganda apparatus whose activities far eclipsed all previous heights of the demagogy of German imperialism. The insidious method it employed to influence the masses, fastened on the social crisis and the nationalist sentiments of the broadest strata of the population.[16]

Nonetheless, despite such a consensus, it has been rightly argued that the functions and assumed effectiveness of Nazi propaganda have not been examined sufficiently closely and critically in the past.[17] The traditional method of analysis has concentrated on the organisation of Nazi propaganda and the manipulative techniques employed.[18] Without attempting to assess the reception of propaganda, writers on the subject have generally assumed that Nazi propagandists invariably achieved their goals. Even Robert Herzstein's impressively detailed study referred to Nazi propaganda as 'the war that Hitler won'.[19] More recently, however, by placing the study of propaganda in relation to wider interpretative questions about the Third Reich, historians have begun to challenge previously held views about the effectiveness of Nazi propaganda.[20]

Before discussing the role that propaganda played in the Nazis' rise to power, there are two common misconceptions that I would like to identify. There is a widely held belief that propaganda implies nothing less than the art of persuasion, which serves only to change attitudes and ideas. This is undoubtedly one of its aims, but often a limited and subordinate one. More often, propaganda is concerned with reinforcing existing trends and beliefs, to sharpen and focus them. A second basic misconception is the entirely erroneous conviction that propaganda consists only of lies and falsehood. In fact it operates with many different kinds of truth – the outright lie, the half truth, the truth out of context. Moreover, many writers on the subject see propaganda as essentially appeasing the irrational instincts of man, and this is true to a certain extent; but because our attitudes and behaviour are also the product of rational decisions, propaganda must appeal to the rational elements in human nature as well. The preoccupation with the former ignores the basic fact that propaganda is ethically neutral – it may be good or bad. The first task for the student of propaganda is to divest the word of its pejorative and derogatory associations. We need to think of propaganda in much wider terms; whenever public opinion is deemed important, there we shall find an attempt to influence it. In all political systems policy must be explained in one form or another, the public must be convinced of the efficacy of government decisions; and rational discussion is not always the most useful means of achieving this, particularly in the age of 'mass man'. Therefore, in any body politic, propaganda is not, as is often supposed, a malignant growth, but is an essential part of the whole political process. E. H. Carr has written: 'Power over opinion is therefore not less essential for political purposes than military and economic power, and has always been associated with them. The art of persuasion has always been a necessary part of the equipment of a political leader.'[21]

Propaganda was not 'invented' by Joseph Goebbels, although it is largely as a result of Nazi propaganda that the term has come to have such pejorative associations. The following chapters attempt to reappraise the relationship between politics, propaganda and public opinion in the Third Reich. The structure of the book can be conveniently divided into the theory and practice of propaganda.

The first two chapters look at the theory and organisational structure of Nazi propaganda. I have quoted extensively from the speeches of Hitler and Goebbels on the subject and also referred to the vocabulary of the legislative machinery set up to shape and control the mass-media (examples of both are reproduced in full in the 'Selected Documents' section). I make no apologies for using these speeches; they represent not simply 'official' thinking on the subject and thus the rationalisation for measures undertaken, but, equally importantly, a direct contact between the Führer and his Propaganda Minister and the German people, both before and after the Nazi *Machtergreifung* ('seizure of power'). As such, they serve as examples of propaganda in 'action' – a living fusion of theory and practice that sheds important light on the Nazi mentality.

The final two chapters analyse the differentiated reactions of the public to the major themes and campaigns conducted by the State, both in peace-time and in war. One of the major obstacles to assessing the German public's responses to these campaigns is the absence of public opinion surveys and other contemporary methods of quantifying reactions to major issues. In attempting to understand what Germans really felt during these years, the historian is faced with a number of problems which render accurate measurement of public opinion virtually impossible. Elections and plebiscites tended to be rigged and the media tightly controlled. Nevertheless, as I hope to demonstrate, it would not be strictly true to say that public opinion ceased to exist. The Nazi leadership was acutely aware of the constant need to gauge public moods and regularly received detailed feedback reports from the public opinion and morale gathering agencies.

In the past few years two key sources have been exploited more fully in an attempt to understand the regime's problems of political control and mobilisation. The first is the various reports on civilian morale and public opinion conducted from 1939 by the Security Service (*Sicherheitsdienst* or SD) of the Schutzstaffel (SS) and later, under cover, by the RMVP (Propaganda Ministry) itself.[22] The second is the *Deutschland-Berichte* (Sopade), underground reports from the Social Democratic Party's contacts, both those stationed in Germany and those travelling through it from outside, who passed on their observations in the form of lengthy monthly reports to the SPD headquarters in exile.[23] These reports, which cover the period 1934–40, encompass every conceivable topic but are particularly concerned with popular attitudes to the regime. Although both sources have their drawbacks and need to be used critically, nevertheless they have greatly contributed to our understanding of questions relating to the popular base of Nazism and specifically to the ongoing debate about the 'power' or otherwise of Nazi propaganda. I shall be referring to both of these sources in the following analysis.

1

THE CONQUEST OF THE MASSES

The art of propaganda lies in understanding the emotional ideas of the great masses and finding, through a psychologically correct form, the way to the attention and thence to the heart of the broad masses.

Adolf Hitler, *Mein Kampf*

The title of this chapter is somewhat misleading, implying as it does the manipulation or seduction of millions into voting for the Nazi Party in apparent disregard of their own best interests. The assumption being that these voters, who might otherwise have resisted Nazism, were 'mesmerised' by a well-functioning propaganda machine. The danger of such an approach is that it concentrates on the 'techniques of persuasion' at the expense of a detached analysis of the programme put forward by the NSDAP to solve fundamental economic and social problems. Such an approach leads to the inevitable conclusion that to vote for the Nazi manifesto was an 'irrational' act. This does not solve the question of why millions of Germans acted in such an apparently irrational way. It seems clear that many groups, rather than being 'seduced' by Nazi propaganda, perceived voting for the NSDAP as being in their own interests and that Nazi propaganda served to reinforce such beliefs. Similarly, other groups remained stubbornly resistant to the Nazi message, and no amount of skilful propaganda could persuade them otherwise. To over-emphasise the importance of propaganda would be to diminish the failure of the Weimar system to solve prevailing economic and social problems and of political opponents of the NSDAP to provide viable alternatives. If, as seems likely, many Germans reluctantly voted for the Nazi Party because there seemed to be little credible alternative, then that is not necessarily the outcome of propaganda alone, but the failure of the Weimar system.[1] It is therefore imperative to re-examine the manner in which propaganda disseminated the Nazi programme and to distinguish between, on the one hand, supporters and opponents of the NSDAP and, on the other, those who remained indifferent.

The basic contention of this book is that propaganda played an important part in mobilising support for the NSDAP in opposition and maintaining the party once in power. But propaganda alone could not have sustained the Nazi Party and its ideology over a period of twelve years. There is now considerable evidence to suggest that Nazi policies and propaganda reflected (many of) the aspirations of large sections of the population. Propaganda in Nazi Germany was not, as is often believed, a 'catch-all' process. The 'revolutionary' aim of the Nazi regime to bring about the *Volksgemeinschaft*, the true harmony of classes, highlights the remarkably ambitious nature of its propaganda. Nevertheless, the 'success' of propaganda should not be measured purely in terms of its ability radically to change opinions and attitudes. Propaganda is as much about confirming as about converting public opinion. Propaganda, if it is to be effective, must in a sense preach to those who are already partially converted. Writing before the Second World War, Aldous Huxley observed:

> Propaganda gives force and direction to the successive movements of popular feeling and desire; but it does not do much to create these movements. The propagandist is a man who canalises an already existing stream. In a land where there is no water, he digs in vain.[2]

If we look at propaganda as a means of reinforcing existing attitudes and beliefs, then the continuing 'success' of propaganda during the Third Reich in creating a largely acquiescent public points to the conclusion that a 'consensus' of sorts had been achieved. In this sense, the regime's propaganda was pragmatic enough to recognise that its policies could be maintained provided sections of the community who were opposed to Nazism remained quiescent. Coercion and terror would play an important restraining role here. But, nevertheless, it is my contention that, once in power, the economic programme put forward by the Nazis and the insidious use made of propaganda in a 'closed' environment were enough to ensure at least 'passive' support for the regime.

Before discussing the nature of Nazi propaganda in opposition, it might be useful to begin with a brief outline of the political performance of the Nazi Party during the final years of the Weimar Republic. In 1928, a mere 810,127 electors voted for the NSDAP; four years later, in 1932, this figure had increased to a staggering 13,765,781. Support for the Nazis in national elections between May 1928 and September 1930 rose from 810,127 (2.6 per cent of the total) to 6,379,672 votes (18.3 per cent). By July 1932 the NSDAP was the largest party in the Reichstag, with 37.3 per cent of the total vote, and this was to help pave the way for Hitler's assumption of the Chancellorship in January 1933. As economic and social conditions deteriorated between 1928 and 1930, membership of the NSDAP also continued to grow, although not to the same extent as the explosion of the Nazi vote. In October 1928 Nazi Party membership had reached 100,000;

in September 1930, 300,000 and by the end of 1931, membership exceeded 800,000. One can see therefore that the most rapid increase in membership occurred after the election victories of 1930 and was thus the result, not the cause, of the Party's electoral breakthrough.

The appeal of National Socialism is understandably one of the most closely studied issues in European history. Historians have been concerned to explain why millions of Germans voted for the NSDAP in free elections. As we have seen, their success has been attributed in large measure to successful manipulation by a well-functioning propaganda machine. The skilful exploitation of propaganda techniques has been cited by historians of widely different political persuasions and approaches as having played a crucial role in mobilising support for the Nazis. In this context, attention has by and large been focused on the dynamics of the Nazi Party, its parades, its symbols, the uniforms and banners, the bands, the marching columns of the SA, etc., which 'captured the imagination' of the masses. In the light of such consensus, it would appear that one of the most important factors contributing to the Nazis' rise to power was the cumulative effect of their propaganda; certainly the Nazis themselves were convinced of its effectiveness. In *Mein Kampf* (*My Struggle*), Adolf Hitler devoted two chapters to the study and practice of propaganda. Although Hitler regarded the First World War as the starting-point for an examination of propaganda, he had become aware of its importance while still a student in Vienna in the years before 1914. Hitler was not an original theorist of propaganda techniques, but he was quick to learn the art of stimulating the hopes and fears of his audience into positive action. To this end he acknowledged his debt to the Austrian 'Socialist-Marxist' organisations. 'And I soon realised', Hitler wrote, 'that the correct use of propaganda is a true art which has remained practically unknown to the bourgeois parties.' Profoundly influenced by the Allies' propaganda in the First World War, Hitler was firmly convinced that propaganda was a 'frightful weapon in the hands of experts', and he was scathing in his condemnation of the failure of German war propaganda. During the war, he declared, 'what we failed to do, the enemy did with amazing skill and really brilliant calculation. I, myself, learned enormously from this enemy war propaganda.'[3] Hitler therefore resolved, early in his political career, 'to fight poison gas by poison gas'.

Hitler could not have anticipated being offered the opportunity to practise his propaganda skills so soon after the end of the war. During the war Hitler had been wounded twice and in October 1918 he was badly gassed and spent three months recuperating in Pasewalk hospital in Pomerania. At the end of the war, amid considerable revolutionary fervour in Germany, he returned to a Munich undergoing violent political upheavals and was eventually, in the summer of 1919, assigned by the Reichswehr (army) to inform on extremist groups in Munich. It is supremely ironic that the German army should turn Hitler into a propagandist by giving him the task of inculcating nationalist and anti-Bolshevik sentiments into the troops. Making the most of the conditions in which he found himself, Hitler discovered that he was a talented demagogue:

> I started out with the greatest enthusiasm and love. For all at once I was offered an opportunity of speaking before a large audience; and the thing that I had always presumed from pure feeling without knowing it was now corroborated; I could 'speak' . . . And I could boast of some success: in the course of my lectures I led many hundred, indeed thousands, of comrades back to their people and fatherland. I 'nationalized' the troops . . .[4]

In 1925, when *Mein Kampf* was first published, Hitler's thoughts on war propaganda were largely a reflection of the prevailing nationalist claims that Allied propaganda was responsible for the collapse of the German empire in 1918. In fact the evidence does not support this; in many respects German propaganda during the First World War was more advanced than that of the British.[5] However, Hitler's account of the German débâcle in 1918 and the failure of German counter-propaganda throughout the war became the 'official' truth and was subsequently repeated by the younger generation of National Socialists and by right-wing politicians in general. According to this view, 'in the Wilhelmine age the German intelligentsia had lived in complete ignorance about the nature of propaganda'.[6]

Convinced of the essential role of propaganda for any movement set on obtaining power, Hitler saw propaganda as a vehicle of political salesmanship in a mass market; he argued that the consumers of propaganda were the masses and not the intellectuals. In answer to his own question, 'To whom should propaganda be addressed? To the scientifically trained intelligentsia or to the less educated masses?', he answered emphatically: 'It must be addressed always and exclusively to the masses.' Hitler made no attempt to hide his contempt for the masses; they were malleable and corrupt, they were 'overwhelmingly feminine by nature and attitude' and as such their sentiment was not complicated 'but very simple and consistent'. In *Mein Kampf*, where Hitler laid down the broad lines along which Nazi propaganda was to operate, he assessed his audience as follows:

> The receptivity of the great masses is very limited, their intelligence is small, but their power of forgetting is enormous. In consequence, all effective propaganda must be limited to a very few points and must harp on these in slogans until the last member of the public understands what you want him to understand by your slogan.[7]

The function of propaganda, Hitler argued, was 'to see that an idea wins supporters . . . it tries to force a doctrine on the whole people'. To achieve this, propaganda was to bring the masses' attention to certain facts, processes, necessities, etc., 'whose significance is thus for the first time placed within their field of vision'. Accordingly, propaganda for the masses had to be simple, it had to concentrate on as few points as possible, which then had to be repeated many times, with emphasis on such emotional elements as love and hatred. 'Persistence is the first and most important requirement for success.' Through the continuity and sustained uniformity of its application, propaganda, Hitler concluded, would lead to results 'that are almost beyond our understanding'.[8] Therefore unlike the Bolsheviks, Hitler did not make a distinction between agitation and propaganda. In Soviet Russia agitation was concerned with influencing the masses through ideas and slogans, while propaganda served to spread the Communist ideology of Marxist-Leninism. The distinction dates back to Plekhanov's famous definition, written in 1892: 'A propagandist presents *many* ideas to one or a few persons; an agitator presents *only one or a few* ideas, but presents them to a *whole* mass of people.' Hitler, on the other hand, did not regard propaganda as merely an instrument for reaching the party elite, but rather as a means for the persuasion and indoctrination of all Germans. This distinction led E. K. Bramsted to conclude that propaganda for the Nazis 'had not a specific, but a total validity'.[9]

Hitler's theories on propaganda were first put into practice in 1925 in the NSDAP newspaper, the *Völkischer Beobachter*. The Nazis had bought the newspaper in 1920 with a small circulation in and around the Munich area, but following the failure of the *Putsch* in 1923, the newspaper had disappeared from newspaper stands until 26 February 1925 – the official date of the 're-establishment' of the Party. Within two months of its re-launch it had become a daily newspaper, and its circulation began to rise until in 1929 it had reached a figure of 26,715. Unlike the long, detailed articles and academic discussion of economic and social problems which characterised the political presses of the Weimar Republic, the *Völkischer Beobachter* went in for short hyperboles on typical National Socialist themes; the evil of Jewry and Bolshevism, the humiliation of the Versailles Treaty, the weakness of Weimar parliamentarianism, all of which were contrasted with Nazi patriotic slogans such as *Ein Volk, ein Reich, ein Führer* ('One people, one nation, one leader') – later to be used to great effect in 1938 with the *Anschluss* (the union of Austria with Germany). Convinced more than that propaganda was a powerful weapon in the hands of an expert, Hitler appointed Joseph Goebbels head of party propaganda in April 1930 with the mission to centralise the Party's propaganda machinery and present the Nazi's remorseless march to electoral victory under the leadership of the Führer. In many respects propaganda is easier in opposition than in power, and Goebbels proved a skilled orchestrator of the Party's propaganda resources. However, until 1929, the technical facilities at Goebbels' disposal were rather limited and the Party still relied heavily on Hitler and a few other Party figures, speaking at public meetings. The instruments of mass communication which are commonly associated with authoritarian police states – mass-circulation press, radio, film and television – were largely absent from the Nazis' initial rise to prominence. Under Goebbels' direction, however, the Party showed an increasing opportunism as regards learning and adapting new propaganda techniques.

The situation began to change, albeit slowly, in 1927. It is probably no coincidence that this is when Goebbels first revealed his skill as a propagandist. In November 1926 Goebbels had been appointed *Gauleiter* of Berlin and began immediately to reshape the Party organisation in the German capital. Although nationally the NSDAP's paid-up membership was only 72,590, in July Goebbels launched a weekly newspaper, *Der Angriff* (*The Attack*), which, as the title suggests, was set up to attack political opponents and exploit anti-Semitic feelings by claiming that Jews were responsible for most of the ills of the Weimar 'system'. Its challenging motto on the front page read: 'For the Oppressed! Against the Exploiters!' Towards the end of 1930, *Der Angriff* was appearing daily and had become closely associated with a relentless campaign of personal abuse and criticism levelled by Goebbels at 'establishment' figures (invariably Jewish) associated with the Weimar Republic. A recurring slogan was *Deutschland erwache, Jude verrecke*! ('Germany awake, Jewry be dammed!')

Violent anti-Semitism permeated the pages of the newspaper, and the Jews became the scapegoats for all of Germany's and the world's, problems. The vehemently anti-Semitic cartoons of Hans Schweitzer ('Mjölnir') were a striking feature of the paper, which often read more like an agitational pamphlet. Some of the most important propaganda motifs of the Third Reich first appeared in the pages of *Der Angriff*. Horst Wessel murdered by the German Communist Party in 1930 and the subject of a major Nazi feature film (*Hans Westmar*, 1933) became the archetypal Nazi hero; much of his legend, a major plank of Nazi mythology, began on the pages of *Der Angriff*. Other Nazi propaganda themes – the 'Unknown SA man' and the 'myth of resurrection and return' – also feature regularly in the newspaper.[10]

The essentially negative anti-parliamentarianism and anti-Semitism of National Socialist propaganda allowed Goebbels to use the paper as a vehicle for the dissemination of one of the most important positive themes in Nazi propaganda, namely the projection of the 'Führer-myth', which depicted Hitler as both charismatic superman and man of the people. *Der Angriff*'s circulation, however, was limited to Berlin, and the Party still lacked a national newspaper network. In the September 1930 elections, for example, the Nazis had six daily newspapers, and only the *Völkischer Beobachter* could claim to be a national newspaper with a Munich and Berlin edition. To some extent, this was offset by the fact that it was in 1927 that Alfred Hugenberg, the press baron and leader of the right-wing Conservative National People's Party (DNVP), bought the largest and most prestigious German film company, Ufa (Universum-Film-Aktiengesellschaft). From now on the social and political activities of the NSDAP were captured more regularly by Ufa newsreels and shown to the German public on the large national network of Ufa cinemas. Until this time National Socialist propaganda had been characterised by the comparatively skilful use of rhetoric and by controlled manipulation of meetings, which depended for its success on the organisational skills of local Party cells to stage its own meetings and disrupt those of its political opponents. In December 1930, for example, Nazi demonstrations organised by Goebbels succeeded in preventing a performance at the Marmorhaus in Berlin of the American anti-war film *All Quiet on the Western Front* (*Im Westen nichts Neues*) which as a novel had already antagonised the right by its claim that the German army, far from having been stabbed in the back at home, had lost the First World War at the front. Subsequent attempts to screen the film led to repeated riots. The censor eventually banned the film on the grounds that it was 'likely to endanger Germany's reputation abroad'. It was obvious, however, that the ban arose solely on account of the Nazi demonstrations. The film immediately became a *cause célèbre*. The events surrounding *All Quiet on the Western Front* caused a storm in the newspapers; all the Scherl Verlag papers, controlled by Hugenberg, supported the demonstrations and the subsequent banning.[11]

Therefore, in the final stages of the Nazis' rise to power, circumstances conspired to make the rise easier. Not only did Hugenberg's press and film empire help legitimise the Party, but German industry was also providing valuable financial resources which allowed the Party to escalate its propaganda campaigns. Moreover, the technical means for propaganda had been developed to such an extent that during 1930 microphones and loudspeakers became a standard feature at all Nazi rallies for the first time. As we have already seen, the NSDAP's electoral breakthrough occurred between 1928 and 1930. How can one explain this dramatic increase in the Nazi vote, and what role did propaganda play in securing this electoral success?

Recent research into Nazi voting patterns suggests that after 1928 the NSDAP performed best in the predominantly Protestant and rural districts of the North German plain; whereas the large cities and urban conurbations, together with predominantly Catholic rural areas in the west and south, proved more resistant to the Nazi appeal. These are, of course, broad generalisations and it is quite clear that manual workers in the cities, together with Catholics, were prepared to vote for the NSDAP as well. The conclusion that can be drawn from electoral figures about social composition shows that, despite the disproportionate number of Protestant, rural and middle-class supporters, the NSDAP could justifiably claim to represent a wider range of economic and social groups than any other political party. The short explanation for this was that individuals and groups were prepared to desert traditional alliegances and vote for the Nazis for different reasons. Most historians would agree, however, that the Nazi movement, or rather the *Hitlerbewegung* (Hitler movement), as it was appropriately labelled at the time, successfully integrated the German middle class. First, it won support from the 'old middle class' of small retailers, self-employed artisans, peasant farmers, pensioners and those on fixed incomes. Second, it also appealed to the 'new middle class' of white-collar, non-manual employees. Under the Second Reich these two groups had shared a sense of their own identity that made them the backbone of the nation. They were known collectively as the *Mittelstand*, the healthy core in the middle of German society. With the collapse of the German empire in 1918, the values and assumptions that had shaped and buttressed the *Mittelstand* were suddenly removed. The Weimar Republic represented an acute threat to their status. Some looked to the Nazis as the saviour of capitalism that would restore the old status quo; while others, particularly among younger white-collar workers, saw National Socialism as a 'revolutionary' movement bent on destroying archaic social hierarchies and replacing them with a new social order.[12]

As the economic crisis deepened and class tension increased, the various sections of the *Mittelstand* came together within the Nazi movement. The *Hitlerbewegung* was the 'mobilisation of disaffection' and as such far more successful than the traditional political parties who had become discredited through their association with the Republic and its failure to redress genuine or imagined grievances. There can be little doubt that under Goebbels' direction, the NSDAP exploited these grievances for the purposes of propaganda. By means of an efficient propaganda apparatus which Goebbels had been building up since 1928, the Party was in a strong position to make a highly effective response to the growing sense of crisis and through its propaganda to appeal to both the interests and the ideals of the *Mittelstand*. Indeed, some historians have suggested that towards the end of 1927, with the fall in agricultural prices and following its failure in the 1928 Reichstag elections, there was a significant reorientation in the Party's propaganda away from the industrial working class in the urban conurbations towards a series of campaigns aimed at the *Mittelstand* in the rural areas.[13] By the early part of 1932 Goebbels was confident enough to write: 'The election campaign is ready in principle. We now only need to press the button in order to set the machine into action.'

The 1928 elections brought to power the so-called 'Grand Coalition' consisting of the Social Democratic Party (SPD) together with a number of middle-class parties. Within two years this much heralded coalition, which had been elected with such high expectations, had collapsed and Hitler would be asked to form a government. In January 1933, General Kurt von Schleicher's government, which had attempted to conciliate both centre and leftist interests within the Weimar system, was unable to secure a majority in the Reichstag and resigned. On 30 January, the President, Field Marshal Hindenburg, accepted a cabinet with Hitler as Chancellor, von Papen as Vice-Chancellor and nationalists including Nazis in other posts. Hitler owed his appointment as Chancellor not to the victory at a national election. Instead, in Alan Bullock's phrase, he was 'jobbed into office by a backstairs intrigue'.

Hitler was thus brought into power in 1933 by an establishment that believed it could use the National Socialist Party to maintain its power and influence. For some time deeply anti-democratic elites had been looking for an authoritarian replacement to the Weimar Republic and the marginalisation of the equally despised SPD. Following the Wall Street Crash in October 1929, the rapid deepening of the economic crisis in 1930, and the Nazi electoral success of September 1930, the writing was on the wall for the Republic. A key moment in this transition from democracy to authoritarianism was the setting up of the Brüning government in March 1930 after the collapse of the 'Grand Coalition'. Under Brüning there was talk of the restoration of the monarchy and a Bismarck-style system of government (where parliament is used merely as a rubber stamp for executive decision-making). Hindenburg made it clear from the start that if Papen's minority government was defeated by the Reichstag, then it would be dissolved and Germany would be governed by presidential decree which had been built into the constitution under Article 48. When Brüning's first cabinet was comprehensively defeated in July 1930 over its financial bill, Hindenburg responded by dissolving the Reichstag. This represented a crucial moment in Hitler's rise to power. It also marks the shift from parliamentary government to presidential government.

When landowning interests persuaded Hindenburg to dismiss Brüning, Franz von Papen, their own choice, was prepared to risk a civil war by using the police and military to suppress political parties and impose a new authoritarian constitution. Evidence of this can be seen in Papen's coup d'état against the Prussian government controlled by a coalition of Social Democrats and the Centre Party in July 1932. With unemployment exceeding six million and the Weimar Republic sinking into its death throes, the 1932 elections were fought in a growing atmosphere of political violence and disorder. After the Reichstag elections held on 31 July the NSDAP emerged as the largest party with 37.3 per cent of the vote and 230 seats. In an audience with Hindenburg on 13 August, Hitler refused the post of Vice-Chancellor and insisted upon full responsibility for government, which Hindenburg rejected.

In fact in the 6 November 1932 elections, the Nazi vote fell by two million, or about 4 per cent, with their Reichstag seats reduced from 230 to 196. The chief beneficiaries were the conservative nationalists who gained eight hundred thousand votes, and the KPD (communists) whose share of the vote rose from 14.5 to 16.9 per cent. While the Nazi vote appeared to be in decline, and the Party's tactics in disarray, the increased support for the Communists had persuaded many industrialists and bankers to transfer their support from the ineffectual conservatives and liberals to the NSDAP, as the only bulwark against the growth of Communism. In November a number of businessmen, headed by Hjalmar Schacht, President of the Reichsbank, appealed to Hindenburg to make Hitler Reich Chancellor. Hindenburg still refused to do so. In December 1932, after further political intrigues, General von Schleicher succeeded von Papen as Chancellor. Von Schleicher (who had served in the Third Foot Guards with Hindenburg's son) attempted to be more conciliatory towards the Left and appeal to a wider mass base of support. However, in January 1933 the ambitious and self-seeking von Papen acted as a power broker between powerful business interests and landowners in political manoeuvres intended to oust von Schleicher. The business interests which actively supported Hitler revolved around the Cologne banker Baron Kurt von Schröder and the Keppler Circle. It was Schröder who persuaded von Papen to meet Hitler at his house in Cologne in January 1933. The negotiations eventually resulted in Hitler becoming Chancellor. Von Papen was now ready to accept Hitler as Chancellor, though the price he demanded was a nationalist-conservative, non-Nazi cabinet, with himself as Vice-Chancellor. On this agreed compromise, von Papen was able to persuade the Reich President that Hitler should be made Chancellor. The fatal miscalculation of Hindenburg and von Papen – indeed of the conservative Right in general – was to believe that Hitler could be 'tamed' once in power. The establishment (which included many in the army) attempted to use Hitler and his party to give itself legitimacy for a new authoritarianism. In reality it served only to legitimise Nazism. Out of a labyrinth of power struggles and intrigues, Hitler emerged the victor.

Nevertheless, despite the political machinations that took place within high politics prior to his appointment, Hitler became Chancellor constitutionally. The suggestion that Hitler and his party somehow 'seized' power is rather misleading. The Nazis themselves are largely responsible for perpetuating this myth by continuing to refer to a *Kampfzeit* ('period of struggle') and to their *Machtergreifung* ('seizure of power'). Having gained power the Nazis used the Reichstag fire of 27 February 1933 as a pretext for suspending civil liberties ('Reichstag Fire Decree') and conducting an election campaign (which had already begun) in circumstances highly favourable to themselves. In the elections of 5 March the NSDAP made further gains, winning 288 seats but failing to secure an overall majority (43.9 per cent).

The Nazis' political success in opposition has frequently been attributed to Goebbels' manipulatory talents. There can be little doubt that Nazi propaganda was quick to seize its opportunity and that it was firmly based on the principles outlined in *Mein Kampf*. It carried through with a ruthless consistency a campaign of propaganda which appealed directly to the emotions rather than to the intellect and was reinforced at all levels by terror and violence. But propaganda alone cannot change social and political conditions; it acts in conjunction with other factors, like organisation. While the Nazis' propaganda machine was important in helping achieve this electoral victory, the NSDAP was in the fortunate political position, unlike almost every other party in the Weimar Republic, of appealing to different groups for different reasons. The Nazi Party recognised not simply the importance of propaganda, but more importantly the need to adapt its propaganda to these different groups. National Socialist propaganda did not destroy Weimar democracy, although it did undermine it. What distinguished the NSDAP from other parties in opposition was its ability to combine the themes of traditional German nationalism with Nazi ideological motifs. This unification of German patriotism and Nazi ideology allowed Hitler, in Jay Baird's words, to 'forge a compelling weapon against what he termed the "immorality of Weimar rationalism", the symbol of cultural decadence, racial impurity, and Jewish putrefaction'.[14] During the 1932 elections campaigns, for example, Goebbels cranked up the party propaganda machinery and skilfully targeted the socialists, communists and Jews as the 'guardian angels of capitalism' (see Plate 1). The Nazis alone were perceived by many groups as representing certain ideas that appeared to transcend Weimar politics. This not only gave them a wider appeal, but it also set them apart from other political parties.

There can be little doubt that the two most important ideas that distinguished the Nazis from other parties and allowed Goebbels' propaganda to mobilise widespread grievances were the notion of *Volksgemeinschaft* (community of the people), based on the principle laid down in the Party programme of 1920 *Gemeinnutz geht vor Eigennutz* ('Common good before the good of the individual') and the myth of the charismatic 'Führer'. The community of the nation was to replace the 'divisive' party system and the class barriers of the Weimar Republic and in effect offer the prospect of national unity without either a bloody revolution or the need to offer too many concessions to the working class. The other element which appears to have been genuinely effective and unique was the projection of Hitler as a 'charismatic' leader. The 'Führer cult' had become synonymous with the NSDAP, and it is significant that the Party referred to itself even on the ballot papers as the 'Hitler movement'. From 1930 onwards, the *panache* of its propaganda in staging political rallies where Hitler could project his leadership and the faithful could give the impression of being a dynamic movement far exceeded that of other parties. The carefully constructed mass rallies, with their marches, banners and flags, when combined with Hitler's speeches, provided Goebbels with the opportunity to synthesise

Plate 1 A 1932 Nazi election poster, directed against the SPD and Jews who are seen striding hand-in-hand. The slogan reads: 'Marxism is the Guardian Angel of Capitalism. Vote national Socialist. List 1.'

Plate 2 The 'Day of Potsdam', 21 March 1933. A deferential Hitler, in morning suit and not in Party uniform, bows to the Reich President Paul von Hindenburg.

the twin concepts of *Volksgemeinschaft* and the 'Führer cult' in one political experience. The mass political rally would continue to play a dominant role in the politics of the Third Reich, where it was seen to be the physical manifestation of a nation's 'triumph of the will'. Significantly, one of Goebbels' first staged events as Propaganda Minister was the opening of the new Reichstag with an elaborate ceremony known as the 'Day of Potsdam' on 21 March 1933. The ceremony was held in the Garrison Church at Potsdam, the shrine of the old Prussian monarchy. President Hindenburg resplendent in the full military regalia of Prussian field-marshal raised his baton to the empty throne of the exiled Kaiser. Hitler, in top hat and morning coat, bowed deferentially before him. The propaganda message was clear. The Nazis were restoring the old imperial glories lost in 1918 by forging a link between the past and the present – between the conservatism of the Prussian tradition and the razzmatazz of National Socialist ritual propaganda. In a symbolic piece of theatrical staging, Hindenburg took the salute for the final parade (which lasted for several hours) while Hitler stood modestly with his ministers some rows behind the old man (see Plate 2).

In the following chapters I intend to expand these points and examine the manner in which Goebbels restructured the means of communication and orchestrated German public opinion in his desire to consolidate the Party's 'conquest' of the masses. First, however, I should like briefly to outline and comment on the implications of Goebbels' own concept of propaganda.

2

GOEBBELS AS PROPAGANDIST

In propaganda as in love, anything is permissible which is successful.

Goebbels[1]

From its very beginning, the Third Reich had set itself the ambitious task of 're-educating' the German people for a new society based upon what it saw as a 'revolutionary' value system. The NSDAP had always rejected the kind of liberal democracy that had evolved in most Western European countries by the beginning of the twentieth century. They fervently believed that the only salvation from the 'degeneracy' of the Weimar Republic was the *Völkischer Staat* which would come about in Germany through a National Socialist type revolution. Coupled with this rejection of democracy, which had failed Germany, was a growing belief that strong leadership was needed to transcend class and sectional interests and provide a new start.

As the custodian of a unique *Weltanschauung* that would maintain the purity of the Aryan race and allow it to find genuine expression, the National Socialist State would be responsible not only for the material welfare of its citizens but for their moral and spiritual welfare as well. It would seek to restore a true consciousness to a people so corrupted by non-Aryans that they were no longer aware of what traditional German values were. This largely explains why all individuals and organisations in this new state were required to be *gleichgeschaltet* (coordinated) in the sense of making them subject to Party control: for the Party was the guardian of the German world view and through the power and will of its leader, the Führer, the 'good' society would be brought into being. For a nation that believed so strongly that it had been wronged at Versailles and was now surrounded by hostile nations, such an appeal provided the basis upon which Nazi propaganda could build up its support. In one of his first declarations of government policy in 1933 Hitler proclaimed:

> In relation to the political decontamination of our public life, the government will embark upon a systematic campaign to restore the nation's moral and material health. The whole educational system,

theatre, film, literature, the press, and broadcasting – all these will be used as a means to this end. They will be harnessed to help preserve the eternal values which are part of the integral nature of our people.[2]

The day following the Reichstag fire on 28 February 1933, the new Chancellor, Adolf Hitler, promulgated an emergency decree signed by President Paul von Hindenburg placing restrictions on individual liberty, including freedom of opinion and freedom of the press. On 13 March, Dr Joseph Goebbels was appointed Minister for Popular Enlightenment and Propaganda (*Reichsminister für Volksaufklärung und Propaganda*). It is not surprising that propaganda in Nazi Germany should have been considered important enough to warrant an entire government ministry; indeed, as we have seen, the story of the Nazi rise to power is often seen as a classic example of political achievement by means of propaganda.

However, after the take-over of power there was some difference of opinion between Goebbels and Hitler as to the exact role of propaganda in the Third Reich. Hitler felt the importance of propaganda would decline once the NSDAP had gained political power. For Hitler, propaganda was important when organised membership was small; but once the Party had acquired the instruments of State power, its significance would decline and organisation would assume a more important role. In *Mein Kampf* he expressed these thoughts as follows:

> Propaganda should go well ahead of organisation and gather together the human material for the latter to work up. . . . When the propaganda work has converted a whole people to believe in a doctrine, the organisation can turn the results of this into practical effect through the work of a mere handful of men.[3]

Not surprisingly, given Goebbels' success in master-minding the Party's election victories in 1933, he disagreed with Hitler's distinction between propaganda and organisation. Goebbels, when he felt inclined to bother with such a distinction, believed that organisation should be limited to what was essential rather than extended to what was possible. Propaganda, on the other hand, would be necessary in power, not only to mobilise mass support for the new *Völkischer Staat*, but also to maintain a heightened level of enthusiasm and commitment for its ideological foundations. What, then, as Minister for Popular Enlightenment and Propaganda, was Goebbels' view of the political function of propaganda in the Nazi system of government?

Goebbels was conscious of the need to draw on the experiences gained in opposition and to benefit from the privileges that political power now bestowed. Unlike Hitler, Goebbels was, however, concerned to show consistency with the 'revolutionary' aims associated with the National Socialist movement. Power, and especially the newly inherited monopoly of the means of communication would not dilute Nazi policies, though they would be fully utilised. In one of his first major speeches after becoming *Reichsminister*, Goebbels declared:

> If we look at the work that lies behind us and at the unparalleled successes we have achieved in the past weeks, we must attribute this mainly to the fact that as a young revolutionary movement we gained a virtuoso mastery of all the means of modern mass influence, and that, rather than directing propaganda from baize tables, we, as true leaders, have come from the people and have never lost intimate contact with the people. I think that one of the most important advantages of the new Government propaganda consists in the fact that the activity of the men who have hitherto been responsible for National Socialist propaganda can now be made to bear fruit for the new state. ... A government that wishes to conduct propaganda must gather round it the most able brains in mass public influence and resort to the most modern methods to achieve this mass influence.[4]

Clearly Goebbels believed that propaganda was to have a central role, particularly in the initial stages of *Gleichschaltung*, and the Ministry for Popular Enlightenment and Propaganda was to be the means of coordinating the political will of the nation with the aims of the State. Outlining his views on the new Ministry for Propaganda, Goebbels provided a clear indication of the political function of propaganda in the Third Reich and reaffirmed its essential role in filling the void that had hitherto existed between government and people:

> I see the setting-up of the new Ministry for Popular Enlightenment and Propaganda as a revolutionary act of government, in so far as the new Government has no intention of abandoning the people to their own devices and locking them up in an airless room. This Government is, in the truest sense of the word, a People's Government. It arose from the people and will always execute the people's will. ... We want to give the people their due, albeit in a different form than has been the case under parliamentary democracy. I see in the newly established Ministry for Popular Enlightenment and Propaganda a link between Government and people, the living contact between the National Government as the expression of the popular will and the people themselves. In the past few weeks we have experienced a growing political coordination (*Gleichschaltung*) between the policy of the Reich and the policy of the *Länder* [states] and I see the first task of this new Ministry as establishing a coordination between the Government and the whole people.[5]

Such a speech is at odds with Hitler's intention that propaganda was to give way to organisation. For Goebbels, propaganda was to be an active force cementing the nation together. In the National Socialist State it was not enough simply to tolerate the Government; Goebbels believed that the people needed to be mobilised into a total commitment to the *Völkischer Staat*. Such wholehearted support could be more profitably achieved through 'creative' propaganda than through coercion or force of arms. Addressing the 1934 NSDAP Rally in Nuremberg, Goebbels reaffirmed the importance of successful propaganda:

> May the bright flame of our enthusiasm never be extinguished. It alone gives light and warmth to the creative art of modern political propaganda. It arose from the very heart of the people in order to derive more strength and power. It may be a good thing to possess power that rests on arms. But it is better and more gratifying to win and hold the heart of the people.[6]

According to Goebbels, however, the only measure of propaganda was the extent to which it achieved its objectives. 'In propaganda as in love', Goebbels observed, 'anything is permissible which is successful.' It would not be too much of an exaggeration to suggest that by Goebbels' own criteria, his ultimate aim was nothing less than complete identification between the people and the National Socialist programme of 'national revolution'. ('The new Ministry has no other aim than to unite the nation behind the ideal of the national revolution.') Goebbels anticipated propaganda providing the contact between government and the people. But how did the Minister for Propaganda view the masses? Here one finds a striking similarity to the views expressed by Hitler in *Mein Kampf*. According to Hitler, propaganda for the masses had to be simple, it had to aim at the lowest level of intelligence, it had to be reduced to easily learned slogans which then had to be repeated many times, concentrating on such emotional elements as love and hatred. Goebbels agreed with these sentiments and the Propaganda Ministry disseminated propaganda of this kind both before and after the outbreak of war. Goebbels was not particularly concerned about the historical roots and antecedents of the term propaganda. In opposition, his propaganda techniques had largely been determined by Hitler's thoughts and wishes and the desire to gain power by any means. Much of Nazi propaganda was extemporised and opportunistic. However, one source that did make a profound impression upon his theory of propaganda was the late nineteenth-century French sociologist, Gustave Le Bon, whose work *The Crowd* analysed how the masses could be manipulated in an age of mass democracy. Le Bon's elitist contempt for the crowd offered Goebbels tantalising insights into how they could be managed: 'The substitution of the unconscious action of crowds for the conscious activity of individuals is one of the principal characteristics of the present age . . . Men are ruled by ideas, sentiments, and customs . . . crowds display a singularly inferior mentality . . . The part played by the unconscious in all our acts is immense, and that played by reason very small'.[7] Like Le Bon, Goebbels (and Hitler) despised the gullible malleability of the masses. Le Bon argued that to be successful, politicians needed to study crowd behaviour in order to exploit their psychology. In particular Le Bon believed in the essential conservatism of crowds and their fear of change. A fearful, disoriented crowd – or nation – could therefore be manipulated to serve the interest of the propagandist. A skilled orator, according to Le Bon, could move the individual in the crowd to acts of extreme savagery or noble heroism. Rudolf Semmler, one of Goebbels' aids in the Propaganda Ministry, confirmed in his diary that Le Bon continued to exert an influence over Goebbels even during the Second World War: 'Goebbels thinks that no one since the Frenchman Le Bon has understood the mind of the masses as well as he.'[8]

In a revealing passage from his wartime diaries (which were more a public rather than a personal testament), he noted:

> Again I learned a lot; especially that the rank and file are usually much more primitive than we imagine. Propaganda must therefore always be essentially simple and repetitive. In the long run basic results in influencing public opinion will be achieved only by the man who is able to reduce problems to the simplest terms and who has the courage to keep forever repeating them in this simplified form, despite the objections of the intellectuals.[9]

Goebbels maintained that one of the key functions of propaganda was to bring certain subjects within the field of vision of the masses. This meant that the population had to be orientated towards specific 'information'. In order to achieve this, the successful propagandist should know his audience both as individuals and as a group. Propaganda in this sense required considerable skill and understanding of human psychology. It is for this reason that Goebbels continued to dislike the pejorative connotations commonly associated with the concept of propaganda:

> Propaganda is a much maligned and misunderstood word. The lay-man uses it to mean something inferior or even dispicable. The word 'propaganda' always leaves a bitter after-taste. But if you examine propaganda's most secret causes, you will come to different conclu-sions: then there will be no more doubting that the propagandist must be the man with the greatest knowledge of souls. I cannot convince a single person of the necessity of something unless I have got to know the soul of that person, unless I understand how to pluck the string in the harp of his soul that must be made to sound. It is not true that propaganda presents merely a blueprint; it is not true that the propagandist does no more than administer complex thought processes in rough form to the mass. Rather, the propagandist must

not just know the soul of the people in general, but he must understand the secret swings of the popular soul from one side to another. The propagandist must understand how to speak not only to the people in their totality, but also to individual sections of the population: to the worker, the peasant, the middle class. He must understand how to speak to different professions and to different faiths. The propagandist must always be in a position to speak to people in the language that they understand. These capacities are the essential preconditions for success.[10]

It is supremely ironic that Joseph Goebbels, who, as Reich Minister for Popular Enlightenment and Propaganda, did more than anyone to create such a 'bitter after-taste', should set himself the mission of rescuing propaganda from such misconceptions. It is the purpose of the following chapters to examine the extent to which Goebbels was successful in orchestrating German public opinion by analysing the major themes and campaigns that were employed both before and after the outbreak of war. But first we need to look at the organisational structures within which propaganda was disseminated.

3

RESTRUCTURING THE MEANS OF COMMUNICATION

THE MINISTRY FOR POPULAR ENLIGHTENMENT AND PROPAGANDA

It was during the early part of 1933 that Goebbels was making the final plans for a Ministry of Propaganda. However, because Goebbels was so involved in the forthcoming elections on 5 March, it was decided to delay announcing the creation of the new ministry until after the Nazis' electoral success was guaranteed. From Goebbels' own account of his rise to power it is quite clear that the decision to create such a ministry had been agreed for some time:

> We are thinking of a Ministry of Public Education within which film, radio, art, culture and propaganda would be combined. Such a revolutionary organisation will be under central control and firmly embody the idea of the Reich. This is a really big project, as big as the world has seen. I am to start at once working out the structure for this Ministry.[1]

Goebbels is said to have been initially unhappy with the open use of 'Propaganda' in the title on the grounds that it was psychologically counter-productive. Given his voluminous writings on the subject and that he felt confident enough to form the Nazi Party Reich Propaganda Directorate in 1930, this claim, which is based on little substantive evidence, seems out of character to say the least. The Ministry for Popular Enlightenment and Propaganda (Reichsministerium für Volksaufklärung und Propaganda – RMVP), was established by a presidential decree, signed on 12 March 1933 and promulgated on the following day, which defined the task of the new ministry as the dissemination of 'enlightenment and propaganda within the population concerning the policy of the Reich Government and the national reconstruction of the German Fatherland'. In June Hitler was to define the scope of the RMVP in even more general terms, making Goebbels responsible for the 'spiritual direction of the nation'. Not only did this vague directive provide Goebbels with room to out-manoeuvre his critics within the Party; it also put the seal of legitimacy on what was soon to be the ministry's wholesale control of the mass-media. Nevertheless, Goebbels was constantly involved in quarrels with ministerial colleagues who resented the encroachment of this new ministry on their old domain.

Analysing the political function of propaganda in the Third Reich is further complicated by the fact that it was simultaneously channelled through three different institutions: the RMVP, the Central Propaganda Office of the Party, and the Reich Chamber of Culture (see figure on p. 30). Moreover, the political structure of the Third Reich was based on the twin pillars of the Party and the State. According to Hitler, it was the task of the State to continue the 'historical development of the national administration within the framework of the law', while it was the function of the Party to 'build its internal organisation and establish and develop a stable and self-perpetuating centre of the National Socialist doctrine in order to transfer the indoctrinated to the State so that they may become its leaders as well as its disciples'.[2] The creation of the the RMVP in March 1933 was a significant step towards the merging of the Party and the State. Goebbels continued to be head of Party Propaganda, but he greatly strengthened both his own position within the Party and the scope of propaganda by setting up this new ministry – the first of its kind in Germany.

Two days after his appointment as Minister for Propaganda Goebbels outlined his view of the role of the new ministry in a revealing speech (for the full text, see Document 1) to representatives of the German press:

> We have established a Ministry for Popular Enlightenment and Propaganda. These two titles do not convey the same thing. Popular enlightenment is essentially something passive; propaganda, on the other hand, is something active. We cannot be satisfied with just telling the people what we want and enlightening them as to how we are doing it. We must replace this enlightenment with an active government propaganda that aims at winning people over. It is not enough to reconcile people more or less to our regime, to move them towards a position of neutrality towards us, we would rather work on people until they are addicted to us.[3]

A few days later Goebbels defined the task of his new ministry as 'achieving a mobilisation of mind and spirit in Germany. It is, therefore, in the sphere of the mind what the Defence Ministry is in the sphere of defence' (see Document 2). With the creation of the RMVP, propaganda became primarily the responsibility of the State, although its departments were to be supported and reinforced by the Party's Central Propaganda Office (Reichspropagandaamt), which remained less conspicuous to the general public. Indeed, the two institutions would often merge into one apparatus: not only would their respective organisations and responsibilities correspond closely, but many of the leading positions in the Ministry

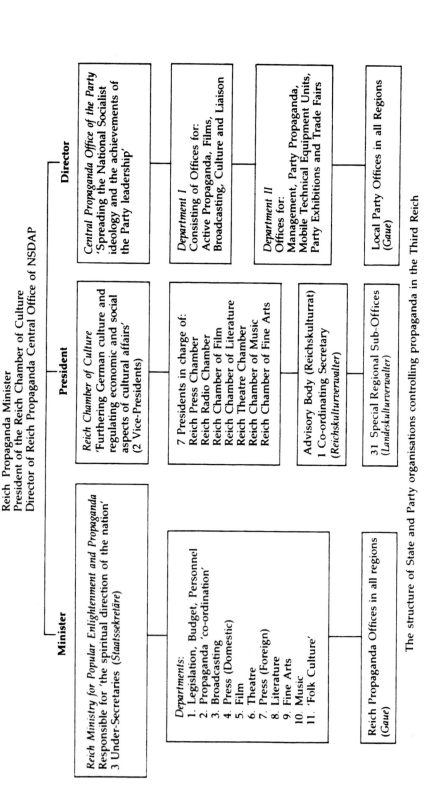

Dr Joseph Goebbels
Reich Propaganda Minister
President of the Reich Chamber of Culture
Director of Reich Propaganda Central Office of NSDAP

Minister

President

Director

Reich Ministry for Popular Enlightenment and Propaganda
Responsible for 'the spiritual direction of the nation'
3 Under-Secretaries (*Staatssekretäre*)

Reich Chamber of Culture
'Furthering German culture and regulating economic and social aspects of cultural affairs'
(2 Vice-Presidents)

Central Propaganda Office of the Party
'Spreading the National Socialist ideology and the achievements of the Party leadership'

Departments:
1. Legislation, Budget, Personnel
2. Propaganda 'co-ordination'
3. Broadcasting
4. Press (Domestic)
5. Film
6. Theatre
7. Press (Foreign)
8. Literature
9. Fine Arts
10. Music
11. 'Folk Culture'

7 Presidents in charge of:
Reich Press Chamber
Reich Radio Chamber
Reich Chamber of Film
Reich Chamber of Literature
Reich Theatre Chamber
Reich Chamber of Music
Reich Chamber of Fine Arts

Department I
Consisting of Offices for:
Active Propaganda, Films, Broadcasting, Culture and Liaison

Department II
Offices for:
Management, Party Propaganda, Mobile Technical Equipment Units, Party Exhibitions and Trade Fairs

Reich Propaganda Offices in all regions
(*Gaue*)

Advisory Body (Reichskulturrat)
1 Co-ordinating Secretary
(*Reichskulturverwalter*)

31 Special Regional Sub-Offices
(*Landeskulturverwalter*)

Local Party Offices in all Regions
(*Gaue*)

The structure of State and Party organisations controlling propaganda in the Third Reich and the *Reichspropagandaleitung* were held by the same officials. Originally Goebbels had planned only five departments for the new ministry, to embrace radio, press, active propaganda, film, and theatre and popular education, but by April 1933 it had acquired its basic structure and was divided into seven departments. During the war even Goebbels' staunch anti-bureaucratic stance could not prevent the RMVP from inclusion in the process of expansion and bureaucratisation, and the number of departments actually increased to fourteen. However, in the context of this study I have confined my discussion to the more important departments. Accordingly, the division of labour within the ministry can be broken down along the following lines. The wide variety of responsibilities of the departments points to a remarkably comprehensive organisational structure:

Department I: Legislation and Legal Problems; Budget Finance, and Accounting.

Department II: Co-ordination of Popular Enlightenment and Propaganda ('active propaganda'); Regional Agencies of the Ministry; German Academy of Politics; Official Ceremonies and Demonstrations; National Emblems; Racial Questions; Treaty of Versailles; Opposing Ideologies; Youth Organisations; Public Health and Sport; Eastern and Border Questions; National Travel Committee.

Department III: Radio; National Broadcasting Company (Reichsfunkgesellschaft).

Department IV: National and Foreign Press; Journalism; Press Archives; News Service; National Association of German Press.

Department V: Film; Film Picture Industry; Film Censorship, Newsreels.

Department VI: Theatre.

Department VII: Music, Fine Arts; People's Culture.

The RMVP began with only 350 administrative and executive officials. Goebbels retained a notoriously low opinion of civil servants and once confided in his diary that 'just as you cannot expect a cow to lay eggs, so you cannot expect a bureaucrat to look after the interests of the State properly'.[4] As a new creation, the RMVP was from the beginning staffed by fanatical young Nazis, generally with better educational qualifications than the average Nazi activist. Goebbels had declared that his staff should never exceed 1,000, and he also agreed to meet the costs of the RMVP from radio licences. Fortunately for the new minister, the purchase of radios increased dramatically during the Third Reich, and it has been estimated that over 80 per cent of the ministry's current expenditure was recovered from this source.[5] Goebbels saw the RMVP as the main policy and decision-making body, providing directions and delegating responsibilities to the numerous subordinate agencies that lay under its control. The most important of these was the Reich Chamber of Culture (Reichskulturkammer).

THE REICH CHAMBER OF CULTURE

Kulturpolitik (cultural policy) was an important element in German life, but the Nazis were the first party systematically to organise the entire cultural life of a nation. As the RMVP ominously proclaimed when it announced the Theatre Law of 15 May 1934: 'The arts are for the National Socialist State a public exercise; they are not only aesthetic but also moral in nature and the public interest demands not only police supervision but also guidance.' The Reich Chamber of Culture was set up by a law promulgated on 22 September 1933 (see Document 4). It represented a triumph for Goebbels in his bitter struggle with the Nazi 'ideologist' Alfred Rosenberg, who before 1933 had claimed responsibility for cultural matters through the establishment of his 'Combat League for German Culture'. The Reich Chamber of Culture allowed the Minister of Propaganda to organise the various branches of the arts and cultural professions as public corporations. Seven individual areas were organised as separate chambers: literature, theatre, music, radio, film, fine arts, and the press. Goebbels was designated president of the Reichskulturkammer (RKK), with power to appoint the presidents of the subordinate chambers. The creation of the RKK is an excellent example of the process of *Gleichschaltung*. This was the term employed by the Nazis when they came to power, and referred to the obligatory assimilation within the State of all political, economic and cultural activities (or 'nazification'). The RKK acted as an agent of this 'coordination' in that it allowed the RMVP to exert its control over almost all aspects of German cultural life. As Minister for Propaganda, Goebbels acted as president of the seven chambers, and through him their jurisdiction spread down to both the nation's regional administration (*Länder*) and the Party's own specifically political areas (*Gaue*). This not only facilitated the RMVP's control over individual chambers but, equally importantly, allowed the ministry to co-ordinate its propaganda campaigns.

The chief function of each chamber was to regulate conditions of work in its particular field. This involved the keeping of a register and the issuing of work permits. Nobody refused such a permit could be employed in his or her profession. To be refused membership of the chamber, therefore, spelt professional ruin. To those sympathetic to the regime, on the other hand, enforced membership of such an immense organisation represented financial security and public recognition. The law which established the RKK conferred on Goebbels the power to exclude all those who were considered racially or artistically objectionable. This also included professional organisations. In February 1933, two members of the Prussian Academy of Arts who were critical of the Nazis were forced to resign: Käthe Kollwitz and Heinrich Mann. Thirteen other members resigned in protest, including Thomas Mann, Alfred Döblin and Ricarda Huch. In July, the Bauhuas school of architecture was closed in Berlin.

As the Nazi revolution was to bring about a new consciousness, which would transcend the political structure, it followed that artists too had a revolutionary role to play. In one of his first speeches as Minister for Propaganda Goebbels outlined the future role of German art:

> Modern German art's task is not to dramatise the Party programme, but to give poetic and artistic shape to the huge spiritual impulses within us. . . . The political renaissance must definitely have spiritual and cultural foundations. Therefore it is important to create a new basis for the life of German art.[6]

Under the Nazis, art was seen as an expression of race and would underpin the political renaissance that was taking place. Whereas Modernism was associated with 'decadent' Jewish–Liberal culture, art under National Socialism would be rooted in the people as true expression of the spirit of the People's Community (*Volksgemeinschaft*). At the height of his power, Hitler gave a succinct summary of his concept of culture and the role of artists in a speech delivered on 18 July 1937 at the opening of the House of German Art in Munich (see Plate 3), which was intended to house officially approved art:

> During the long years in which I planned the formation of a new Reich I gave much thought to the tasks which would await us in the cultural cleansing of the people's life; there was to be a cultural renaissance as well as a political and economic reform. . . . As in politics, so in German art-life, we are determined to make a clean sweep of empty phrases. . . . The artist does not create for the artist. He creates for the people, and we will see to it that the people in future be called to judge his art. No one must say that the people has no understanding for a really valuable enrichment of its cultural life. . . . The people in passing through these galleries will recognise in me its spokesman and counsellor. It will draw a sigh of relief and gladly express its agreement with this purification of art. . . . The artist cannot stand aloof from his people.[7]

This speech (which can be read in full in Document 8) defined what was and what was not artistically desirable in the Third Reich. Moreover, it was believed that, by establishing the seven chambers under the umbrella of the RKK, such a control mechanism would allow the regime largely to dispense with a formal system of censorship, since artists had either been purged or, if they remained, would exercise self-censorship for fear of losing their livelihood. In practice the regime became increasingly sensitive to artistic criticism of any kind, and Goebbels was eventually persuaded that once a work of art had been officially approved it was not the function of critics to criticise it. On 13 May 1936 Goebbels issued a proclamation which banned the writing of critical reviews on the same evening as the performance (*Nachtkritik*). Justifying his position, the Minister for

Plate 3 Otto Hirth (1940), *The House of German Art and its Extension.*

Propaganda declared: 'Artistic criticism no longer exists for its own sake. In future one ought not to degrade or criticise a well-meaning or quite respectable artistic achievement for the sake of a witty turn of phrase.'[8] Such measures were clearly intended as a warning to critics not to question, by means of hostile reviews, officially approved artistic works (which would range from a piece of sculpture to a feature film). However, on 27 November 1936 Goebbels decided to ban all art criticism by confining critics to writing merely 'descriptive' reviews (*Kunstbetrachtungen*) (see Document 7). In future all critics would need a special licence from the RKK, and these licences would only be given to critics over the age of thirty. The day following Goebbels' famous order, his press chief at the RMVP, Alfred Ingemar Berndt, informed the Reich Chamber of Culture:

> Judgement of art work in the National Socialist State can be made only on the basis of the National Socialist viewpoint of culture. Only the Party and the State are in a position to determine artistic values. . . . If a licence has been issued by those who are appointed to pass judgement on art, the reporter, may of course, employ the values thereby established. This situation will arise only rarely, however.[9]

It can be seen that art criticism was never an aesthetic but always a political question. In practice art criticism came more and more to resemble publicity material distributed by the State to promote a particular venture or activity. Although the ban met with some hostility (especially abroad), the first manifestation of such a mentality occurred as early as 10 May 1933, a few months before the RKK was established, in Berlin's Opernplatz, with the barbarous ceremony of the 'Burning of the Books' (see Plate 4). Twenty thousand works of 'undesirable and pernicious' writers were thrown on a ceremonial bonfire, and Goebbels made a speech, broadcast on German radio, in which he referred to such writers as 'the evil spirit of the past', and declared:

> the age of extreme Jewish intellectualism is over . . . the past is lying in flames . . . the future will rise from the flames within our hearts . . . Brightened by these flames our vow shall be: the Reich and the Nation and our Führer Adolf Hitler: Heil! Heil! Heil![10]

Revealingly there were book burning episodes taking place in all German universities at the same time that were not orchestrated by Goebbels. Largely initiated by the German Students' Association but eagerly supported by right-wing nationalist groups, local authorities and the police, public libraries were also ransacked without protest. The poet Heine whose works were consumed by the flames, had written: 'Where books are burnt, in the end people are also burnt.'

From now on the State would determine what was 'good' and what was 'bad' literature. However, since its establishment Goebbels and the RMVP

Plate 4 The 'Burning of the Books' in front of the Opera House, 10 May 1933.

had become embroiled in a struggle for power with Alfred Rosenberg, who had set up a Party agency, the 'Reich Office for the Encouragement of German Literature' and vied with Goebbels for ultimate control of censorship. Rosenberg was the Nazis' self-styled 'official' ideologist and author of *The Myth of the Twentieth Century* (1930). He had established the League of Struggle for German Culture in 1929 and was elected to the Reichstag in September 1930 the year he became editor (later publisher) of the *National Socialist Monthly* – the political and cultural journal of the NSDAP. In 1934 Hitler appointed Rosenberg 'the Führer's representative for the comprehensive intellectual and ideological indoctrination of the NSDAP'. In November 1933, Goebbels had requested all State governments to consult with the Reich Chamber of Literature before banning books. The matter was finally resolved – much to Rosenberg's irritation – by a decree of 25 April 1935 which established the supreme authority of the Reich Chamber of Literature, who were now empowered to draw up an 'index' of all 'damaging and undesirable literature', which threatened 'the National Socialist cultural aspirations'. If the police now wished to ban or confiscate a work of literature, they were obliged to request its inclusion in this 'confidential' index. The balance of power between Goebbels and Rosenberg was controlled by Hitler and had shifted decisively in Goebbels' favour. The League of Struggle for German Culture was prevented from gaining further control in cultural affairs. By 1935, the League (sometimes referred to as the 'Combat League'), was incorporated into the Nazi Labour Front and had lost its significance within the Nazi cultural system. Although Rosenberg continued to exert some ideological influence over Party education, by 1939 he was largely a spent force, though he remained a constant thorn in the side of Goebbels.

Kulturpolitik in the Third Reich had a 'revolutionary' role in an attempt to create a 'people's culture' which would express the new art forms of the National Socialist revolution. Government statistics regularly purported to show the increasing number of 'people's theatres', 'people's films', 'people's sculpture', 'people's radios', etc., all of which were intended to reflect the manner in which art was being brought to the people and expressing the 'national community'. Objectivity and opinion, however, were eliminated, and replaced by a definition of truth as defined by the Nazi regime. Conformity of opinion and action were also secured within the *Kunstwelt* itself. Addressing the opening of the 'Week of German Books' (an annual event) in Weimar in October 1936, Goebbels argued that writers, for example, should no longer follow their own whims but feel obliged to work for the nation: 'Now the pen has been compelled to serve the nation like the sword and the plough', he declared.[11]

In order that art should reflect the ideological precepts of National Socialism, it was imperative that artists themselves should be sympathetic towards the aims and ideals of the new regime. Accordingly a 'cleansing' process of *Entjudung* eliminated Jews and other political undesirables from working in German cultural life. The striking feature of the 'nazification' of German cultural life was the alacrity with which intellectuals, writers, artists and academics eagerly collaborated in the process. In some cases this could be put down to idealism but more often than not 'self-coordination' (*Selbstgleichschaltung*) was an opportunistic means of career advancement. The result of these measures was inevitably an overwhelming cultural mediocrity that produced 'safe', conventional art, rather than the vibrant 'people's culture' that the regime purported to encourage. In 1941 Goebbels was forced to admit at a press conference: 'The National Socialist State has given up the ambition of trying to produce art itself. It has wisely contented itself with encouraging art and gearing it spiritually and intellectually to its educative function for the people.'[12] Before taking up these issues and analysing the themes disseminated by the regime, I should first like to discuss the major channels of communication and the manner in which they were 'coordinated' into the Ministry for Propaganda, the RKK, and the Central Propaganda Office of the Party.

RADIO

When Goebbels became Minister for Propaganda, the newspaper and film industries were still privately owned; the broadcasting system, however, had been State-regulated since 1925 by means of the Reich Radio Company (*Reichsrundfunkgesellschaft* – RRG). Under this system, 51 per cent of the capital was owned by the Ministry of Posts, which also appointed a Radio Commissioner (*Reichsfunkkommissar*). However, the RRG had little say over programme content, which was the responsibility of nine regional broadcasting companies, who owned the remaining 49 per cent of the capital.[13]

Although the Nazis had failed to gain access to this medium while in opposition, once in power the 'coordination' of German radio proved comparatively easy, despite a few initial setbacks. From the moment he assumed power, Goebbels recognised its propaganda potential and he was determined to make the most of this relatively new medium. In his address to representatives of the press on 15 March 1933, Goebbels had revealed that the radio would have the responsibility of bringing the people closer to the National Socialist State. He hinted that the Nazis had already gone some way to achieving this, because

> our radio propaganda is not produced in a vacuum, in radio stations, but in the atmosphere-laden halls of mass gatherings. In this way every listener has become a direct participant in these events. I have a vision of a new and topical radio, a radio that really takes account of the spirit of our time . . . a radio that is aware of its great national responsibility.

Goebbels clearly saw in radio an instrument not only to create uniformity but also to guide public opinion towards the Nazi concept of 'national community' as the ideological obverse to the class conflict that had been such a feature of Weimar politics. The theme of *Volksgemeinschaft* also figured prominently in his first address to managerial staff of German radio in the Haus des Rundfunks on 25 March 1933 (see Document 2). Goebbels began by flattering his audience ('I hold radio to be the most modern and the most important instrument of mass influence that exists anywhere'), and he continued: 'I am also of the opinion – and one shouldn't say this out loud – that in the long term radio will replace newspapers.' The Minister for Propaganda concluded his speech by declaring:

> I am placing a major responsibility in your hands, for you have in your hands the most modern instrument in existence for influencing the masses. By means of this instrument you are the creators of public opinion. If you perform this well, we shall win over the people. . . . As the piano is to the pianist, so the transmitter is to you, the instrument that you play on as sovereign masters of public opinion.[14]

In his efforts to consolidate his control over radio, Goebbels' immediate problem was to break down the federal structure, over which the Reich possessed limited economic and political control. He also had to contend with resistance from Hermann Göring, who, as Prussian Minister of the Interior, supported the independence of the regional authorities for radio. Thus before Goebbels could assert his new ministry's control over radio, indeed over all rival agencies, he was obliged to persuade Hitler to issue a supplementary decree on 30 June 1933 which laid out in detail those responsibilities which were to be transferred to RMVP from other ministries and rival agencies. The regulations stated:

> The Reich Minister for Popular Enlightenment and Propaganda is responsible for all influences on the intellectual life of the nation; public relations for the State, culture, and the economy, for instructing the domestic and foreign public about them and for the administration of all the institutions serving these purposes.[15]

Although this decree stated unequivocally that responsibility for radio now rested with the RMVP, to clear this matter up still required a personal letter from Hitler (dated 15 July) to the *Reichsstatthalter* (Governors), who had assumed control of *Länder* governments on behalf of the Reich. In fact it would take several months more before the whole broadcasting system was unified, on 1 April 1934, under a drastically purged 'Reich Radio Company', which would in theory be subordinate to Department III of the RMVP. The nine regional stations now became merely branches (renamed 'Reich Radio Stations') with general managers centrally controlled by the Ministry for Propaganda. Once this organisational structure had been established, the RMVP could then implement what it termed *Rundfunkeinheit*, complete unity in all radio matters. This entailed a 'pooling-together' of all broadcasting resources, very much on the model of fascist Italy. The first important step towards integrating the technical, commercial and listening side of radio came with the formation on 8 July 1933 of the RRG under the new Director of Broadcasting, Eugen Hadamovsky, a former motor mechanic, who had originally formed a 'voluntary' organisation called the 'National Socialist Radio Chamber' on 3 July. Six months later this would become the official Reich Chamber of Radio. Hadamovsky was also given the additional title of Reich Transmitter Leader (*Reichssendeleiter*) and in his capacity as overlord for broadcasting he established a direct link to Goebbels and was largely responsible for approving all important broadcasts. Eugen Hadamovsy was described by Willi A. Boelcke (an aid in the RMVP) as a man 'with the uncontrollable enthusiasm of the born fanatic'.[16] Sadly from Goebbels point of view, he was also largely incompetent. In an attempt to neutralise his incompetence, Goebbels appointed Dr Heinrich Glasmaier as Reich Superintendent of the Greater German radio network. Glasmaier proved no better than Hadamovsky and in 1942 Glasmaier was deprived of his authority and Hadamovsky was shunted sideways to the Reich Propaganda Central Office where he could do less harm.

Mention must also be made of the 'German Wireless Service' (DDD) under the leadership of Hans Fritsche. The DDD was responsible for all news broadcasts and was attached not to the radio but to the press department of the RMVP. Fritsche was no Party apparatchik and in fact had worked for the Hugenberg telegraph company and later became director of the radio news service where he had his own broadcasting slot surveying the political press. Taking no chances, Fritsche joined the Party on 1 May 1933 and remained in control of all German news broadcasts until his appointment as head of the press department in 1938. In 1942 Goebbels promoted him to head of the Ministry's radio division and Goebbels' commissioner for the political restructuring of the Greater German Radio where he was able to issue daily radio communiques to all Reich propaganda offices. Fritsche represented the continuity between Weimar and Nazi politics. On the other hand, Hans Flesch, who had been responsible for modernising radio broadcasting during Weimar with his pioneering live reporting and audience participation, was not retained but instead sent to a concentration camp.

Membership of the RRG now became compulsory for everyone connected with broadcasting, whether radio engineers or salesmen of wireless sets. Within a year, however, control of the manufacturing side of the industry would be removed from the Reich Chamber of Radio and transferred to the Reich Ministry of Economics. The Chamber would also be frustrated in its attempts to implement legislation (*Reichsrundfunkrecht*) that would secure complete control of broadcasting for the RMVP. Although a working compromise would eventually be reached between the RMVP and the radio industry in the form of a voluntary liaison committee, the original concept of an integrated 'radio unity' can be seen to have been hopelessly illusory.[17]

Despite these setbacks, the new masters of German broadcasting never lost their faith in the medium. It was a faith confirmed as early as 1934 by the results of the radio campaign to reincorporate the Saarland into Germany. During the Weimar Republic, radio had been used by successive governments as a means of contacting German-speaking minorities (*Volksdeutsche*) living abroad. Under the Treaty of Versailles, the future of the Saar was to be settled by a League of Nations plebiscite in 1935. In January 1934, however, Goebbels had pre-empted this by setting up a specific office to coordinate propaganda broadcasts into the Saar area with the innocuous title of the Westdeutsche Gemeinschaftsdienst. He also distributed cheap radio sets and encouraged National Socialist listeners' associations to organise community listening to important Nazi events. The content of these broadcasts was based on highly charged emotional appeals to past German grievances. In January 1935, 91 per cent of those who voted in the plebiscite opted for the return of their province to a National Socialist Germany.

Although the Nazis were unlikely to lose in the plebiscite, there can be little doubt that Goebbels' broadcasts played a decisive part in achieving such a clear majority. It should be noted that in conjunction with these broadcasts the Nazis instigated a ruthless campaign of 'whispered propaganda' (*Flüsterpropaganda*). This was a typical Nazi psychological device, intended to convince the voter that the Party knew how individuals voted and therefore, by implication, that they would be punished or rewarded accordingly. Needless to say, the success of the Saarland campaign convinced Nazi agitators that the planned use of radio propaganda could achieve almost any political goal. Not surprisingly, radio was used extensively for propaganda purposes in the following year for the 1936 Berlin Olympic Games. The extensive radio coverage provided by the Nazis together with their impressive technical know-how made an indelible impression on foreign audiences and on journalists reporting the Games.

The technical mobilisation of German radio as the 'voice of the nation' is a history of remarkable accomplishment. To increase the number of listeners, the Nazis persuaded manufacturers to produce one of the cheapest wireless sets in Europe, the VE 3031 or *Volksempfänger* ('people's receiver'). The 'people's radio' was heavily subsidised so that it would be affordable to all workers. In fact two versions of radio receivers were quickly produced: one for 75RM, and the *Volksempfänger* for 35RM payable in instalments. A poster issued by the RMVP advertising the *Volksempfänger* showed one of these uniform radio sets surrounded by thousands of people, with the caption: 'All Germany listens to the Führer with the People's Radio.' One-and-a-half million sets were produced during 1933, and in 1934 the figure for radio sets passed the 6 million mark, indicating an increase of more than 1 million in a single year. The long-term aim was to install a set in every home in Germany. Indeed, by the beginning of the war over 70 per cent of all households owned a wireless set – the highest percentage anywhere in the world. The 'people's receivers' were designed with a limited range, which meant that Germans who purchased them were unable to receive foreign broadcasts. Great emphasis was placed on the encouragement of community listening, changing listeners' thinking from what Hadamovsky referred to as 'the anarchic intellectualism of the individual to the organically developed spirituality of the community'.[18] Moreover, in order to ensure the widest possible listening audience, local Party branches were encouraged to organise community listening. On these occasions an army of National Socialist radio functionaries (*Funkwarte*) took charge of the event and staged what came to be referred to as 'National Moments' (*Stunden der Nation*). When a speech by a Nazi leader or an important announcement was to be made, this network of radio wardens established loudspeakers in public squares, factories, offices, schools, even restaurants. Sirens would howl and professional life throughout the nation would stop for the duration of the 'community reception' in an effort to persuade the individual citizen to identify with the nation. The radio warden was also responsible for popularising the radio and encouraging people to share their sets with friends and neighbours. In addition, these wardens, who were invariably Party members, forwarded criticism of and requests for specific programmes. A leading Nazi radio propagandist compared communal listening with the total experience of worship in a church.[19] More sinisterly, the wardens also monitored for compliance; it being forbidden to move from one's desk or machinery until the broadcast had finished. The radio warden became notorious during the war, when he reported those Germans listening to foreign broadcasts (see Chapter 5).

The radio soon came to be regarded as the Nazi regime's principal propaganda medium for the dissemination of National Socialist ideas and the creation of a single public opinion. In order to achieve these objectives, special emphasis was placed on political broadcasts. Listeners soon learned to associate signature tunes with various Party leaders who would make regular speeches over the radio. Hitler's speeches were preceded by his favourite march, the *Badenweiler*; Goebbels' annual eulogy on Hitler's birthday was accompanied by Wagner's 'Meistersinger' overture, and the Führer's speech on Heroes' Day by Beethoven's 'Eroica' symphony. It has been estimated that in 1933 alone, fifty speeches by Hitler were transmitted. By 1935, Hitler's speeches reached an audience of over 56,000,000. The radio was, not surprisingly, described as 'the towering herald of National Socialism', the means of expression of a united State. In his desire to create 'one single public opinion' Goebbels maintained that it was imperative that this 'spiritual weapon of the totalitarian State' should enjoy the confidence of the people. With the radio, he declared, 'we have destroyed the spirit of rebellion'.

Although the radio continued to play an important part in the Nazis' propaganda arsenal, it was not without its shortcomings. The first disappointment was the discovery that Hitler, if confined in the studio without an audience, was uncomfortable, and ineffective as a speaker. Accordingly from October 1933, when he announced Germany's departure from the League of Nations, until the end of the war Hitler did not speak in a studio again. Instead his speeches would be transmitted from public meetings (often specially assembled for the purpose), where he gained direct contact with an audience and was thus provided with the essential stimulus for his oratory.

The second disappointment was that in the middle of the war the intense concentration on political broadcasting was proving to be counter-productive with the average listener. Radio wardens were reporting that listeners were so bored that they were switching off. Therefore in 1942 Goebbels decided that almost 70 per cent of transmissions should be devoted to light music in order to guarantee a large audience for the important political bulletins. Indeed, the most popular wartime radio programme was *Wunschkonzert*, a request show of songs, music and words designed to link the home and fighting fronts. Thus there were limits to radio's ability to create uniformity of opinion and action. But Goebbels learned to mix the content of transmissions accordingly, and this corresponded to his wider belief as Minister for Propaganda in mixing entertainment with propaganda. Despite these drawbacks, there can be little doubt that the most impressive achievement of Nazi broadcasting lay in the creation of such a mass listening public. Neither fascist Italy nor the Soviet Union used the radio to such a degree on its less literate population.

PRESS

The *Gleichschaltung* of the press proved infinitely more complicated for the Nazis than the radio, which had, for some time, experienced a degree of State involvement. The press, on the other hand, was associated with a whole plethora of political parties, pressure groups, religious bodies and private companies. In 1933 Germany could boast more daily newspapers than the combined total of Britain, France and Italy.

According to O. J. Hale,[20] the Third Reich adopted a three-pronged approach to the control of the press: first, all those involved in the press industry were rigorously controlled; second, the Party's publishing-house, the Eher Verlag, gradually acquired the ownership – directly or indirectly

– of the vast majority of the German press; and, finally, the RMVP controlled the content of the press by means of the State-controlled press agency (Deutsches Nachrichtenbüro) and daily press briefings and directives. The response of the publishers and journalists to the Nazi take-over is most revealing. The publishers' association (*Verein deutscher Zeitungsverleger*), effectively 'coordinated' themselves. They immediately sought a *modus vivendi* with the new regime by first of all replacing politically 'unacceptable' members and then appointing Max Amann, the head of Eher Verlag, as chairman of their organisation, under the revised title of the 'Association of German Newspaper Publishers' (*Reichsverband deutscher Zeitungsverleger*). On 15 November 1933, Amann was appointed president of the Reich Press Chamber to which the publishers were affiliated. The Reich Association of the German Press (Reichsverband der deutschen Presse) likewise felt compelled to appoint the Nazi press chief, Otto Dietrich, as their chairman. On 30 April 1933, the Association announced that membership would be compulsory and that all members of the Association would be screened for their 'racial and political reliability'.

In his speech to the press of 15 March 1933, Goebbels referred to the press as a piano on which the Government could plan to influence the public in whatever direction it desired. However, although the Nazis looked upon the press as an instrument of mass influence, they were aware that their success had been due more to the spoken than to the printed word. In order to reassure his audience, Goebbels presented himself to the press as a fellow-journalist who had experienced the frustrations of working in opposition to the Government of the day: 'If opposition papers claim today that their issues have been forbidden, they can talk to me as a fellow-sufferer. There is, I think, no representative of any newspaper banned fifteen times, as mine was!' According to Goebbels, the press must not 'merely inform; it must also instruct'. He argued that there was 'no absolute objectivity', and the press should expect to receive not simply information from the Government but also instructions: 'We want to have a press which cooperates with the Government just as the Government wants to cooperate with the press. . . . We do not want a state of daily warfare.' He also urged the press to change its style of reporting in order to reflect the 'crusading' spirit of the time: 'The reader should get the impression that the writer is in reality a speaker standing behind him.' Newspapers in the Third Reich were to capture the atmosphere of the emotion-laden mass meetings. In this respect, the Party newspaper, the *Völkischer Beobachter*, would give the lead.

One of the most important tasks confronting the RMVP when it came to power was the elimination of alternative sources of information. However, the fact that the German press was not centralised like its British counterpart proved a major obstacle. The lack of a 'national' press, together with long-standing regional loyalties, persuaded Goebbels to undertake the

Gleichschaltung of the German press in gradual stages. This would have the dual advantage of allowing Nazi journalists to be trained for their future role and, more importantly, of not suddenly breaking readers' habits.

The emergency decree issued immediately following the Reichstag fire on 28 February 1933 allowed the regime to suspend publication and include the spreading of rumours and false news as treasonable offences. The Reichstag fire served as the pretext for the suppression of the Communist and Social Democratic press, which was either destroyed or taken over by Nazi newspapers. Catholic and other middle-class democratic dailies soon followed, as Nazi-controlled advertising agencies switched their contracts to the Nazi press. However, some liberal papers, notably the *Frankfurter Zeitung* and the *Berliner Tageblatt*, were still permitted to publish. So too, for a while, was the flourishing *Generalanzeiger* press, which showed little interest in politics; but its confessional character posed a moral threat and its popularity a competitive one. The Nazis disapproved of both and eventually undertook measures to prohibit them.[21] At the beginning of 1933, the Nazis owned fifty-nine daily newspapers with a combined circulation of only 782,121, which represented only 2.5 per cent of the population. By the end of the year, they had acquired a further twenty-seven dailies and increased their circulation by 2.4 million copies per day. In 1934, they would acquire the large Jewish publishing firm of Ullstein. By 1939 the Eher Verlag, largely as a result of Amann's ordinances, controlled, either directly or indirectly, two-thirds of the German press. Many of these papers retained their old names so that their readers would be unaware of the change of ownership. The elimination of many non-Party newspapers was followed by the fusion of Germany's two principal news agencies, Wolff's Telegraphisches Büro and Hugenberg's Telegraphen-Union, into a new official agency, the Deutsches Nachrichtenbüro (DNB). It was soon providing over half the material which appeared in the German press, and newspapers were often confined to simply publishing verbatim a story put out by the news agency.

The other important instrument of political control over the newspaper industry was the Reich Press Chamber, and particularly the professional institutions under its tutelage. The Reich Association of the German Press became a corporate member of the Press Chamber, which not only acted as a kind of labour exchange for the profession by keeping registers of 'racially pure' editors and journalists, but also regarded the 'regulation of competition' within the industry as a perfectly legitimate function. The Press Chamber was determined to imbue all members with a strong National Socialist bias and to educate a new generation of journalists along strict Party lines so that they would, in Goebbels' words, 'take a stand for the new Reich and its Führer, not because they have to, but because they wish to do so'.

Having regulated both entry into the profession and the flow of news from its source, Goebbels then tackled the problem of editorial policy and content. From 1933 the press department of the RMVP took over the daily press conferences which had been a regular feature of journalistic life during the Weimar Republic. The content of the newspapers was rigidly controlled through the very detailed directives issued by the RMVP, which even covered the length of articles on particular topics and where they should be placed in the paper. Admission to these conferences was now severely controlled along Party and racial lines. As one senior journalist for the *Frankfurter Zeitung* observed:

> The press conference *with* the Reich Government established in 1917 was changed by the National Socialists on their seizure of power in Germany in 1933 into a 'press conference of the Reich Government'. So it was now an institution of the Government. There it gave directives, laid down language variations, and brought the 'press into line'. . . . Before 1933, these press conferences were run by journalists and the Government was their guest; after they were run by the Government.[22]

Such restrictions were soon to be reinforced by the so-called 'Editors' Law' (*Schriftleitergesetz*) of 4 October 1933 (see Document 5). From now on editors of newspapers and political periodicals would be made responsible for any infringement of Government directives. In effect, the law reversed the roles of the publisher and the editor, reducing the publisher to the position of a business manager.[23] The obligatory character of all directives and decrees was stressed repeatedly, ruling out editorial independence. Clause 14 of the regulations obliged editors to keep out of the newspapers everything 'which is calculated to weaken the strength of the Reich abroad or at home, the resolution of the community, German defence, culture or the economy, or to injure the religious sensibilities of others, as well as everything offensive to the honour or dignity of a German'. By turning the individual editor into the regime's censor, this piece of legislation went a considerable way towards achieving uniformity of the press by transforming journalism into a public corporation. Editors and journalists could now only work if they were officially accredited, and Goebbels, as Minister for Propaganda was appointed president of the Press Association with the power to veto any journalist entering the profession. A system of professional courts was set up to enforce the law with the power to reprimand, fine or expel offenders.[24]

Once some degree of uniformity had been achieved, Goebbels believed it important that the content of the press should not become lifeless. This proved difficult given the fact that newspapers were restricted to publishing Government directives. Therefore the themes commonly associated with Nazi propaganda – charismatic leadership, appeals to national unity, anti-Semitism, etc. – were supplemented by special appeals and special campaigns aimed at securing repeated gestures of conformity from the people. Such appeals and campaigns were ideally suited to the medium of the press. They would take the form of a positive discussion of the deeds of the Führer, or of some aspect of the Volk community life, such as the 'Strength through Joy' programme. A particular favourite of Goebbels was the campaign to obtain more public money for the 'Winter Help' schemes. This invariably manifested itself in the slogan 'A Sacrifice for the Community', by which housewives and workers were urged to restrict their eating consumption to the *Eintopfgericht* ('one-pot meal') in order to conserve food, especially meat ('the meal of sacrifice for the Reich'). Alternatively, there was the annual 'National Day of Solidarity', which developed out of 'Winter Help' and which was a sort of plebiscite for the regime. Here the press was urged to stress not only the amount of money that was collected for the community, but also the uniqueness of the event and the voluntary character of the donations. The German public's response to these campaigns is analysed in Chapter 4.

The press was also instrumental in the Nazis' virulent anti-Semitic campaigns. Sections of the press, particularly *Der Stürmer* and the *Völkischer Beobachter*, continued to depict the Jew as barbaric and 'subhuman' and denounced alleged Jewish 'criminality' and the 'conspiracy' of foreign Jews against Germany. Campaigns waged in these papers might be used to prepare the public for some forthcoming anti-Jewish legislation. The press was also directed to answer foreign criticism of their racial policy by means of counter-attacks which were also intended to heighten people's awareness of their Aryan origins and characteristics. Anti-Semitic propaganda became so omnipresent that in terms of everyday journalism few news items or articles could be published without such a slant.

Quantitatively as well as qualitatively, the national press declined during the Third Reich. When the Nazis came to power there were approximately 4,700 daily newspapers, reflecting a variety of political persuasions. The NSDAP controlled less than 3 per cent of all German dailies and periodicals; in 1944, 82 per cent of the remaining 977 newspapers were firmly under the Party's control. Between 1933 and 1938 a total of 10,000 periodicals and learned journals had been reduced to 5,000, a decline symbolising the basic anti-intellectualism of National Socialism in general.

The overriding feature of the press until the outbreak of war at least was the deliberate sacrifice of speedy reportage of news in favour of staggeringly comprehensive, but unwieldy, press directives. In many respects Nazi propagandists favoured broadcasting at the expense of the press. Hitler, who was a voracious newspaper reader, is said to have been hostile to the press and to journalists. Not only did he believe that pictures and spoken words had greater impact than printed words, but he also resented the press for its vehement criticism of him during the years when the Nazis were in opposition. Although he rarely received journalists, he would occasionally praise the press for their performance. The most celebrated occasion was on 10 November 1938, when he addressed 400 representatives of the German press in Munich. Complimenting them for their work preceding the Munich Conference, Hitler went on to describe the role of press propaganda both abroad and at home as 'decisive' in the acquisition of the Sudetenland by Germany: 'Gentlemen, this time we have actually obtained 10 million men with over 100,000 square kilometres of territory through propaganda in the service of an idea. This is something momentous.'[25] Goebbels, on the other hand, who recognised good journalism, was never entirely happy about the drab uniformity of the German press which was the outcome of his policy. He nevertheless defended the press laws by arguing that the free expression of opinion could seriously threaten the National Socialist State, and continued to reject suggestions that problems should be frankly discussed in the press. His directives became so minutely detailed that the papers were virtually written for the editors by the Ministry for Propaganda. The Government straitjacket so destroyed journalistic initiative that Goebbels was prompted to remark in his diary: 'No decent journalist with any feeling of honour in his bones can stand the way he is handled by the press department of the Reich Government . . . Any man who still has a residue of honour will be very careful not to become a journalist.'

FILM

Hitler and Goebbels shared an interest in film. Shortly after his appointment as Minister for Popular Enlightenment and Propaganda, Goebbels declared that the German cinema had been given the mission of conquering the world as the vanguard of the Nazi troops. Film propaganda was Goebbels' special interest, for he believed in the power of the cinema to influence people's thoughts and beliefs, if not their actions.

As early as the 1920s the National Socialists had infiltrated their members into many spheres of public life.[26] The entire organisation of the Party, the division into administrative sectors and the structure of leadership were built up as a state within a state. The Nazis were therefore well placed to take control of a film industry which had to a large extent prepared itself to be controlled. The *Gleichschaltung* of the German cinema was affected behind the scenes by a process of which the ordinary citizen was largely unaware. To achieve this end, a plethora of complex laws and decrees and an intricate state machinery were instigated to prevent non-conformity. Pursuing a policy that was to become traditional in the Third Reich, the Party organisation was kept separate from State administration at both national and regional levels, while at the same time remaining closely linked with it.

During 1932 the industry was still recoiling from the continuing effects of the recession in world trade and the advent of talking films, which involved considerable expenditure at a time when total receipts were falling, companies were going bankrupt and cinemas were changing hands at an alarming rate.[27] The German film industry responded with the so-called 'SPIO-Plan' of 1932; SPIO (*Spitzenorganisation der deutschen Filmindustrie e.V.*) was the industry's main professional representative body, and its principal concern was to strike a satisfactory relationship between the production, distribution and exhibition sectors, while at the same time retaining the traditional structure of the industry. Significantly, SPIO was dominated by the large combines (particularly Ufa), and it was no surprise that they should produce a plan that discriminated so blatantly against the German Cinema Owners' Association (*Reichsverband Deutscher Lichtspieltheater e.V.*), whom they accused of flooding the market with too many cinemas, price-cutting and retaining a disproportionate share of total receipts. The Cinema Owners' Association retorted by complaining, quite justifiably, that they were expected to exhibit films they were given regardless of their suitability in terms of box-office appeal.

In the months following Hitler's appointment as Chancellor in January 1933 the divisions within the Party which had flared up in 1932 became an issue again. Certain organisations – such as the Nazi 'trade union', the *Nationalsozialistische Betriebszellen Organisation* (NSBO), and the Fighting League for German Culture (*Kampfbund für deutsche Kultur* – KfdK) – put forward radical solutions to the film industry's problems, demanding centralisation and the banning of all films which offended the *völkische Weltanschauung*. Goebbels, on the other hand, was more realistic and appreciated that the *Filmwelt* did not welcome these forces of Nazi extremism. He was unwilling to undertake an immediate nationalisation of the industry, not only on ideological grounds but for the pragmatic reasons that Alfred Hugenberg, who owned the largest film company, Ufa, was a member of the new cabinet as Minister of Economics and that the Party in general depended on big business for its finances.

However, on 9 February 1933, at the Cinema Owners' annual conference, the Nazi elements demanded that their leader, Engl, should be elected to the Association's board. Their argument that the small owners faced bankruptcy in the face of unfair competition from the large combines seemed to be confirmed when the SPIO-Plan was published nine days later. On 18 March the entire board of the Cinema Owners' Association resigned, thus giving Engl and the NSDAP complete control. They responded by demanding that all cinema owners express unconditional loyalty to Engl's leadership within two weeks.[28]

Cinema owners were not the only sector of the industry to be effectively 'coordinated' in this manner; throughout March and April the NSBO had been active in all spheres of film production – from cameramen to film actors and composers. When the Nazis banned all trade unions in early May, the industry's 'official' trade union DACHO (*Dach-Organisation der*

Filmschaffenden Deutschlands e.V.) was dissolved and absorbed into the NSBO, which was itself transferred automatically to the German Labour Front (*Deutsche Arbeitsfront*), the only permissible trade union; DACHO therefore had little chance of preventing its own dissolution, though there is no evidence of any united stand being organised.

The film industry presented a number of structural, economic and artistic problems for the builders of the new German society. Significant of the high estimation of the cinema in the Third Reich is the fact that the Reich Film Chamber (*Reichsfilmkammer*) was founded by Goebbels some months before the Reich Chamber of Culture, of which it became a part. The creation of the *Reichsfilmkammer* (RFK) on 14 July 1933 is an excellent example of the process of coordination in that it allowed the RMVP to exert its control over both film-makers and the film industry as a whole. The structure of the RFK was scarcely changed after it had been incorporated into the Reich Chamber of Culture (RKK). Its head and all-responsible president was subordinate only to the president of the RKK, that is, the Minister for Propaganda. The first president of the RFK was Dr Fritz Scheuermann, a financial expert who had been involved in secret plans to implement the recommendations of the SPIO-Plan, which had been merged with the RFK in July. Scheuermann was assisted by a vice-president, Arnold Räther, who was also head of the Film Office of the NSDAP Propaganda Office. There was an Advisory Council (*Präsidialrat*) consisting of financial experts from the RMVP and the banks; and specialist advisory councils taken from the individual *Fachgruppen*, as the former SPIO elements were now called. The various sections of the industry were grouped together into ten departments. These ten departments controlled all film activities in Germany. The centralisation, however, did not lead to what the Minister of Propaganda claimed – the harmonisation of all branches of the industry – but it did harm the substance of the German film by limiting personal and economic initiative and artistic freedom.

It must also be remembered that the *Filmwelt* greeted the Nazis with some misgivings. The industry was not entirely convinced that it could expect much constructive assistance from the new regime. To offset these fears and also to gain control over film finance, a Filmkreditbank (FKB) was established. It was announced on 1 June 1933 as a provider of credit for the crisis-ridden film economy, which had been badly hit by the costs of installing equipment for the new 'talking movies' and the effects of the slump on film audiences.

The idea of the Filmkreditbank had originally been proposed in the SPIO-Plan with the aim of encouraging independent production by lending money to approved film-makers at highly competitive rates. In practice the FKB was to create the beginnings of the National Socialists' disastrous film policy and to result in the dependence of private film producers on the Nazi

State. However, at the time of its inauguration the FKB was greeted with great enthusiasm from all sides of the film industry. By 1936, the FKB was financing over 73 per cent of all German feature films. The result was that the smaller companies' share of the market continued to decline as the process of concentration was relentlessly increased. This proved a further step towards creating dependence and establishing a State monopoly in order to destroy independent initiative.

The Filmkreditbank functioned to all intents and purposes as a normal commercial undertaking, except that it was not expected to make large profits. It took the form of a private limited-liability company formed out of the Reichskreditgesellschaft, SPIO (acting as a cover for the Reichsfilm-kammer), and a number of the main banks. However, within a year the banks transferred their shares to the RFK and on Goebbels' personal initiative the president of the latter became the Filmkreditbank's chairman. The procedure for securing finance from the bank was that a producer had to show that he could raise 30 per cent of the production costs as well as convincing the FKB that the film stood a good chance of making a profit. The film then became the property of the bank until the loan was repaid. Thus private finance was excluded from all freedom of credit and opportunities for profit. Within a short time this financial body would also become an important means of securing both economic and political conformity. The FKB, acting on behalf of the Government, could refuse all credit at the preproduction stage until a film reflected the wishes of the regime. Significantly, there is no evidence to suggest that the film industry was unwilling to accept this form of self-censorship.

Apart from regulating the financing of films, one of the main purposes of establishing the Reichsfilmkammer was the removal of Jews and other *entartete Künstler* (degenerate artists) from German cultural life, since only racially 'pure' Germans could become members. Whoever wished to participate in any aspect of film production was forced to become a member of the RFK. By 1936, the Party had begun publishing a new illustrated film magazine, *Der deutsche Film,* with the intention of disseminating Party policy relating to the film industry through consciously anti-Semitic propaganda. Statistics were published in film magazines and books, which purported to expose an overwhelmingly Jewish influence in film production. Although the industry had been heavily dependent on Jewish artists and executives, these figures were a gross exaggeration. However, because Nazi propaganda identified Jewish influence with the downfall of German culture, it was only to be expected that the Party would use the struggle in the film industry to stir up racial hatred. Not surprisingly, these policies resulted in the emigration of all those who either could not or would not submit to such conditions. The loss of talent was severe, but the Nazis were able to retain a reservoir of talented actors, technicians and artistic staff.

On 28 March 1933, Goebbels introduced himself to the *Filmwelt* at a SPIO-DACHO function at the Kaiserhof. Goebbels presented himself as an inveterate film addict (which he was), and showed considerable ingenuity in mitigating many of the industry's fears caused by the already extensive exodus. Films, he said, were to have an important place in the culture of the new Germany (for the full text of the speech, see Document 3). But he warned that film-makers must, in future, learn to regard their profession as a service, and not merely as a source of profit. Goebbels went on to mention four films that had made a lasting impression on him. They were *Battleship Potemkin, Anna Karenina, Die Nibelungen* and *Der Rebell*. According to Goebbels, the German cinema was in a state of spiritual crisis which 'will continue until we are courageous enough radically to reform German films'. National Socialist film-makers, he argued, 'should capture the spirit of the time'. What was not required in these films was 'parade-ground marching and the blowing of trumpets'. In calling for the industry's cooperation in this new venture Goebbels concluded by declaring that with this new conviction 'a new moral ethos will arise', allowing it 'to be said of German films, as in other fields, "Germany leads the world!"'.

To consolidate his position, Goebbels still desired more power than he had hitherto secured through the Reichskulturkammer legislation. He also needed some form of legal confirmation to be able to supervise films in the early stages of production. Goebbels settled both these issues by creating a revised version of the Reich Cinema Law (*Reichslichtspielgesetz*), which became law on 16 February 1934. This legislation attempted to create a new 'positive' censorship by which the State encouraged 'good' National Socialist films instead of merely discouraging 'bad' ones (the full text of the law and subsequent amendments is reprinted in Document 6).

The new Cinema Law anticipated three different channels through which this positive censorship could be achieved: a compulsory script censorship, an increase in the number of criteria according to which the Censorship Office (*Filmprüfstelle*) might ban a film, and an enlarged system of distinction marks (*Prädikate*) awarded by the regime to worthy films.

The most significant innovation of the Cinema Law was the institution of a pre-censor (*Vorzensor*), a role undertaken by an RMVP official called the Reich Film Director (*Reichsfilmdramaturg*). If a producer wished to make a film, he had first to submit a 'treatment' to the *Dramaturg*, who was appointed directly by Goebbels. If this was passed, the full scenario could be written, and this would have to be approved before shooting could begin. In most cases the *Dramaturg* could supervise every stage of production. The orders issued and the changes suggested by him were binding. As the representative of the RMVP, he could even interfere with the censorship exercised by the Censorship Office in Berlin.

The new film legislation greatly extended the powers of censorship, which it prescribed in some detail. It replaced the original law of 12 May

1920, which had regulated films during the Weimar Republic. Although the Weimar censorship was initially a democratic one – 'films may not be withheld on account of political, social, religious, ethical, or ideological tendencies' – the intervention of the censor was permitted when 'a film endangers public order or safety . . . or endangers the German image or the country's relationship with foreign states'. The examination of films was delegated to two censorship offices (*Prüfstellen*), in Berlin and in Munich. Each office had two chairmen, who examined films with the aid of four assessors drawn from the teaching and legal professions and the film industry itself. However, the 1934 law joined the two *Prüfstellen* together and incorporated them as a subsidiary office of the RMVP. The procedure by which the Censorship Office reached its decision was also revised. Under the 1920 law, decisions were arrived at by means of a majority vote and if a film was banned its producer could appeal to the Supreme Censorship Office (*Oberprüfstelle*). After 1934 the power to decide whether or not a film should be exhibited rested entirely with the chairman.

According to Paragraph 4 of the 1934 Cinema Law, all kinds of films were to be submitted to the censor. Public and private screenings were made equal in law. Even film advertising in the cinemas was censored. For each print of a film a censorship card had to be issued which contained the official report on the film together with an embossed stamp of the German Eagle. In all matters concerning censorship, the Minister for Propaganda had the right of intervention. He could either appeal to the *Oberprüfstelle* or, by circumventing the *Prüfstelle*, he could forbid the release of various films directly. In the Second Amendment to the Cinema Law, of 28 June 1935, Goebbels was given extra powers to ban any film without reference to the *Prüfstelle* if he felt it was in the public's interest. Not only was the entire censorship apparatus centralised in Berlin, but the previous right of local governments to request re-examination of films was now the exclusive prerogative of the RMVP.

In addition to direct censorship, the film industry depended on a system of distinction marks (*Prädikate*), which was really a form of negative taxation. During the Weimar Republic these distinction marks were considered an honour and an opportunity to gain tax reductions. Under the Nazis, however, a film had to obtain a *Prädikate* not only to benefit from tax deductions but to be allowed to be exhibited at all. Films without these distinction marks needed special permission to be shown. A further incentive was that producers with a *Prädikate* now received an extra share of the film's profits. By 1939, there were eleven distinctions, ranging from 'politically and artistically especially valuable' to 'culturally valuable'. 'Film of the Nation' (*Film der Nation*) and 'valuable for youth' (*Jugendwert*) differed from the others in that they carried no tax relief. However, these were special awards which greatly enhanced a film's status. Furthermore, they were decisive for selection in schools and Nazi youth organisations.

After 1938 no cinema owner was allowed to refuse to exhibit a film with a political distinction mark if a distributor offered one.

The *Prädikate* system not only produced certain financial advantages but also helped to establish the appropriate expectations and responses on the part of cinema audiences. These distinction marks were naturally a key to the political and propaganda content in the description of films. 'Politically valuable' clearly reflected a political message that was completely accept-able to the Party, whereas 'artistically valuable' was understood in the sense of cultural propaganda and was given only to the prestige films and those reserved for export.

Secure in the knowledge that film censorship had been reorganised according to the principles of the NSDAP, Goebbels now embarked on his next project, the nationalisation of the film industry. In fact this would be carried out in two stages, largely through a process of which the ordinary citizen was totally unaware. When the Nazis came to power there were four major film companies operating in Germany. To have nationalised them immediately would have damaged their contacts with foreign distri-butors, which in turn would have reduced the not inconsiderable revenue and foreign currency earned from Germany's film exports. It seemed advisable, therefore, to proceed warily with the nationalisation of the cinema industry and not alarm the outside world unnecessarily. However, as German film exports continued to decline under the Nazis and produc-tion costs continued to increase, the RMVP decided secretly to buy out the major shares in the film companies and to refer to them as *staatsmittelbar* (indirectly State-controlled), rather than State-owned. Germany's military victories in 1939/40 had created a German-dominated film monopoly in Europe which the RMVP believed it could only exploit if the film industry produced 100 films per year. Towards the end of 1941 it became increasingly clear that this target was not being reached. The only solution, it was decided, lay in a complete take-over by the State. To this end the nationalisation of the film industry was completed in 1942. On 10 January 1942 a giant holding company, Ufa-Film GmbH (called Ufi to distinguish it from its predecessors) assumed control of the entire German film industry and its foreign subsidiaries. Every aspect of film-making was now the immediate responsibility of Ufi. The Reichsfilmkammer had become merely a bureaucratic administrative machine and Ufi, thanks to its vertical organisation, was a mere receiver of orders from the RMVP. This repre-sented an enormous concentration of a mass medium in the hands of the National Socialist State and, more specifically, of the Minister for Popular Enlightenment and Propaganda. With his task completed Goebbels could sit back and reflect on the wisdom of his actions:

Film production is flourishing almost unbelievably, despite the war. What a good idea of mine it was to take possession of the films on behalf of the Reich several years ago! It would be terrible if the high profits now being earned by the motion-picture industry were to flow into private hands.[29]

An analysis of the different types of film produced during the Third Reich reveals a good deal about Goebbels' *Filmpolitik*. Of the 1,097 feature films produced between 1933 and 1945, only about one-sixth were overtly propagandist with a direct political content. The majority of these films were 'State-commissioned films' (*Staatsauftragsfilme*), including politically the most important films, which were given disproportionate funding and publicity.

Such films were invariably classified at the time as *Tendenzfilme*. This was a term employed during the Third Reich to describe a certain type of film that exhibited 'strong National Socialist tendencies'. In other words, without necessarily mentioning National Socialism, these films advocated various principles and themes identifiable with Nazism which the Ministry for Propaganda wished to disseminate at intermittent periods. Of the entire production of feature films, virtually half were either love stories or comedies, and a quarter dramatic films like crime thrillers or musicals. Yet all went through the pre-censorship process and all were associated with the National Socialist ideology in that they were produced and performed in accordance with the propagandist aims of the period. In a highly politicised society like the Third Reich, even the apolitical becomes significant in that so-called 'entertainment films' tend to promote the official world-view of things and to reinforce the existing social and economic order. Propaganda is as important in reinforcing existing beliefs as it is in changing them, and even the most escapist entertainment can, as Goebbels noted, be of value to the national struggle, 'providing it with the edification, diversion and relaxation needed to see it through the drama of everyday life'.[30] The comparatively small number of overt political films was supplemented by documentary films and newsreels, which became increasingly important during the war.

Thus the themes that recur in the Nazi cinema are central to their *Weltanschauung*, and these ideas were repeated at carefully chosen intervals. Goebbels therefore chose to keep prestigious film propaganda at its maximum effectiveness by spacing out the films concerned – except, that is, for the newsreels (*Deutsche Wochenschau*), which depended on their ability to capture the immediacy of events. The full-length documentaries were all the more effective for their comparative rarity. Perhaps the two best-known documentaries of the Nazi period are Leni Riefenstahl's *Triumph des Willens* (*Triumph of the Will*, 1935) about the 1934 Party rally in Nuremberg, and *Olympiade* (*Olympia*, 1938), a four-hour record of the 1938 Olympic Games held in Berlin, which proved an ideal vehicle for Nazi propaganda to foreign countries.

Surprisingly enough, there was very little sign of an overall pattern or strategy of film propaganda. It is true that a trilogy of films eulogised the *Kampfzeit* (time of struggle), and glorified the Nazi Movement and its martyrs in 1933 (*SA-Mann Brand, Hitlerjunge Quex, Hans Westmar*). Similarly, in 1940, three films were produced which were intended to prepare the German people for the final solution of the 'Jewish problem' (*Die Rothschilds, Jud Süss, Der ewige Jude*). Equally, 1941 marked the highest concentration of *Staatsauftragsfilme* commissioned by the RMVP. But Goebbels' main concern was to keep the important themes of Nazi ideology constantly before the public by releasing an optimum number of State-commissioned films. In accordance with Hitler's dictum of orientating the masses towards specific topics, a number of these propaganda films attempted, together with carefully coordinated campaigns in the press and radio, to dramatise aspects of the National Socialist programme that were deemed important. Such films would include *Das alte Recht* (*The Old Right*, 1934), the justification of the State Hereditary Farm Law; *Ich für Dich – Du für mich* (*Me for You – You for Me*, 1934), emphasising the importance of *Blut und Boden* (blood and soil) and defining the source of strength of the 'master race' in terms of peasant virtues and the sacredness of German soil; *Ewige Wald* (*Eternal Forest*, 1936), an attempt to create national solidarity and the need for 'living space' (*Lebensraum*); *Der Herrscher* (*The Ruler*, 1937), providing analogies with Hitler's teachings and calling for strong leadership; *Sensationsprozess Casilla* (*The Sensational Trial of Casilla*, 1939), anti-American propaganda designed to ridicule the American way of life; *Heimkehr* (*Homecoming*, 1941), about the sad fate of German nationals living abroad; *Ich klage an* (*I Accuse*, 1941), an exposition of the Nazis' euthanasia campaign.

This strategy illustrates Goebbels' desire to mix entertainment with propaganda. For, unlike Hitler, Goebbels believed that propaganda was most effective when it was insidious, when its message was concealed within the framework of popular entertainment. Goebbels was well aware of this and believed that 'entertainment can occasionally have the purpose of supporting a nation in its struggle for existence, providing it with the edification, diversion and relaxation needed to see it through the drama of everyday life'.[31] In the course of the Third Reich, Goebbels was frequently called upon by the older Party members to justify his *Filmpolitik* and its apparent failure to explicitly glorify the Nazi movement in films. Alfred Rosenberg was Goebbels' most hostile critic, and the Propaganda Minister obviously resented this intrusion into his domain and the fact that he was obliged to defend his policies. In a typical outburst in his diary, Goebbels complained:

Rosenberg is once again criticizing our film production in a recent letter to me. I could answer him with a 'barbed' criticism of the situation in the East: but I am not going to, because the matter seems too trifling to me. In any case one would have thought that Rosenberg would have other matters to bother about, rather than one or other film that has flopped![32]

However, Goebbels did feel compelled to justify his position, and in an earlier entry in his diary he wrote:

> Even entertainment can be politically of special value, because the moment a person is conscious of propaganda, propaganda becomes ineffective. However as soon as propaganda as a tendency, as a characteristic, as an attitude, remains in the background and becomes apparent through human beings, then propaganda becomes effective in every respect.[33]

Goebbels therefore encouraged the production of feature films which reflected the ambience of National Socialism rather than those that loudly proclaimed its ideology. The result of Goebbels' *Filmpolitik* was a monopolistic system of control and organisation which maintained profits and managed to quadruple the annual number of cinema-goers between 1933 and 1942. Film was only one factor in reaching an uncritical audience; but it had an important function, in the sense that when people read newspapers or listened to the radio they were more conscious of the propaganda content. The cinema, on the other hand, was associated with relaxation and entertainment and was therefore all the more dangerous, particularly as the *Gleichschaltung* of the German cinema had been carried out behind the scenes. It is clear that when the Nazis assumed power they thought highly of film as a propaganda weapon. The need for conformity in a police state meant that the film industry had to be reorganised according to the ideals of the NSDAP. Like all forms of mass communication, film had to correspond to the political *Weltanschauung* and the propaganda principles of the Party. The communications media – the press, radio and film – had a circular interrelationship in that they supplied each other with themes in the manner prescribed by the State, and supported each other in their effect by a simultaneous and graduated release of information, which was circulated, controlled and modulated by the State. This control remained of paramount importance to Goebbels and Hitler, both of whom continued to recognise its importance as a source of their 'popularist' appeal. In his diary entry for 20 June 1941, Goebbels recorded: 'The Führer praises the superiority of our system compared with liberal–democratic ones. We educate our people according to a common world-view (*Weltanschauung*), with the aid of films, radio and the press, which the Führer sees as the most important tools of popular leadership. The State must never let them out of her hands.'[34] It is the major propaganda themes disseminated by the Nazi State before and during the war that I now wish to analyse in some detail.

4

PROPAGANDA AND PUBLIC OPINION, 1933–9

Domination itself is servile when beholden to opinion; for you depend upon the prejudices of those you govern by means of their prejudices.

Rousseau, *Emile*

The point has to be made at once that any attempt to quantify public reaction to Nazi propaganda is fraught with difficulties. Accurate measurement of the effectiveness of Nazi propaganda is weakened by the absence of public opinion surveys and the fact that in a society that resorted so readily to coercion and terror reported opinion did not necessarily reflect the true feelings and moods of the public, especially if these views were opposed to the regime. Nevertheless, to state that public opinion in the Third Reich ceased to exist is not strictly true. After the Nazi 'seizure of power' in 1933 the Minister for Propaganda, Joseph Goebbels, stressed the importance of coordinating propaganda with other activities. In a dictatorship, propaganda must address itself to large masses of people and attempt to move them to uniformity of opinion and action. Nevertheless, the Nazis also understood that propaganda is of little value in isolation. To some extent this explains why Goebbels impressed on all his staff at the Ministry for Popular Enlightenment and Propaganda the imperative necessity constantly to gauge public moods. Goebbels therefore regularly received (as did all the ruling elites) extraordinarily detailed reports from the Secret Police (SD) about the mood of the people and would frequently quote these in his diary. Hitler too was familiar with these reports, and his recorded determination to avoid increasing food prices at all costs for fear that this would undermine the regime's popularity suggests a political sensitivity to public opinion. To assure themselves of continued popular support was an unwavering concern of the Nazi leadership, and of Hitler and Goebbels in particular.

To this end, a number of different agencies were engaged in assessing the state of public opinion and the factors affecting public morale. The SD, the Gestapo, the Party, local government authorities and the judiciary all made it their business to gauge the mood and morale of the people. Their reports were based on information received from agents throughout the Reich, who reported on their conversations with Party members or on conversations they had overheard. It has been estimated that by 1939 the SD alone had some 3,000 full-time officials and some 50,000 part-time agents.[1]

It would therefore be an over-simplification to think of the German public as a *tabula rasa* upon which the regime drew whatever picture it wished.[2] In any political system policy must be explained, and the public must either be convinced of the efficacy of government decisions – or at least remain indifferent to them. Nazi Germany was no exception, and as with any other political system, public opinion and propaganda remained inexorably linked. That is not to say that all major decisions taken in the Third Reich were influenced by public opinion. Such a statement is clearly absurd; rather, decision-making and the propaganda justifying policy were conditioned by an awareness of how the public already felt about certain issues. Therefore the 'success' or 'failure' of propaganda was not simply due to the resources and skill of the Ministry for Propaganda and its ability (or otherwise) to coordinate its campaigns, but also depended on the prevailing opinions and prejudices of the German public. Too often in the past historians have been concerned only with the organisational techniques of Nazi propaganda and not with how it was received by the population, the assumption being that simply because propaganda played such a disproportionate role in the Third Reich, by implication it *must* have been highly effective. Clearly Goebbels believed this, but the historian needs to be more sceptical. My aim is to provide a balanced picture of the different reactions of the public to propaganda in the context of the declared aims of that propaganda and the manner in which it was disseminated. By breaking down the aims of Nazi propaganda into specific themes, it is possible to make an informed assessment of the differentiated reactions of the public to various leitmotivs. As a general statement it is fair to say that propaganda tended to be more effective when it was reinforcing existing values and prejudices than when it was attempting to manufacture a new value system, or, indeed, when it was encountering some resistance.[3] This is an obvious point, but giving greater weight to a scheme of differentiation confirms yet again that the Nazi State was no monolith but a mosaic of conflicting authorities *and* affinities.

Recent studies have tended to confirm that National Socialist ideology was neither a hotchpotch of racial nonsense nor merely a means of securing an electoral victory prior to 1933. On the contrary, the Nazis saw their *Machtergreifung* ('seizure of power') as more than simply a change of government: it represented the start of a revolution which would transform German society in accordance with their ideology. The so-called 'Nazi revolution' was essentially compounded of three elements. First, the Nazis utilised the legal authority of the State and its machinery to legitimise their control over the civil service, the police and the armed forces; all those who were unwilling to submit to this new authority were either dismissed or liquidated. Second, there was the widespread use made of terror and coercion in the absence of law and order that allowed Nazi Stormtroopers to seize persons and property at will. The pervasive fear of violence should not be underestimated, for it undoubtedly inhibited the forces of opposition. The menace of violence, was, to some extent, counter-balanced by the positive image of Nazi society presented in the mass-media on an unprecedented scale. Propaganda is thus the third element. A society that was still suffering from a deep sense of national humiliation, and weakened by inflation, economic depression and mass unemployment, was perhaps not surprisingly attracted to a National Socialist revival which proclaimed that it could integrate disparate elements under the banner of national rebirth for Germany.

The 'revolutionary' aims of the Nazi regime highlight the remarkably ambitious nature of its propaganda. From the moment that the Ministry for Popular Enlightenment and Propaganda was established, it set itself the task of re-educating the population for a new society based on National Socialist values. Although Nazism is often thought of as a temporary aberration in the history of a nation, it was in fact based upon various strands of intellectual thought which go back at least a century and which constitute the *völkisch* doctrine, essentially a product of late eighteenth-century Romanticism.[4] The major themes that recur in Nazi propaganda during this period reflect the roots and antecedents of *völkisch* thought: (1) appeal to national unity based upon the principle 'The community before the individual' (*Volksgemeinschaft*); (2) the need for racial purity; (3) a hatred of enemies which increasingly centred on Jews and Bolsheviks; and (4) charismatic leadership (*Führerprinzip*). Both the original doctrine and the manner in which it was disseminated by Nazi propaganda led inexorably to the mobilisation of the German people for a future war. Once in war, these propaganda aims could then be extended in order to maintain the fighting morale of the military and civil population.[5]

THE 'NATIONAL COMMUNITY' (*VOLKSGEMEINSCHAFT*)

The primary goal of Nazi propaganda was radically to restructure German society so that the prevailing class, religious and sectional loyalties would be replaced by a new heightened national awareness. A considerable degree of mysticism was involved in the displacement of such deeply held yet conflicting values by means of a 'national' or 'people's' community (*Volksgemeinschaft*). This desire for unity drew its strength from an idealised past rather than from the present. In an age of industrialisation and class conflict, man (it was argued) had to transform his feeling of alienation into one of belonging to a 'pure' community or *Volk*. In modern times, this notion can be traced back to the *Burgfrieden*, or the myth of the 'spirit of August 1914', when the Kaiser declared: 'I recognise no parties, but only Germans.' By ending domestic political strife in the name of the *Burgfrieden*, the nation apparently became united behind the banner of a fully justified war of self-defence. In August 1914 it seemed that the war had created a new sense of solidarity in which class antagonisms were transcended by some entirely fictitious 'national community'. The *Burgfrieden* could not, however, survive a long war, just as the reconciliation of class tensions was dependent on a swift military victory. In reality the superficial harmony of 1914 was a far cry from the *Volksgemeinschaft* invoked by the Nazis. Nevertheless, the nationalist fervour of 1914, the spirit of a united nation ready and eager for a justifiable war, remained a potent force for the German Right throughout the interwar period and appeared to have come to fruition in the 'fighting community' of 1933.

In order to manufacture a consensus where one did not previously exist, the Nazi propaganda machine would constantly urge the population to put 'the community before the individual' (*Gemeinnutz vor Eigennutz*) and to place its faith in slogans like 'One People! One Reich! One Führer!' (see Plate 5). To this end, the political function of propaganda was to coordinate the political will of the nation with the aims of the State – or, if this proved impossible with certain groups (for example, sections of the industrial working class and Bavarian Catholics), to establish at least passive acquiescence. Propaganda was intended to be the active force cementing the 'national community' together, and the mass media – indeed art in general – would be used to instruct the people about the Government's activities and why it required total support for the National Socialist State. In the years leading up to the war – partly as an antidote to the increasing use of coercion and the subsequent loss of liberty – propaganda eulogised the achievements of the regime. The press, radio, newsreels and film documentaries concentrated on the more prominent schemes: the impact of Nazi welfare services, 'Strength through Joy' (the Labour Front's agency for programmed leisure), and Winter Help. Posters proclaimed the benefits of 'Socialism of the Deed'; newsreels showed happy workers enjoying cruise holidays (see Plate 6) and visiting the 'people's theatre' for the first time; the radio bombarded the public's social conscience with charitable appeals; and the press stressed the value of belonging to a 'national community' and the need for self-sacrifice in the interests of the State. Cheap theatre and cinema tickets, along with cheap radio sets and the cheap 'people's car' (*Volkswagen*) (see Plates 7 & 8), even the 'People's Court' (*Volksgerichtshof*) – all were intended to symbolise the achievements of the 'people's community'.

Propaganda presented an image of a society that had successfully manufactured a 'national community' by transcending social and class divisiveness. But was there a gap between the Nazi propaganda image and

Plate 5 A painting of Hitler in a Renaissance pose with the propaganda slogan:
'One People, One Nation, One Leader'.

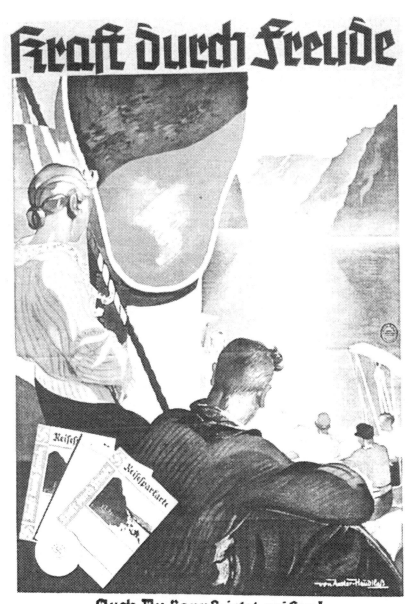

Plate 6 A 'Strength through Joy' poster showing happy workers on a cheap package-holiday.

Plate 7 A poster showing a young couple who have successfully saved for a Volkswagen car.

Plate 8 A stamp issued to promote the 'People's Car' (*Volkswagen*).

social reality? Recent works have suggested that there was, and indeed that the gap between social myth and social reality in the Third Reich grew ever wider. The argument suggests that propaganda of the 'national community' failed to break down objective class and social divisions and, more importantly, failed to destroy an awareness of these divisions.[6] Two sections in particular who are singled out as 'resisting' the blandishments of 'national community' propaganda are the industrial working class and Catholics. I should like, therefore, to concentrate on the relationship between the regime and the industrial working class and, by way of contrast, to look at the response from another important section of the 'community', German youth. I shall be analysing the relationship between the Catholic Church and the Nazi regime in the following section.

The basis for the system of labour relations in force when the Nazis came to power in 1933 had been established during the first years of the Weimar Republic. The right of workers to join trade unions was incorporated in the Weimar Constitution of 1919, and in the same year a new law guaranteed workers a degree of participation in the running of factories by setting up works councils made up of both employers and workers. The trade union movement had established itself in three separate divisions: the Free Trade Unions, which were the largest group and closely associated with the Social Democratic Party; the Catholic Christian trade unions, linked with the Centre Party and influential in the predominantly Catholic industrial areas; and the smaller Hirsch—Düncker unions who traditionally aligned themselves with the liberals.

Determined to control the organisation of labour without compromise, the destruction of the trade unions was carried out by the Nazis in various stages. The Free Trade Unions were the first to be 'coordinated' (gleichgeschaltet) on 2 May 1933. A few days later, the Hirsch—Düncker unions 'voluntarily' coordinated themselves; while the Catholic Christian Trade Unions were given a temporary reprieve since the new regime was in the middle of negotiating a concordat with the Vatican. Once this had been secured at the end of June, they too were disbanded. Meanwhile, on 6 May, Dr Robert Ley, the head of the political organisation of the Party, had announced the creation of the German Labour Front (Deutsche Arbeitsfront – DAF), which not only provided a National Socialist substitute for the trade unions but also served to neutralise the radical Nazi Factory Cells Organisation (NSBO) which had been founded to enable the movement to defeat Marxism on the shop floor. The second phase began in December 1933, when the Labour Front (DAF) was reorganised to allow blue- and white-collar sections to be replaced by so-called 'Reich plant communities'. The reorganisation of industrial relations was brought about by the 'Law for the Ordering of National Labour' of 20 January 1934 and the dissolution of the still autonomous economic interest organisations. The main aim of the new law which governed labour in the Third Reich was to establish a system of labour relations based on the concept of the 'plant community' (*Betriebsgemeinschaft*), formed by the 'plant leader' (employer) and his 'retinue' (employees) with Councils of Trust replacing the former works councils. The first clause of the new law stated: 'The employer works in the factory as leader of the plant, together with employees and workers who constitute his retinue, to further the aims of the plant and for the common benefit of the nation and State.' The intention was to replace industrial conflict with trust and cooperation based on the common ethic of *Volksgemeinschaft*. To this end, the DAF assumed an increasingly powerful role in the sphere of industrial relations and social policy. The DAF had initially been financed from the confiscated funds of trade unions, and although membership was in theory voluntary, by the late 1930s the vast bulk of the workforce had been forced to join under pressure from employers and the State.

The Nazis viewed trade unions as a vehicle of the class struggle and were determined that they should be depoliticised. By 'coordinating' trade unions into the Labour Front they were transforming organised labour into an organ for vocational representation which placed strengthening the national economy above self-aggrandisement. The document enshrining the principles of the Labour Front stated:

> Within it [the DAF] workers will stand side by side with employers, no longer separated into groups which serve to maintain special economic or social distinctions or interests. . . . The high aim of the Labour Front is to educate all Germans who are at work to support the National Socialist State and to indoctrinate them in the National Socialist mentality.[7]

Moreover, by encompassing employers as well as workers, the DAF was intended to become the 'symbol of the nation', to act, in Hitler's own words, as an 'honest broker' between the classes (see Plate 9). It was referred to in a decree of 24 October 1934 as 'the organisation of creative Germans of brain and fist'.

In order to sell *Volksgemeinschaft* as an ideological drawing-card where no labour policy existed, the Nazis chose to appeal to abstract emotions like pride and patriotism and focus less on the worker and more on the ennobling aspects of work itself. Slogans proclaimed that 'work ennobles' (*Arbeit adelt*) and, more grotesquely, 'labour liberates' (*Arbeit macht frei*). An idealised image of the worker was invoked, in an attempt to raise the status of the worker (if not his wages) and fulfil the psychological assimilation of 'the worker' into the life of the nation. In pursuit of this Hitler himself took the lead. The following question and answer were part of an 'ideological' catechism: 'What professions has Adolf Hitler had?' 'Adolf Hitler was a construction worker, an artist and a student.' In the numerous publicity films and posters produced by the *Propagandaamt* of the DAF to advertise

Plate 9 The striking 'futuristic' design outside the headquarters of the German Labour Front (DAF).

the 'victory of the battle for work' Hitler was referred to as the 'first worker of the nation'. May Day was transformed from a traditional Socialist celebration of working-class solidarity into the 'National Day of Labour', a reaffirmation of the national community, when employers and workers would parade side by side throughout Germany and listen to a speech from Hitler. To demonstrate further the Third Reich's esteem for its working population, the press, under the rubric 'workers of the head and hand' (*Arbeiter der Stirn und der Faust*), would celebrate the 'peerage of hard jobs' (*Adel der schweren Arbeit*), 'unfashionable' workers such as rubbish collectors being interviewed in a positive way. The whole notion of *Volksgemeinschaft* implied that every 'pure' German had some claim to equality, regardless of social background or occupational position. This sometimes rested uneasily with other notions like *Leistungsgemeinschaft* ('from each according to his ability'), which implied that equality of status was to extend to equality of opportunity. The DAF and the press were only too eager to extol the virtues of merit, highlighting workers who had advanced from humble beginnings. 'The worker is even more aware', a functionary of the Labour Front announced on the sixth anniversary of Hitler's appointment as Chancellor, 'that he has the opportunity to reach the highest levels in his plant commensurate with his merit.'[8]

By assimilating workers into first the 'factory community' and then the 'national community', the Labour Front was able to boast that it had successfully overcome the alienation and exploitation felt by many modern industrial workers and at the same time provided an opportunity for advancement based on performance and not social background. The DAF's problem, however, was that in view of the priority of concentrating the nation's resources into rearmament, strict limits were imposed on wage increases, which were the obvious way of attempting to win (or bribe) the support of the working class. Therefore inducements of a different kind were sought, and when the DAF was restructured on 27 November 1933, two new organisations were established within its ambit; they were 'Beauty of Labour' (*Schönheit der Arbeit*) and 'Strength through Joy' (*Kraft durch Freude*). Both can be seen as an attempt to improve status and working conditions as a substitute for wage increases.

'Beauty of Labour' initiated a series of propaganda campaigns with slogans coined to publicise good working practices such as 'Fight against noise', 'Good ventilation in the work place', 'Clean people in a clean plant'. These were designed to persuade employers to improve working conditions, and they would be backed up by official Government figures showing, for the benefit of the workers, the increased number of factory inspections and the way in which this had led to improved facilities within the workplace.

Called at first 'After Work', 'Strength through Joy' was to organise the leisure time and activities of the German labour force. Intended to compensate for the loss of trade union rights, the inadequacy of wage increases and the increasing regimentation of life, 'Strength through Joy' prescribed in detail the correct methods, time and content of leisure for the one purpose of enhancing the worker's productivity. Typical was the annual efficiency competition for young apprentices. Furthermore, plants developing the most successful vocational-training schemes received from Dr Ley an 'efficiency' medal. The design was a cog-wheel enclosing a swastika above a hammer, with the initials 'DAF' and below the words 'recognised vocational plant'.[9] Such awards were also used to encourage a sense of community spirit. The reduction of leisure to a mere auxiliary of work was the official philosophy of the Labour Front, although it preferred, of course, to concentrate on the achievements of organisations like 'Strength through Joy' in allowing ordinary workers to participate in a wide range of sporting activities and in luxury pursuits such as sea cruises, and in giving them the prospect of owning one of the new 'people's cars' (*Volkswagen*). Posters urged workers: 'Save five marks a week and get your own car' (see Plate 7). Workers responded enthusiastically and payed in millions of marks to the saving scheme to buy a *Volkswagen*, but they received no cars. Nevertheless, in 1940 a Party official felt confident enough to write:

> It is no exaggeration to say that for millions of Germans 'Strength through Joy' has made the world beautiful again and life worth living again . . . the idea of 'Beauty of Labour' has ensured that the factories are once more worthy of a human being. This too has a deeper significance. People can produce more in clean, airy and bright workplaces.[10]

These, then, are some of the measures implemented to secure the loyalty or acquiescence of the industrial working class. How did workers respond to these programmes? Tim Mason has suggested that Nazi social propaganda was an unmitigated failure among industrial workers. Ian Kershaw, in his detailed analysis of Bavaria, has persuasively argued that the 'national community' idea had little impact in changing behavioural patterns, which continued to be determined by material considerations.[11] But historians like Mason and Kershaw may be giving too much weight to the claims that the Nazis themselves made about their propaganda successes. For while 'national community' propaganda did not achieve its 'revolutionary' goal of destroying class and religious loyalties, there is evidence to suggest that it did have some success (by default, in many instances) in creating a new heightened national awareness – and that this was in itself sufficient to secure for the regime a considerable degree of stability and social integration. Many sections of the community, particularly the petit bourgeoisie and those who were formerly unemployed, viewed *Volksgemeinschaft* not necessarily in terms of a radical restructuring of society involving fundamental social change, but rather as an acceptable insurance policy against the alternative, Marxist–Leninism.

Reports from the Sopade, the Social Democrats' exile organisation, reveal a mixed response to community propaganda and the Nazis' social welfare measures. Workers were clearly aware of the many contradictions that existed. Reports show that social facilities, like factory sports fields and swimming-baths, offered by the DAF had some impact on working-class perceptions of the regime; yet at the same time workers complained that very often they were 'compelled to build these facilities in their spare time without pay'.[12] The 'Beauty of Labour' was seen by many as simply a continuation of paternalistic German business practices and the vogue in the 1920s for increasing productivity through modern 'scientific management' techniques. Similarly, for many workers increased real wages could only be earned through large amounts of overtime. Sopade reported that this had an impact on productivity and on morale, which in turn led to rising absenteeism and sickness rates.[13] On the other hand, Sopade was acknowledging in 1939 that 'Strength through Joy' was very popular: 'It cleverly appeals to the *petit bourgeois* inclination of the unpolitical workers who want to participate in the pleasures of the "top people".'[14] Although few workers could afford to go on the prestigious foreign cruises to Madeira and Scandinavia, by introducing cheap package tours 'Strength through Joy' skilfully exploited a latent consumerism and won a good measure of approval in the process. Similarly, reports suggested that the decision to build a 'people's car' and the setting-up of the *Volkswagen* saving scheme, met with an enthusiastic response and had the dual advantage of overcoming the problem of restricted consumerism by removing money that might otherwise be spent on goods that could not be supplied, and second, achieving a clever diversionary tactic in the sphere of domestic politics: 'This car psychosis, which has been cleverly induced by the Ministry for Propaganda, keeps the masses from becoming preoccupied with a depressing situation.'[15]

For many workers, then, 'national community' propaganda represented more than simply a cosmetic exercise. While perhaps recognising the cynical intentions behind the propaganda, workers were nonetheless prepared to take advantage of the various schemes and benefits and, moreover, to give the regime some credit for introducing them. On the whole, the Sopade reports in the period leading up to the Second World War lend support to the work of the Cambridge economist C. W. Guillebaud, who visited Germany and emphasised the significance of social welfare in the Third Reich, claiming that notions like *Volksgemeinschaft* strengthened support for the regime among the working class.[16] Guillebaud emphasised the solid economic achievements of the regime in solving the twin problems of mass unemployment and economic stagnation. In 1933 well over one-third of the working population was unemployed, a figure reduced to 74,000 by the summer of 1939, by which time there were over 1 million job vacancies. When the Nazi Party came to power in 1933, the national income had fallen by 40 per cent during the previous three years and total industrial production only slightly less. Wholesale prices had fallen by between 15 and 35 per cent, and the real incomes of those who had retained their jobs had fallen by 10–15 per cent. The Nazis approached the 'battle for work', as it was called, as a political rather than an economic problem. In order to restore confidence and give the impression that something positive was being done, priority was given to reducing the number of unemployed. The first step during 1933 was a cynical book-keeping manoeuvre which allowed the Nazis to strike nearly 1 million engaged in voluntary or temporary works schemes from the unemployed register. By the autumn of 1933 the real programme of Government-financed work-creation was started, albeit on a modest scale. Of the £200 million spent on public works up to the end of 1934, over half had been agreed by Hitler's predecessors. The increasing expenditure on armaments, together with the general recovery of the world economy, combined to bring down the number of registered unemployed to 1.7 million in August 1935. The 'battle for work' was won after a fashion, and business confidence, as a result of Schacht's economic and fiscal measures, was gradually restored. That is not to say that such a 'victory' could not have been won more quickly and efficiently.[17] Nevertheless, the experience of the depression had shaped the minds of a generation of workers, and the continuing provision of full employment and the manner in which it was celebrated in mass media continued to offset many of the negative features of the regime. Moreover, despite Göring's attempts to impose a wage freeze in 1938, real incomes generally increased in the period leading up to the outbreak of war, although workers' experiences varied markedly between individual sectors of the economy.

Closely linked to the idea of *Volksgemeinschaft* was the regime's desire to maintain social conformity. By creating a new series of public rituals to celebrate important days in the Nazi calendar, 'national comrades' (*Volksgenossen*) were expected to attend parades and speeches and show their enthusiasm by hanging out flags. To integrate the people more fully into the community required positive and active devices that expressed publicly to Germans themselves and to the outside world the national community in being. To this end the Nazis initiated the 'Winter Help' (*Winterhilfe*) programme for collecting money, food and clothing for distressed families who had suffered as a result of mass unemployment. The reports suggest that during the first years of the regime *Winterhilfe* not only brought genuine relief to many but also functioned as a means of social integration by encouraging the more affluent members of society to aid the poor on the grounds of national and racial affinity. Similarly, the *Eintopf* ('one-pot') meal encouraged families once a month during the winter to have only one dish for their Sunday lunch and donate what they had saved to collectors who came to the door. Propaganda posters referred to the *Eintopf* as 'the meal of sacrifice for the Reich' and urged all *Volksgenossen* to increase the size of their donations as a sign of their gratitude to the Führer. Rituals like 'Winter Help' and the 'one-pot' meal were intended to represent a vivid expression of the newly created 'national community' and proof of loyalty to the regime (see Plates 10 & 11). Increasingly, however, as unemployment ceased to be a problem and 'voluntary' donations were diverted to pay for welfare measures and the rearmament programme, these compulsory gestures of conformity and 'political reliability' met with widespread resentment, to which the authorities responded with tough measures. Later in the war, on the occasion of his anniversary address on 30 January 1942, Hitler referred to the collection campaigns as a 'plebiscite', adding: 'While others talk about democracy, this *is* true democracy.' On 23 December 1942, after defeat at Stalingrad, Hitler issued an order threatening execution to all those who 'enriched themselves by means of articles collected or intended for collection'.

As the war dragged on, with no apparent end in sight, the tendency of the authorities to resort to threats and coercion substantiates (to some extent) the argument put forward by historians who stress the limited effectiveness of Nazi propaganda and the collapse of any form of consensus in Germany. Historians like Mason and Kershaw are surely right when they highlight the failure of the Nazis to achieve complete social conformity. The evidence from the various public-opinion gathering agencies suggests that Germans were not automatically persuaded to put the community before their own self-interest – or, at least, not all the time. Equally, however, by looking for examples of grumblings about and resistance to 'national community' propaganda, it may be that historians are applying different criteria when analysing the bases of consent and resistance in the Third Reich from those applied to other European societies of the period. During the 1930s and 1940s, such discontent could be found in all the modern industrial nations and was certainly not unique to National Socialist Germany. The obvious danger of citing examples of social dissent (as opposed to resistance) is that this may be at the expense of stressing the significance of *Volksgemeinschaft* in terms of integration and stability. As we have seen, the response of the industrial working class to the implementation of the 'national community', and the manner in which it was portrayed in the media, were both varied and complex.

One section of the population which proved particularly receptive to the notion of a 'national community' was German youth. The assault on the individual, so characteristic of the regime, was directed primarily at youth, with the intention of enveloping the individual at every stage of development within a single organisation by subjecting him to a planned course of indoctrination. Addressing the Nuremberg Party Rally in September 1935, Hitler proclaimed:

What we look for from our German youth is different from what people wanted in the past. In our eyes the German youth of the future

Plate 10 Hitler and Goebbels enjoying an *Eintopf* with their guests.

Plate 11 An advertisement encouraging Germans to observe the 'one-pot' meal (*Eintopf*).

must be slim and slender, swift as the greyhound, tough as leather, and hard as Krupp steel. We must educate a new type of man so that our people is not ruined by the symptoms of degeneracy of our day.[18]

From this point of view the teaching profession represented one of the most politically reliable sections of the population and from a very early stage was justly regarded by the NSDAP as a vanguard for their propaganda. Party control over the teaching profession was initially secured through the Führer Decree of 24 September 1935, which allowed political vetting by the Nazis for all civil service appointments. Teachers were also mobilised and controlled by means of their own professional association, the National Socialist Teachers' League (NSLB), which had been established as early as 1929. The NSLB provided political references for all appointments and promotions within the teaching profession, and generally attempted to maintain the political reliability of teachers through a process of ideological indoctrination. By 1937, the NSLB claimed a membership of over 95 per cent of all teachers.[19]

In *Mein Kampf* Hitler laid great stress on organisation, and this included the organisation of leisure-time as well. Indoctrination in schools was therefore reinforced by the 'new comradeship' of the Hitler Youth (*Hitlerjugend* – HJ) and its female counterpart, the League of German Girls (*Bund deutscher Mädel*) (see Plate 12). Writing in 1937, the historian Stephen Roberts, who had spent over a year in Germany observing the system, referred to the 'triumph of Nazi propaganda over teaching':

Again and again in Germany, even in Catholic Bavaria and the Black Forest, I found cases of children whose Roman Catholic parents tried to keep them in the few struggling Church societies that still exist for children. In every case the children wanted to join the *Hitler Jugend*. To be outside Hitler's organisation was the worst form of punishment. The resultant worship was too distressing. Their attitude of mind is absolutely uncritical. They do not see in Hitler a statesman with good and bad points; to them he is more than a demigod. . . . It is this utter lack of any objective or critical attitude on the part of youth, even with the university students, that made me fear most for the future of Germany. They are nothing but vessels for State propaganda.[20]

Such contemporary impressions were certainly encouraged by the German government. However, the belief that the HJ had successfully mobilised all young people is clearly an exaggeration. There is considerable evidence to suggest that by the late 1930s the regimental nature of the HJ was alienating some young people, who were forming independent gangs. The two most documented 'non-conformist' groups who rejected the Hitler Youth, though for different reasons, were the 'Swing Youth' (*Swing-Jugend*) and the 'Edelweiss Pirates' (*Edelweisspiraten*).

Plate 12 Ludwig Hohlwein's poster for the League of German Girls.

The Swing Youth were certainly not anti-fascist. They tended to be the offspring of the urban middle class, with the money and status to reject *völkische* music and listen instead to jazz and swing music, which the authorities labelled as American-influenced *Unkultur* and later banned. The SD reports were concerned less with what was invariably referred to as 'negro music' than with sexual promiscuity, lack of parental discipline and a general cult of 'sleaziness' that surrounded these groups. As one former participant later put it: 'the main problem was not that we were against the Nazis but that the Nazis were against us'. The 'Swing Youth' cultivated a somewhat elitist culture which rejected the strident nationalism of the Hitler Youth but was nonetheless politically indifferent to National Socialism. The Nazis for their part viewed them as a minor irritant.

The Edelweiss Pirates, on the other hand, represented a more serious challenge to the social conformity that the Hitler Youth attempted to instil. The first Edelweiss Pirates sprang up spontaneously towards the end of the 1930s in western Germany. Consisting mainly of young people between the ages of fourteen and eighteen, individual groups were closely associated with different regions but identifiable by a common style of dress with their own edelweiss badge and by a general oppositional attitude towards what they saw as the increasingly paramilitary obligations of the HJ. However although they rejected the authoritarian and hier-archical lifestyle of the Nazis, their non-conformist behaviour tended to be restricted to petty provocation. Fourteen- to eighteen-year-olds could hardly be expected to pose a serious political threat or, indeed, offer a poli-tical alternative. Nevertheless, they represent a very small group of youth who rebelled against regimented leisure and who remained unimpressed by the propaganda eulogising a *Volksgemeinschaft*.[21]

For the vast mass of German youth, however, Nazi propaganda offered youth comradeship and a pioneering role: the ideology of National Socialism represented the triumph of a rejuvenated Germany liberated from outdated fallacies of bourgeois liberalism or Marxist class war. After all, it was to be this generation that would instil the Nazi *Weltanschauung* in their 'national comrades' and lay the foundations for the New Order in Europe. As Hans Schemm, the leader of the Nazi Teachers' League put it: 'Those who have youth on their side control the future.' In a celebrated speech on 6 November 1933 Hitler declared: 'When an opponent says, "I will not come over to your side", I calmly say, "Your child belongs to us already . . . you will pass on. Your descendants, however, now stand in the new camp. In a short time they will know nothing else but this new community."'

Although, as we have seen, the growing regimentation and militarism of the youth organisations isolated some young Germans, the Sopade reports of the 1930s tend to concede that the opportunities for participation, the comradeship and enthusiasm, together with the HJ's anti-intellectualism, generally attracted the support of young people (see Plates 13 & 14).[22] While some parents and teachers complained about the brutalising effects of the HJ, Sopade acknowledged that the contempt for the intellect cultivated by the HJ was a potent drawing-card to youth itself: 'The new generation has never had much use for education and reading. Now nothing is demanded of them; on the contrary, knowledge is publicly condemned.' Fired by nationalist rhetoric, Nazi education stressed the importance of 'character building' and the value of 'experience' (*Erlebnis*), rather than the acquisition of 'knowledge', to the development of the individual.[23] Slogans like 'Youth must be led by youth' appealed to the desire of youth to be independent and to challenge traditional authority figures in the name of the Nazi social 'revolution'.

To this end, concepts like *Volksgemeinschaft* provided a vehicle for the ambitions of a younger generation which had grown frustrated with a discredited establishment that had failed to solve Germany's national problems. The 'battle for work' and the Nazi welfare schemes appeared to hold out opportunities for social advancement which had previously been denied to large sections of the youth population. Although the six months that students were obliged to undertake in the Labour Service was in reality a means of reducing overcrowding in the universities (and providing cheap labour) it served, nonetheless, to heighten an awareness of the needs of the national community. Furthermore, the constant stress on achievement and competition within the youth movement (behind which lay the glorification of the heroic fighter) served to harness and channel young people's enthusiasm and project participation as a dynamic involvement. Nazi feature films, for example, depicted a German society in which class barriers were rapidly being broken down. Typical of the way in which this message was disseminated under the guise of film 'entertainment' was the apparently innocuous comedy film *Der Stammbaum des Dr Pistorius* (*Dr Pistorius' Family Tree*, 1939). The film centres on the activities of the new German youth and the outmoded reactions of parents. A public official and his wife have to learn to accept a daughter-in-law from a craftsman's (cobbler's) family. The father is heard to exclaim: 'Youth today does not know what class-consciousness is!' The Nazis had no qualms about criticising social rank, provided such criticism was not too divisive. *Der Stammbaum des Dr Pistorius* ends with the same parents looking out at the HJ marching in the streets to the song 'Hearts are ready, fists are clenched, ready for the battles ahead', their recognition coupled with a new respect: 'A new generation is coming – it is different from ours . . . Youth today is marching, it is stronger than we are.' In this sense, youth gave a lead to the rest of the nation. Sopade reported:

the young people follow the instructions of the HJ and demand from their parents that they become good Nazis, that they give up Marxism,

Plate 13 Recruitment poster for the Hitler Youth, 'The Hand [Hitler's] that Guides the Reich'.

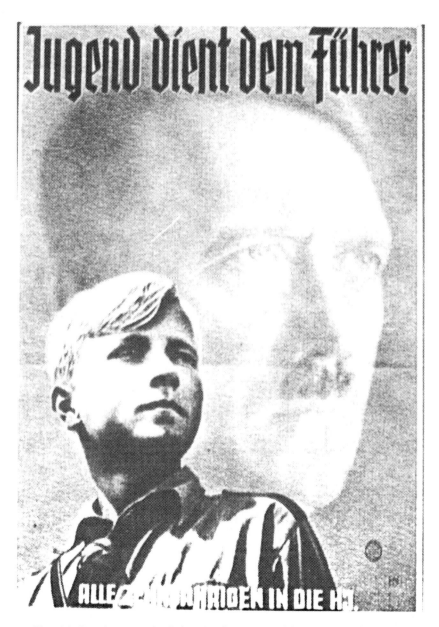

Plate 14 'Youth serves the Führer'. All ten-year-olds join the Hitler Youth!

reactionism, and contact with Jews. It is the young men who bring home enthusiasm for the Nazis. Old men no longer make any impression . . . the secret of National Socialism is the secret of its youth.[24]

To the question 'Did Nazi social propaganda successfully displace traditional political and religious loyalties by means of a "national" or "people's" community?' the answer must be that it 'failed' ultimately to achieve this objective. But the 'success' or 'failure' of *Volksgemeinschaft* should not necessarily be seen in terms of its ability, or otherwise, to destroy old loyalties. On a more limited basis, it was enough that it suspended such allegiances with the ethos of a Nazi *Weltanschauung* that urged the population to put the 'community before the individual'. That is not to say that 'national community' propaganda sustained a heightened commitment to such a radical concept. The outbreak of war did eventually produce a decline in the standing of the Party (though not of Hitler), but German society did not fragment or disintegrate. Schemes like 'Strength through Joy', 'Winter Help', and the 'one-pot' meal could not be maintained indefinitely without resentment setting in. Equally, *Volksgemeinschaft* did not bring an end to people's grievances; they continued throughout the twelve years of the Third Reich, many of them the result of cleavages that existed *before* 1933. However, the implementation of a 'people's community' was widely seen in positive terms that would continue to guarantee at least passive support for the regime. It may not have been recognised as a true 'people's community' in the way in which it was eulogised in the mass-media, but it was apparently tolerable to wide sections of the population. In the sense that it was attempting to disseminate the idea of social and national harmony as the ideological obverse of class conflict, it can be said to have succeeded by default.[25] By turning large sections of the population into passive consumers, the Nazi technique of organisation and atomisation led to a gradual process of depoliticisation which effectively achieved the desired consent. The monopoly of organisations, whether it be the Labour Front, or Strength through Joy, or the HJ, served the same purpose: compulsorily to 'involve' the 'national comrades' so completely that individuals were no longer left to themselves or ultimately to think for themselves. Even anti-Nazi sources such as the pre-war Sopade reports testify gloomily to the widespread political indifference of the population 'who have been persuaded to leave politics to the men at the top'.[26]

THE NEED FOR RACIAL PURITY

The euthanasia campaign

Intrinsic to the idea of a 'national community' was the Nazis' belief in the need for racial purity, an issue dominated by the 'Jewish Question' but one that really encompassed two main enemies: the threat posed by the Jew from within Germany; and the danger of the *Slav Untermenschen* in Poland and Russia. Indeed, in establishing a Marxist-inspired Jewish–Bolshevik conspiracy, propaganda was able at times to fuse these enemies into one. By juxtaposing such enemies as alien *Staatsfeinde* and the NSDAP as the only dynamic bulwark against Marxism, the Party successfully integrated even those elements which might otherwise have had misgivings about National Socialism. Sopade recorded that the anti-Communist campaigns, intensified after 1936 and aimed at deep-rooted anti-Marxist fears, proved particularly effective with all sections of the population.[27]

The underlying consideration of racial propaganda was the desire to bring the nation to a common awareness of its ethnic and political unity. In *Mein Kampf*, Hitler set out the need to implant racial attitudes:

> The whole organisation of education and training which the People's State is to build up must take as its crowning task the work of instilling into the hearts and minds of the youth entrusted to it racial instincts and understanding of the racial idea. No boy or girl must leave school without having attained a clear insight into the meaning of racial purity and the importance of maintaining the racial blood unadulterated. Thus the first indispensable condition for the preservation of our race will have been established and the future cultural progress of our people assured.[28]

Racial teaching within the educational system, and propaganda in general, preached hatred of Jews and Slavs and proclaimed the superiority of the so-called Aryan race. A song of the period exclaimed: 'That is the meaning of life, that God is astir in one's blood, but God is present only in pure blood.'[29] The need for racial purity centred on two interrelated themes; one was *Blut und Boden* ('blood and soil'), and the other was *Volk und Heimat* ('a people and a homeland'). Like anti-Semitism, 'blood and soil' remained a consistent theme during the Third Reich. David Schoenbaum has noted that it could be rationalised 'strategically as a means of resisting Polish encroachment, sociologically as the basis of certain egalitarian virtues and a kind of social stability, economically as an alternative to imports and loss of foreign currency reserves'.[30] For committed National Socialists, however, the superior virtue of rural life and the need for 'living space' in the east were ends in themselves, and required no such rationalisations.

Thus the concept of 'a people and a homeland' sprang directly from the doctrine of *Blut und Boden*, which attempted to define the source of strength of the *Herrenvolk* (master race) in terms of peasant virtues, the Nordic past, the warrior hero, and the sacredness of the German soil, the last of which could not be confined by artificial boundaries imposed arbitrarily by a treaty such as Versailles. The reason for this is clear: the so-called ideology of the Nazi 'revolution' was based upon what were presumed to be Germanic traditions; while the revolution looked to the future, it tried to recapture a mythical past and with it old traditions which to many people provided the only hope of overcoming the chaos of the present. Therefore, the type of nationalism espoused by the National Socialist was an attempt to recapture a morality attributed to the *Volk*'s past. It was the purpose of Nazi *Kultur* to give this morality form and substance in a manner acceptable to the Party hierarchy.

As a result of Nazi racial propaganda, certain stereotypes emerged which were essential in transforming the ideology into a unifying element. Artists in the Third Reich had an important part to play here, for they were required to give expression and shape to such beliefs. This was achieved in two ways: first, propaganda attacked modern degenerate trends in painting and sculpture, from Expressionism to Cubism; second, such *Unkultur* was replaced by 'official' Nazi art which purported to represent the healthy instincts of the Germanic utopian community of the master race (*Herrenvolk*). Nazi writers argued that the purest contemporary race was the Aryan, a race whose inward qualities were intrinsically linked to its external appearance. In practice this meant the idealisation of blonde Nordic stereotypes, described by one race theorist as 'blond, tall, long-skulled, with narrow faces, pronounced chins, narrow noses with high bridges, soft fair hair, widely spaced pale-coloured eyes, pinky-white skin'.[31] Not surprisingly, this limited the range of subjects that could be depicted: the virtues of the peasantry symbolised the importance of the doctrine of 'blood and soil', usually in the form of some idyllic pastoral setting (urban and industrial life did not correspond to such a utopian vision). This was accompanied either by lantern-jawed storm troopers in steel helmets and with clenched fists and swastika banners, or by examination of the naked human form with the intention of revealing the animate beauty of the Nordic racial type. It followed from this that portraiture and nude studies could only be termed German if they depicted the German body. Similarly, this emphasis on racial types led Nazi musicologists into the domain of primordial musical expression.[32] Moreover, documentary films in this mode, like Leni Riefenstahl's *Olympiade* (1938), which celebrated the Aryan body, can be seen as a counterpart to the sculpture of Arno Breker and the paintings of Adolf Ziegler (known throughout the art world as the 'Reich master of pubic hair'), which combined to erase all 'ugliness' from the popular consciousness.

The obsession with the German utopian community of the *Herrenvolk* often led the Nazis to draw an equation between fitness to survive and physical fitness (see Plate 15). This was in part attributable to the generally anti-intellectual prejudices of the movement, and in part to a misapplied social Darwinism. Walther Darré, the Minister for Agriculture, drew a typical parallel between breeding horses and humans:

Plate 15 A poster showing the ideal Nazi family: 'If you need counsel or aid, turn to your local Party organisation'.

We shall gather together the best blood. Just as we are now breeding our Hanover horse from the few remaining pure-blooded male and female stock, so we shall see the same type of breeding over the next generation of the pure type of Nordic German.[33]

The Nazis threw their entire weight behind the existing movement in favour of increased physical training and racial instruction in schools and youth organisations. Secondary schools were required to teach heredity, racial science, and family as well as population policies. Intrinsic to each of these was an ideological instruction in biology. Witness this extract, written by a biologist, on the need for a 'new biology':

Racial eugenics works in the same way, namely, the education of the student in a national sense. . . . It should be repeatedly emphasised that the biological laws operative in animals and plants apply also to man; for example, that the knowledge acquired from studying the genetics of these organisms can, in a general way, be applied to man. Thus, the teaching of animal breeding and plant cultivation can effectively prepare the way for conceptions of racial biology.[34]

Given the Nazis' obsession with health and hygiene, it should come as no surprise to discover the existence of their eugenics policies. Indeed, eugenics legislation was a logical outcome of National Socialist thought and propaganda, which had always stressed the importance of achieving a pure and healthy race. At the Nuremberg Party Rally in 1929 Hitler had cited ancient Sparta's policy of selective infanticide as a model for Nazi Germany: 'If every year Germany had 1 million children and eliminated 700,000–800,000 of the weakest, the end result would probably be an increase in national strength.'[35] Although Hitler's intentions were a matter of public record, he was never able to implement these ideas, despite setting out the legislative machinery for such an operation should the occasion arise.

Only a few months after coming to power, the Nazis set about justifying the eradication of inferior human material. The first people to be exterminated were not Jews but unhealthy Germans. On 14 July 1933, the new Government approved the 'Law for the Prevention of Hereditarily Diseased Offspring', which permitted the compulsory sterilisation of people suffering from a number of allegedly 'hereditary' illnesses. In order not to jeopardise the successful conclusion of the Concordat with the Holy See, the publication of the decree was delayed until 25 July. Although in theory this measure was discretionary, in practice it had a compulsory flavour about it. It came into effect on 1 January 1934; sterilisation was permitted in cases of hereditary imbecility, schizophrenia, hereditary deafness, hereditary epilepsy, manic depression, Huntington's chorea, chronic alcoholism and extreme physical malformation. During 1934,

32,268 sterilisations were carried out; the following year the figure increased to 73,174, and, in 1936, 63,547 persons were sterilised. In 1935, the German bishops initially ruled that, since the main purpose of marriage was procreation, sterilised persons could no longer partake of the sacrament of matrimony. However, the decision was swiftly reversed when it became clear that Catholic officials had helped enforce the law and that such a decision might alienate the growing number of Catholics who had actually been sterilised. Individual priests who protested against the sterilisation law incurred immediate penalties, and the regime responded by proclaiming that it was no longer prepared to tolerate any further sabotage of the law.[36]

The Nazi attitude towards the Churches was confused and inconsistent, and characterised by fundamental hostility in outlook and considerable local persecution. At first the Nazis attempted to identify National Socialism with Christianity but later declared the two beliefs to be irreconcilable. Even though Hitler may have been fundamentally hostile to the Christian Churches by 1933, he had no definite idea of how to proceed against them. In 1933, 62.7 per cent of the population (i.e., over 40 million people) belonged to one of the country's twenty-eight independent Protestant Churches, and 32.4 per cent of Germans (almost 22 million people) were Catholic.

When the NSDAP gained power in 1933 it was not seen by either the Protestant or the Catholic Church as a particular call for protest or resistance. On the contrary, both Churches viewed the overthrow of the pluralist, 'decadent' Weimar Republic with delight and looked forward in anticipation of a restoration of traditional German values. Protest by church leaders that did take place was invariably directed against certain interests of the National Socialist authorities, but not against the state; indeed, most forms of muted protest were accompanied with the affirmation that the protest served the state. By and large, church leadership observed the Nazi's actions in the social and political spheres with sympathy, as exemplified by the 12 November 1933 pastoral letter by the Bavarian bishops, which speaks of saving the German people from the 'horrors of Bolshevism'. 'Resistance' or 'dissent' by church leaders was confined to matters of the Church. There was strict division between the sphere of the Church, in which the State was not to become involved, and the sphere of the State, in which the Church was not to become involved.

The Protestant Church, weakened by serious internal divisions, was obliged in July 1933 to accept a new constitution which rapidly became the means of forcing the Church under State control. It was further weakened by a radical break-away movement known as the 'German Christians', who adopted Nazi paramilitary form and style and called for a new 'People's Church' that could identify with the *Volk*. Accusing the two main branches of the Protestant Church – the Lutheran and the Reformed – of having lost touch with the people, the German Christians, campaigning for control under the slogan 'the swastika on our breasts and the cross in our hearts', gradually began to undermine the fabric of the established Protestant Church. The Roman Catholic Church, despite the Concordat of 20 July (that had largely emasculated ecclesiastical resistance), also lost much of its authority, although it was allowed to retain its autonomous organisation. Hitler viewed with concern both the struggle within the Protestant Church and, in particular, the continuing ability of the Roman Catholic Church to represent an alternative 'ideology'. Confirming in 1936 that the State would continue to take precedence over the Church in religious matters, Hitler made the following remarks about his relationship with the Roman Catholic Church:

> Do not suppose that I am going to make the same mistake as Bismarck did. Bismarck was a Protestant and therefore did not know how to get the better of the Catholic Church. Providence has caused me to be a Catholic, and I know how to handle the Church. If she will not accommodate herself to us, I will let loose upon her a propaganda that will exceed her powers of healing and of sight. I will set in motion against her the press, the radio, and the cinema . . . I know how to handle these fellows and how they are to be caught out. They shall bend or break – but, since they are no fools, they will bow their heads.[37]

For their part, the Churches responded by seeking an accommodation with the regime. As Sopade observed in the summer of 1934: 'The attitude of opponents *within* the Church to the regime is inconsistent. Their struggle is not least directed towards improving the position of the Churches within the system.'[38] The Catholic Church was in a stronger position because it was less divided and also more cosmopolitan. Since Bismarck's *Kulturkampf* of the 1870s, German Catholics had sought to maintain their position within Germany. The history of relations between the regime and the Catholic Church in the years leading up to 1939 is the 'history of the attempt by the Church to assert the privileges granted to it by the Concordat and the attempt by the regime to erode them'.[39] Nothing illustrates this tension between Church and State more vividly than the attempt by the Nazi regime to implement its 'euthanasia' programme.

On 1 September 1939, the day that Poland was invaded, Hitler issued an order to kill all persons with incurable diseases. The idea of compulsory 'euthanasia' had been in Hitler's mind for some time, but he had held back because of expected objections from the Catholic Church. The start of the war seemed the most propitious moment for inaugurating this radical eugenic programme. After the war, at the Nuremberg doctors' trial, Dr Karl

Brandt, the *Reichskommissar* for health, testified: 'In 1935 Hitler told the Reich Medical Leader, Dr Gerhard Wagner, that, if war came, he would take up and carry out this question of euthanasia because it was easier to do so in wartime when the Church would not be able to put up the expected resistance.'[40] Such a programme would also provide much-needed hospital space for the wounded. Thus the euthanasia programme was in direct line of succession to the sterilisation measures enacted in the early months of the regime.

Interestingly enough, as in the summer of 1941, so in the autumn of 1939, centrally organised and systematic killing was preceded by local initiatives. Between 29 September and 1 November 1939, SS units shot about 4,000 mental patients in asylums in Poland. The first euthanasia installation opened in December 1939 and the victims were shot. As the programme expanded, gassing in rooms designed as showers was introduced; or lethal injections might be administered. It is estimated that between December 1939 and August 1941 at least 72,000 perished in institutions which operated under such fictitious names as the 'Charitable Foundation for the Transportation of the Sick' and the 'Charitable Foundation for Institutional Care'.

Although corporately neither the Churches nor the legal profession protested (the notable exception being the 1937 Papal Encyclical 'With Burning Anxiety'), individual clergy and lawyers did. Most notably, Bishop Galen of Münster, in a sermon delivered on 3 August 1941, revealed in detail how the innocent sick were being killed, while their families were misled by false death notices. The next of kin were notified that the patients had died of some ordinary disease and that their bodies had been cremated. Often they received warnings from the Secret Police not to demand explanations and not to 'spread false rumours'. Galen branded these deeds as criminal and demanded the prosecution for murder of those perpetrating them. Bishop Galen's disclosures struck a responsive chord and copies of the sermon were distributed throughout the Reich. His popularity made it impossible for the Government to proceed against him, although some officials did propose that his 'treasonable actions' warranted the death penalty. Goebbels feared that the 'population of Münster could be regarded as lost during the war, if anything were done against the bishop, and in that fear one safely could include the whole of Westphalia'. Hitler contemplated action against Galen at a later date: 'he may rest assured that in the balancing of our accounts no "t" will remain uncrossed, no "i" left undotted'.[41] This remained an idle threat, for as Michael Burleigh has reminded us, Galen survived them all.

The regime had underestimated the possibility of such a public reaction and the far-reaching nature of its impact. The BBC made propaganda capital out of it by means of numerous broadcasts, the RAF dropped copies of the sermon over Germany and it made the front cover of the *Daily*

Express. Burleigh quotes from a lonely outpost in northern Lapland, where a Nazi army captain, who thought 'euthanasia' was the logical corollary of sterilisation, wrote home: 'the sermons of our querulous bishop have even penetrated here. A few of my soldiers have been sent copies of them from home. In this way, despite the war, the Churches have occasioned a certain disquiet among the soldiers.' Shortly after Galen's sermon, the euthanasia programme was officially halted by a *Führerbefehl* (command from the Führer) of 24 August 1941. These public protests helped to form and consolidate public opinion, contributed to the general feeling of outrage, and led to the suspension of the euthanasia campaign. Thus the public conscience could still assert itself even in 1941 when an issue affected the lives of Germans and their families. But the whole question of 'mercy killings' would not rest there; realising their mistake, and determined to keep the issue alive, the Nazis attempted to re-educate the public through the medium of feature film. On 29 August 1941, Tobis, one of the major film companies, released *Ich klage an* (*I Accuse*), one of the most insidious of all Nazi propaganda films, in that it attempted to portray an emotionally sympathetic case for 'mercy killings'. The plot concerned a pioneering professor of pathology, whose young wife develops multiple sclerosis, a condition diagnosed by the family doctor, one of the wife's former admirers. The doctor starts out as a convinced opponent of euthanasia, but these convictions are shaken through the device of a sub-plot in which a baby whose life he once saved becomes horribly deformed. Meanwhile the husband, confronted with the inability of modern medicine to alleviate his wife's slow and painful deterioration, resolves to overdose her. He is accused of murder and the final scene is a courtroom drama in which the Nazi case for 'mercy killings' of people suffering from incurable diseases is rehearsed (by some of the most popular actors of the German cinema). The response from cinema audiences was generally positive, and the SD claimed that the working class ('the simple worker') in particular supported a change in the law sanctioning 'mercy killings' of the incurably sick and mentally handicapped. According to the SD, the poorer sections of the community were more conscious of their financial burdens and less likely to be swayed by religious or moral arguments than by the purely materialistic consideration of whether they could afford to care for sick people.

The film proved less popular in Catholic areas, where clergy actively discouraged people from seeing it. Although the film's 'agonised reasonableness' was recognised as 'extremely seductive', the clergy saw the film (quite correctly) as an attempt to refute Galen's sermon. Protestants, on the other hand, proved less hostile; indeed, the SD recorded some 'positive' attitudes from the Protestant Church. Doctors (particularly the younger ones) and the legal profession generally welcomed the idea, with the proviso that safeguards should be incorporated into any further legislation.[42]

The commercial success of *Ich klage an*, which was seen by over 18 million people, together with the findings of the SD reports, reveals an alarming flight from reality, a willingness on the part of German audiences to delegate responsibility, and a reluctance to face the moral implications of their actions. In fact the *Führerbefehl* did not bring an end to the euthanasia campaign; it merely 'halted' the mass gassing of mental patients – albeit after the original global target of 70,000 had been surpassed. They continued to be murdered in 'wild euthanasia' killings through starvation or lethal medication.[43] The insidiousness of *Ich klage an* was that it highlighted the existence of a social problem that it claimed was in the process of being solved. It is interesting to note that similar methods were employed with regard to film propaganda to coincide with the preliminary stages of the 'final solution' to the 'Jewish Question'. The subsequent disaster which befell the Jews, the culmination of a virulent and unrelenting anti-Semitic propaganda, did not give rise to the same ostensible debate or public outcry.

Although the need for racial purity would eventually be dominated by the 'Jewish Question', the racial-eugenics components of the Nazis social policy did eventually have a profound effect on Germans themselves. Although the Nazis could not openly admit as much, the implication of *Rassenpolitik* was that before there could be a 'solution' to the Jewish problem 'unfit' Germans would first have to be eliminated.

The 'Jewish Question'

Even under National Socialism and the relentless fanaticism demanded by such a regime, some form of diversion was needed as a focus for national unity. Hatred of the enemy was manipulated to fulfil this need, as it is probably the most spontaneous of all reactions and, in order to succeed, need only be addressed to the most simple and violent of emotions and through the most elementary means. It consists of attributing one's own misfortunes to an 'outsider'. A frustrated people needs to hate, because hatred when shared with others is the most potent of all unifying emotions. Whether the object of hatred is the Bolshevik, the Jew or the Anglo-Saxon, such propaganda has its best chance of success when it clearly designates a target as the source of all misery or suffering.

The Nazi attitude to the Jews is an excellent example of this facet of propaganda. It cannot be argued rationally that anti-Semitism was a result of National Socialism or that Joseph Goebbels' propaganda made Germans anti-Semitic, but the fact remains that the Third Reich was responsible for an attempt at genocide of unparalleled scope and brutality. This situation may be attributed partly to the effects of propaganda itself, which could depend upon widespread latent anti-Jewish feeling, and partly also to the closed political environment within which that propaganda was necessarily working. Thus when Hitler came to power he needed the Jews as a permanent scapegoat on which those in the movement could work off their resentment; the Jew was manipulated to fulfil a psychological need for Germany. Nazi propaganda simply used the historical predisposition of the audience towards an anti-Semitic explanation for Germany's cultural, economic and political grievances. Therefore an important negative function of anti-Semitic propaganda was to divert the population from the economic and social measures that the regime had promised but had failed to deliver. It proved increasingly significant for retaining the loyalty and unity of the Party that, in the absence of positive features, the administration could still point to negative goals being fulfilled.

Prejudice against Jews derived largely from a profound ignorance. Forming less than 1 per cent of the population, Jews had for the most part been successfully assimilated into the German community for generations. In 1933 only 20 per cent of Germany's half a million Jews still retained their distinctive Jewish garb, and these so-called 'Eastern Jews' tended to live together in certain quarters of major cities like Frankfurt, Berlin and Breslau. Only a relatively small percentage of the German population, therefore, came regularly into contact with Jews. The Nazis, nevertheless, claimed that Jews had dominated the cultural and economic life of Germany. While it is true that Jewish artists were prominent in the cultural life of the Weimar Republic, Jewish involvement in commercial and professional life does not bear out such claims. In certain professions there was a higher proportion of Jews than of Aryans. For example, just under 17 per cent of all lawyers were Jews (but rarely was a judge Jewish); 17 per cent of all bankers – a percentage that had declined since the end of the nineteenth century – and almost 11 per cent of all doctors were Jews. While it is true that in the clothing and retail trades Jewish influence was pronounced, statistics show quite clearly that Jews did not exert a disproportionate dominance. However, because Nazi propaganda identified Jewish influence with the downfall of German culture and economic life, it was only to be expected that they would grossly exaggerate Jewish influence to stir up racial hatred. Even children's text books taught young children the importance of racial consciousness (see Plate 16).

Some recent works on this topic have controversially maintained that anti-Semitic propaganda was by no means as effective as had previously been assumed.[44] The relative success of elements within the Catholic Church in forcing the regime to suspend its secret euthanasia campaign has been cited to support the claim that Christian and humanitarian values had not been destroyed by the regime.[45] While the euthanasia issue did prompt an unparalleled episcopal protest against 'mercy killings', the SD reports revealed, as we have seen, that the campaign was not without

'Here is the Jew. You see it right away,
the greatest scoundrel in the whole
nation! He thinks he is very beautiful,
but he is really ugly.'

'The German is a proud man who
can work and fight. He is beautiful
and full of courage. That is why
the Jew hates him forever.'

Plate 16 A page from the anti-Semitic children's book 'Don't Trust a Fox on the Green Heath and never Trust the Word of Jew' (*Trau keinem Fuchs auf grüner Heid und keinem Jud bei seinem Eid!*) written by Elvira Bauer and published in 1934.

its supporters. The fact that 'mercy killings' were only spasmodically continued after the *Führerbefehl* of late 1941 is attributable not only to the forceful reaction of the Catholic Church, but perhaps more importantly to the military reverses that were shortly to occur and the fact that it coincided with the preliminary stages of the 'final solution to the Jewish Question'. Moreover, the 'euthanasia issue' involved not Jews but 'unhealthy' Aryans. Although anti-Semitism was in principle unacceptable to the Churches, latent anti-Semitic prejudices shared by clergy and parishoners in both the Protestant and Catholic Churches continued to undermine their defence of Jews. While anti-Semitism may have involved many Germans who could not find any rational argument for Jew-baiting in a crisis of conscience, such revisionist interpretations go perhaps too far. The Sopade reports confirm that a plurality of attitudes towards Jews – ranging from virulent hatred to apathy and indifference – continued to exist during the Third Reich and that these attitudes were shaped as much by geographical, class and religious affiliations as by propaganda. There is also evidence to suggest that in the early years of the regime Nazi propaganda encountered some resistance from Germans who were not persuaded to break off commercial or professional contacts with Jews.

Anti-Semitism was not only the core of Nazi ideology, but the Jewish stereotype that developed from it provided the focal point for the feeling of aggression inherent in the ideology. Before 1939, anti-Semitism was propagated chiefly by means of the educational system and the press. Three major campaigns were waged, in 1933, 1935 and 1938. Immediately after the Nazi electoral victory in March 1933, rank-and-file Party activists went on the rampage assaulting Jews and damaging Jewish shops. Their demand was for a 'Jewish-free' economy, which they sought through a coordinated boycott of Jewish business interests. However much Hitler privately sympathised with these sentiments, once in power he was obliged to contain such crude and visceral anti-Semitism in the interests of public order, political stability and economic recovery. Furthermore, he was constrained by the interjections of President Hindenburg and Foreign Minister Neurath to limit the boycott to a one-day protest. Similarly, the decision in April 1933 to dismiss Jewish civil servants ('Law for the Restoration of the Professional Civil Service') was successfully emasculated by Hindenburg, when the cabinet was reluctantly forced to accept exemptions for all Jews who had been appointed before August 1914 and for all those who had fought in the First World War, or whose fathers or sons had died in the war. The cabinet also approved a parallel 'Law Concerning the Admission to the Legal Profession', published on 11 April, which incorporated the 'Aryan clause' on lawyers.

Although Hitler remained in the background while intimidation of Jews continued unchecked, his long-standing anti-Semitism never wavered. He continued to view Jews as harbingers of 'crime, corruption and chaos'.

They also posed a danger. In *Mein Kampf* he referred to Jews as a 'noxious bacillus' that had to be removed from German blood and soil:

> Bearing in mind the devastation which Jewish bastardisation visits on our nation each day, and considering that this blood poisoning can be removed from our national body only after centuries, if at all . . . This contamination of our blood, blindly ignored by hundreds of thousands of our people, is carried on systematically by the Jew today.[46]

It is one thing to have anti-Semitic prejudices, quite another to be able to implement such beliefs. Did Hitler conclude that he could 'realise the unthinkable' and exterminate the Jews or did the 'Final Solution' emerge gradually as a series of *ad hoc* pragmatic responses to changing political, economic and military circumstances?

Throughout 1934 Jews would continue to experience harassment at a local level, but it remained a year of relative freedom from State-encouraged terror and persecution. This was to change from March 1935, when there were widespread reports from various parts of the Reich of Jewish boycotts taking place. Since Hindenburg's death and the culling of the SA in the 'Night of the Long Knives', Hitler was now in a stronger position to respond positively to rank-and-file calls for increased anti-Jewish legislation. The result was the 'Law for the Protection of German Blood and German Honour', announced at the Party Rally in Nuremberg in September 1935, which outlawed marriage between Jews and Gentiles and forbade sexual relations between them outside marriage. Under the so-called 'Nuremberg Laws', Jews were also denied German citizenship and were forbidden to fly the German flag. The law, which served to protect not only 'German blood' but also 'German honour', provided wide scope for the legal interpretation of 'miscegenation' and laid Jews open to denunciation and framing. The fascination of many anti-Semites with the sexual aspect of the legislation was an important feature of Nazi anti-Semitic propaganda and found its most pornographic expression in Julius Streicher's semi-official broadsheet *Der Stürmer*, which specialised in denunciations of alleged Jewish moral and sexual practices by juxtaposing 'Aryan' maidens with 'Jewish' seducers. Streicher claimed that it was the only paper that Hitler read from cover to cover.

Despite being deprived of their rights as German citizens, Jews had, up until the end of 1937, managed for the most part to retain control of their businesses. But indications of a more radical anti-Semitic policy multiplied in the autumn of 1937. In September, at the Party Rally, Hitler made his first outspoken public attack on Jews for two years. By the end of 1937 Germany's economic position had become much stronger and Hitler had begun to purge conservatives in the government, including Schacht, the Minister for Economics, who for some time had been criticising the speed of rearmament and pointing out the serious damage to the German economy produced by excesses of anti-Semitic propaganda. He was replaced by the less outspoken and more pliable Walther Funk, whom Göring, as plenipotentiary for the Four-Year Plan and a friend of big business, incorporated immediately into his Four-Year Plan organisation. In the following months pressure increased on Jewish businesses to sell out to their Aryan competitors at knock-down prices. The big industrial concerns were only too eager to eliminate Jewish competition and proceed to the 'Aryanisation' of the economy. Göring facilitated this process by issuing decrees in December 1937 which reduced the foreign exchange and raw materials quotas for Jewish firms and, in March 1938, which banned Jewish firms from receiving public contracts.

The *Anschluss* with Austria in March 1938 not only accelerated the unlawful seizure of Jewish businesses by local Party officials; it also served to galvanise Göring, who issued a further decree in April ordering Jews to register all property above 5,000 RM in value and forbidding them to sell or lease such property without permission. The position of German Jews deteriorated further still with the *Reichskristallnacht* ('Night of Broken Glass') of 9–10 November 1938, when Party activists unleashed by Goebbels and the RMVP burned down synagogues and vandalised thousands of Jewish shops. This was in response to the assassination of Ernst vom Rath, an official in the German Embassy in Paris, who was shot dead by a young Polish Jew either in revenge for the mistreatment of his parents by the Nazis, or, as is now being claimed, because of a homosexual relationship with vom Rath. Although Goebbels attempted to depict the *Kristallnacht* as a spontaneous uprising against Jews, the savagery of the outburst, which resulted in ninety-one Jews being murdered and over 20,000 arrested and thrown into concentration camps, left the German public in a state of shock. Although there was widespread disapproval of what had occurred, most citizens seemed to object to the unchecked vandalism and wanton destruction of property. Little objection was raised to a spate of discriminatory decrees which followed, aimed at formalising the extensive 'Aryanisation' of German economic life and creating a 'Jewish-free' economy.[47]

Although considerable foreign objections were raised to the Nazis' anti-Semitic campaigns (particularly after the *Reichskristallnacht* of 1938), the kind of propaganda which depicted the Jew as an evil, money-grabbing Communist raised little opposition within Germany. Nor were serious objections raised to the Nuremberg Laws of 1935, which deprived Jews of most of their rights as citizens. On the contrary, it would seem that many Germans viewed the new laws as a stabilising and necessary measure to limit Jewish influence and intermarriage. It is significant that the civil service in particular welcomed such discriminatory legislation, which placed anti-Semitism on a sound 'legal' foundation.[48]

By the late 1930s the increasingly fanatical tone of propaganda reflected the growing radicalisation of the regime's anti-Semitic policies. Not only had racial propaganda convinced the population that a 'Jewish Question' existed, a point acknowledged by Sopade as early as 1935,[49] but Jews, as we have seen, were now being openly driven from public posts and their property confiscated. The Jewish stereotype depicted in Nazi propaganda served to reinforce anxieties about modern developments in political and economic life, without the need to question the reality of the Jewish role in German society. In November 1937 'The Eternal Jew' exhibition opened in Munich and ran until 31 January 1938, claiming to show the 'typical outward features' of Jews and to demonstrate their allegedly Middle Eastern and Asiatic characteristics. The exhibition also attempted to 'expose' a world-wide 'Jewish-Bolshevik' conspiracy. The striking poster for the exhibition revealed an 'eastern' Jew wearing a kaftan and holding gold coins in one hand and a whip in the other. Under his arm is a map of the world with the imprint of the hammer and sickle (see Plate 17). The exhibition attracted 412,300 visitors, over 5,000 per day. The SD reports claimed that it helped to promote a sharp rise in anti-Semitic feelings and in some cases violence. The massive increase in the circulation of the obnoxious and virulently anti-Semitic *Der Stürmer* was an indication of this trend.

An important function of Nazi propaganda was to disseminate Nazi racial 'ideology'. Press directives had ensured that racial issues would figure prominently in the daily newspapers. Goebbels had even suggested that not a week should pass without a discussion of racial-political questions. Emphasis would often be placed on Jewish aspects of 'criminality' against German interests. Before the proclamation of the Nuremberg laws, for example, a 'public enlightenment' programme had been instigated to demonstrate the history of Jewish 'crimes' and 'conspiracies'. A similar campaign followed the *Reichskristallnacht*. Nothing illustrates this intention more clearly than the use the Nazis made of film. To this end a number of films were prepared, in coordination with campaigns in the other media, in an attempt to make the German people aware of the 'dangers' posed by Jewry and also to rationalise any measures that were or might be taken by the administration, either publicly or in secret.

Anti-Jewish characters and themes recur throughout the cinema of the Third Reich. In the early *Kampfzeit* (time of struggle) films, the Jews are shown to have deliberately fragmented German society by creating a rift between worker and Government. It is the Jews who prompt the Poles to commit atrocities against German minorities (*Heimkehr*, 1941); and it is a Jew who attempts to assassinate the Iron Chancellor (*Bismarck*, 1940). However, the first two anti-Jewish films, *Robert und Bertram* and *Leinen aus Irland* (both 1939), caricature the subhuman Jew within the framework of comedy. In the same year Goebbels forbade the term 'anti-Semitic' and replaced it by 'defence against Jews' or 'opposition to Jews'.

Plate 17 The poster for the 'Eternal Jew' exhibition, 1937.

Deportation of the Jews from Austria and Czechoslovakia to Poland began on a small scale in October 1939, and by February 1940 some Jews were being deported as a result of 'local initiatives' from Germany to the East, although this was stopped for a while owing to the strains on limited food supplies in the *General Gouvernement* (the remainder of German-occupied Poland, governed by Hans Frank). In 1940, three major anti-Semitic films, *Die Rothschilds*, *Jud Süss* (*Jew Süss*) and *Der ewige Jude* (*The Eternal/Wandering Jew*), were released to justify these measures and to convince the German population that a 'Jewish Question' did exist and needed to be 'solved'. These films, together with an intensification of anti-Jewish accusations in the radio and press, were intended to inflame and justify such a situation. They achieved their purpose by the grotesque distortion of Jewish characteristics, while bluntly declaring themselves to be 'merely factual reportage' and by no means intended as propaganda. In May 1940 Goebbels informed all film-makers and critics: 'Films in which Jews appear are not to be labelled as anti-Jewish. We want it to be made perfectly clear that such films are not determined by any tendentious considerations, but reflect historical facts as they are.'

Jud Süss, a story of Jewish machination in eighteenth-century Württemberg which ends with the hanging of Süss and the banning of all Jews from Stuttgart, was hailed in the press as a 'decisive breakthrough in creating cinematic art out of our National Socialist ideology'. Himmler was so impressed with the film that he ordered every SS man to see it. The parallel between Württemberg in 1738 and Germany in 1940 could not have been missed by film audiences. According to the SD on the reception of the film, it succeeded in bringing together themes and archetypes that created the desired antipathy towards Jews – and it did so under the guise of entertainment which resulted in a great box-office success. Newspapers reporting on the film referred to 'a phantom that was caught in time', and the *Völkischer Beobachter* saw it as a fight to the end between the 'polluting Jewish spirit and a healthy German national core'. In his diary Goebbels commented favourably on the reception of the film and held *Jud Süss* to be an example of the power of the cinema to persuade.[50]

However, the most notorious of all anti-Semitic films is *Der ewige Jude* (*The Eternal/Wandering Jew*), described by the Allied Commission after the war as 'one of the most striking examples of direct Nazi anti-Semitic propaganda, probably the vilest and subtlest of its kind ever made for popular consumption'. The film received its première two months after *Jud Süss*, in November 1940. It was subtitled 'A cinematic contribution to the problem of world Jewry'. Produced by the Deutsche FilmHerstellungs und Verwertungs, a euphemism for the Reich Propaganda Department, this documentary film was directed by Fritz Hippler (head of the film section of the RMVP) from an idea and with a commentary by Dr Eberhard Taubert.

The concept of the 'eternal or wandering Jew' was older than National Socialism; it derived from the Christian legend of Ahasver, a Jew who prevented Jesus from resting while he was carrying the cross. Thereafter he had to travel the world without release of death. Nazi propaganda saw in this proof that other races had already persecuted the Jews. In 1937 they set up an exhibition in Munich of 'degenerate art' under the heading of the 'Eternal Jew'. The point of resurrecting and amplifying this old legend was to demonstrate that Jews had no feelings or civilised qualities. These accusations are repeated in *Der ewige Jude*; by appealing to primitive, medieval conceptions of a wandering Jew bearing great epidemics of the plague in an effort to desecrate other races, the film attempts to strengthen existing prejudices and to create new ones. Because it was believed that the Jew never revealed his true face, the facts could be distorted and presented as revelations. The film runs through the whole gamut of Nazi allegations against Jews, and these can be seen as a five-pronged attack, which begins with scenes of the Warsaw ghetto, designed to show the reluctance of Jews to undertake creative labour and continues with the migration of Jews and their attempts to assimilate with European peoples; the development of Jewish banking-houses; the destructive influence of Jews in the Weimar Republic; and an attack on the nature of Jewish religion and its teaching, culminating in the slaughter of animals for kosher meat.

Like most effective propaganda films in documentary format, *Der ewige Jude* moves from the general to the specific. Thus by the time the film has come to make detailed allegations against the Jews, the audience is already in an anti-Semitic frame of mind and receptive to the virulent ending. By a mixture of half-truths and blatant lies the spectator is gradually won over to at least a passive receptiveness to Nazi racial theories. Context is thus important to the internal structure of the film, but it is also important in terms of the material used. Scenes of the Warsaw ghetto are accompanied by a commentary claiming that the Jews have always lived like this. In fact these scenes were shot in Warsaw and Lodz, where the Nazis had herded together almost half a million Jews, sometimes thirteen to a room, *en route* for Auschwitz. The ghetto life depicted in the film is thus entirely a creation of the National Socialists themselves. The cynicism of the exercise is confirmed by evidence that the more ruthlessly realistic shots of the ghettos were excised from the finished film lest they should arouse sympathy for the suffering Jews amongst the German population.

He who is not convinced by these 'rational arguments' cannot fail to be affected by the thorough-going emotional exploitation of the ending. The culmination of the final section is the Jewish slaughter of animals for kosher meat; after a title warning 'all sensitive *Volksgenossen*' not to look at the following pictures, we are shown some 'original' film of Jewish ritual slaughter. The emotional effect of its presentation quite overshadows the scenes of violence and the final execution in *Jud Süss*. The slaughter scenes are introduced by a narrative which claims: 'The following pictures are genuine. They are among the most horrifying that a camera has ever recorded. We are showing them even though we anticipate objections on the grounds of taste. Because more important than all objections is the fact that our people should know the truth about Judaism.'

Press cuttings from the 'Jewish-controlled press' show how, before 1933, the National Socialist campaign against ritual slaughter was hindered by liberal and socialist newspapers who defended such dubious practices. The solution to kosher slaughter is shown as a rationalisation for the Nuremberg Race Laws, which are read out in some detail, followed by Hitler's speech to the Reichstag on 30 January 1939 ('Should the international Jewish financiers succeed once again in plunging the nations into a world war, the result will not be the victory of Jews but the annihilation of the Jewish race in Europe'). The film ends with an idealised sequence of blond Nordic stereotypes against a background of sky, Nazi salutes and close-ups of flags and banners, with a final warning that the Aryan race will only triumph if racial purity is preserved: 'The eternal law of nature, to keep the race pure, is the legacy which the National Socialist movement bequeaths to the German people in perpetuity. It is in this spirit that the nation of German people marches into the future.'[51]

An interesting aspect of *Der ewige Jude* is that by using the extract from Hitler's notorious Reichstag 'prophecy' of 30 January 1939 the Party appeared for the first time to be publicly associating Hitler with a radicalisation in the Jewish Question, without mentioning details of the 'final solution'. Throughout the 1930s Hitler's public pronouncements on the Jewish Question are cautious and surprisingly few, and generally confined to the more popular 'legal' type of discrimination found in State legislation. He had, in fact, taken great pains to distance himself from the violent and generally unpopular pogrom associated with the *Kristallnacht* of 1938. At the height of his popularity Hitler's hatred of the Jews, although well known, was of secondary importance to the fact that he was widely perceived as an outstandingly successful politician (see the section on 'Charismatic leadership' below). Hitler's views, as far as the general public was concerned, were more closely associated with legal measures that attempted to exclude Jews from economic and social life. Party activists, on the other hand, interpreted his writings and speeches as 'ideological metaphors' which provided authorisation to implement a 'final' solution to the 'Jewish problem'. By allowing himself to be shown in 1940 in such a virulently anti-Semitic film as *Der ewige Jude*, Hitler appeared to be deliberately associating himself with the more radical elements in the movement.[52]

In 1941 the Party's Propaganda Department produced a poster containing the most inflammatory extract from Hitler's 'prophecy' speech. The poster, which is reproduced in Plate 18 reads: 'Should the international

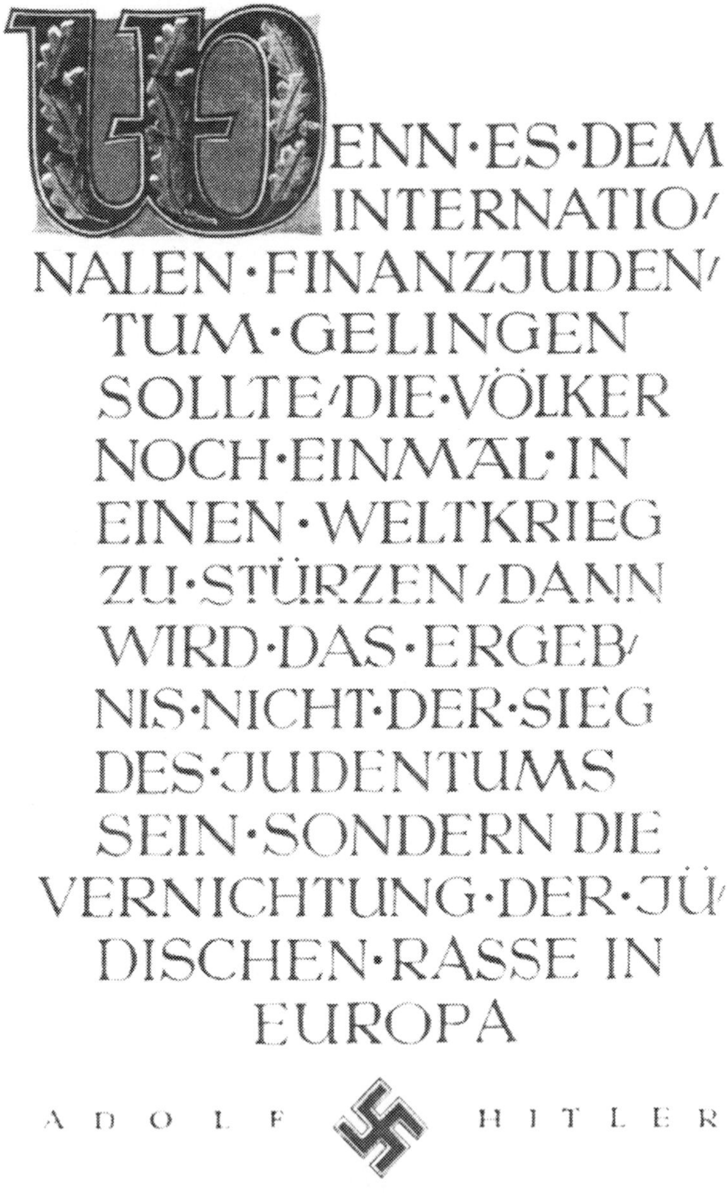

WENN·ES·DEM
INTERNATIO-
NALEN·FINANZJUDEN-
TUM·GELINGEN
SOLLTE-DIE·VÖLKER
NOCH·EINMAL·IN
EINEN·WELTKRIEG
ZU·STÜRZEN-DANN
WIRD·DAS·ERGEB-
NIS·NICHT·DER·SIEG
DES·JUDENTUMS
SEIN·SONDERN DIE
VERNICHTUNG·DER·JÜ-
DISCHEN·RASSE IN
EUROPA

A D O L F H I T L E R

Plate 18 The 1941 poster of Hitler's 'prophecy' speech to the Reichstag: 'Should the international Jewish financiers succeed once again in plunging the nations into a world war, the result will not be the victory of Jews but the annihilation of the Jewish race in Europe' – Adolf Hitler

Jewish financiers succeed once again in plunging the nations into a world war, the result will not be the victory of Jews but the annihilation of the Jewish race in Europe – Adolf Hitler'. The poster was distributed to Party branches throughout the Reich.

Using 'documentary proof', *Der ewige Jude* was intended as definite evidence which underlined not only racialist theories expressed in films such as *Die Rothschilds* and *Jud Süss*, but also the more vehement anti-Semitism found in magazines such as *Der Stürmer*. By contrasting Jewish individualism and 'self-seeking' with the National Socialist ideal of a 'people's community' (*Volksgemeinschaft*), and by showing that Jews were only motivated by money, it was possible to demonstrate that Judaism was the total antithesis of the cherished values of the German cultural tradition as interpreted by Nazi ideology. But, more importantly, the constant analogy made with rats and parasites suggested that the Jew differed from the Aryan not only in body but, more significantly, in soul, for the Jew had no soul. The implication was that here was a menace which had to be 'resisted'. Thus the conclusion to be drawn from watching the film was that the killing of Jews was not a crime but a necessity: Jews, after all, were not human beings but pests which had to be exterminated. *Der ewige Jude* represents a form of National Socialist 'realism' depicting not so much what was, but what ought to have been, in accordance with the preconceived notions of Nazi racial 'ideology'. Having previewed the film before its release, Goebbels wrote in his diary: 'Scenes so horrific and brutal in their explicitness that one's blood runs cold. One shudders at such barbarism. This Jewry must be eliminated.'[53]

The use of film for this purpose – to prepare rather than to justify – was a new departure in propaganda techniques and a measure of the success the Nazis felt they had achieved in attaining their main purpose of mobilising mass support of the population for the Party and its leader. Reports from the SD, sent back to the Propaganda Ministry, suggested, however, that the Germans were rather tired of anti-Semitism by the time *Der ewige Jude* was released. *Jud Süss* had been very effective, but it had also been enough. So *Der ewige Jude* finished up being shown on the one hand to the populations of the occupied countries and on the other to guards at the concentration camps before a new batch of victims arrived for processing and extermination. It would not have done for them of all people to think of the Jews as human beings.

The purpose of illustrating anti-Semitic propaganda by means of film is to demonstrate that propaganda had its limitations, even when it could depend upon the existence of extensive latent anti-Jewish feeling for its campaigns. The public's reaction to anti-Semitic films reveals that propaganda had considerable success in persuading the population that a Jewish 'problem' existed, but equally that there was a limit to their tolerance of the type of virulently anti-Semitic propaganda to be found in films like

Der ewige Jude and publications like *Der Stürmer*. Germans did not wish to visit the cinema to be 'entertained' by films like *Der ewige Jude* – and they made this perfectly clear. Moreover, although years of Nazi propaganda had unquestionably hardened anti-Jewish feelings, there still remained a question-mark in Goebbels' mind as to whether such propaganda had persuaded Germans to condone open violence against Jews.

To the extent that Goebbels thought it unnecessary to repeat such an exercise, the trilogy of anti-Semitic films released in 1940 achieved their purpose. From the Nazi point of view, the Jew provided an important escape valve from serious political and economic problems. The 'image' of the Jew in the mass media as 'self-seeking' and 'parasitic' was outside the range of serious intellectual analysis, and that was its strength. In this way, racial propaganda was able to rationalise any doubts that may have existed, minimise possible dissent, and at the same time provide the emotional basis for a totalitarian solution to the 'Jewish Question'. In fact the only evidence of anti-Semitism to be found in film propaganda during the final years of the war can be seen in the *Deutsche Wochenschauen* (German newsreels). Occasionally the newsreels would contain some element of anti-Jewish propaganda, but generally such propaganda did not figure even in the newsreels.

The explanation as to why overtly anti-Semitic propaganda did not figure so prominently after 1941 is closely related to the wider policy decisions that had already been taken by this time. The German public's reaction to the largely unplanned *Kristallnacht* of 1938 had convinced the Nazi leadership that during 1940 anti-Jewish propaganda would have to be intensified in order to prepare people for the future treatment of Jews in Germany and in the occupied territories. At the same time anti-Jewish policy would have to be better coordinated, more centralised and less public in its vulgar, 'rabble-rousing' attempts to solve the Jewish Quesion. Once it was agreed that there was a Jewish 'problem', solving it could be carried out by the SS, with the public largely excluded.

The radicalisation of German foreign policy had led to the invasion of the Soviet Union. Operation Barbarossa was a war of extermination. With the entry of the USA into the war in December 1941 Hitler's huge military gamble was effectively lost. But Hitler was also engaged in another war – the systematic genocide of the Jews. This aimed at more than the population in Poland and Russia and involved nothing less than the Jewish population of Europe, estimated by the SS at approximately 10.5 million. Although the logistics of extermination would be delegated to the SS, locating Hitler's precise role in the 'cumulative radicalisation' of anti-Jewish policy is both complex and crucial. At one level this embraces the question of a so-called 'Hitler order', and its corollary, the degree of complicity of the German population in the Final Solution. The notion of 'collective guilt' and the argument that the German people were Hitler's 'willing executioners' have been given an added poignancy in recent years with the publication of Daniel Goldhagen's controversial and flawed best seller *Hitler's Willing Executioners* (see Postscript).

Many historians agree that the 'final solution of the Jewish Question' began with the German invasion of the Soviet Union on 22 June 1941. The war in the East removed all remaining restraints against 'licensed barbarism'. Ever since he wrote *Mein Kampf* Hitler continued to insist that the Jews were behind Communism. The war with the Soviet Union provided him with an opportunity to crush both. Within a few months of the attack, what had been hitherto a hesitant and improvised campaign of mass murder, was placed even more firmly under the central control of the SS, directed by Heinrich Himmler and his deputy Reinhard Heydrich. (The SS had control of the Jewish Question since January 1939.) The growing involvement of the SS represents the connection between bureaucratic organisation and charismatic leadership that will be discussed later in this chapter. The architect of the genocide, Heinrich Himmler, who had set up the first concentration camp in Dachau in 1933, had been outraged at the shambles of *Kristallnacht*. This former poultry farmer had proved himself to be a fanatical disciple of Hitler's race theory and, moreover, deferential to Hitler's will. In October 1939 Hitler appointed him Reich Commissar for the Strengthening of German Racial Identity (*Reichskommissar für die Festigung des Deutschen Volkstums*) and he was given absolute control over the newly annexed part of Poland. In the same year Reinhard Heydrich was appointed head of the Reich Security Head Office (RSHA) which incorporated the Gestapo, the criminal police and the Security Service (SD). Between them, these two men rapidly accumulated enormous power together with the necessary administrative apparatus, manpower and technology to coordinate and implement the systematic extermination of European Jewry.

Four months after the invasion of the Soviet Union in October 1941, Heydrich, assisted by Adolf Eichmann, organised the mass deportation of Jews from Germany and Austria and annexed parts of Poland to the *General-Gouvernement* (the part of Poland not annexed by Germany). The removal of Jews from the annexed parts of Poland was intended to make way for ethnic Germans, mainly from the Baltic. However, this created huge ghettos in areas like Lüdz and Warsaw and it soon became clear that because of the numbers involved the strategy could not succeed. The lack of an overall plan of extermination at this stage is highlighted by the fact that sections of the SS were considering a bizarre Foreign Office proposal to ship European Jews to Madagascar in the Indian Ocean (although not necessarily for resettlement). On 31 July 1941, following the attack on the USSR, Heydrich had been given responsibility by Göring for carrying out the 'total solution of the Jewish question in those territories of Europe which are under German influence' – with Himmler as the supreme overseer. Interestingly, the document charging him with taking on these responsibilities refers to both 'total' solution (*Gesamtlösung*) and 'final' solution (*Endlösung*). By this stage *Einsatzgruppen* (specially selected SS units) with the cooperation of the Wehrmacht, were shooting Jews in the Soviet Union. In Germany Party activists were demanding to have Jews from the Reich deported. With the ghettos bursting at the seams it was decided in the late summer of 1941 that mass extermination by poison gas was the solution. In December 1941 the first killing installations using mobile 'gas vans' were operating at Chelmno in the Warthegau (a part of western Poland annexed to the Reich). However the 'final solution' to the 'Jewish Question' was not implemented until after the Wannsee Conference of 20 January 1942 finally coordinated measures for mass extermination. The conference had been convened by Reinhard Heydrich and appropriately enough given the circumlocutory language used to disguise mass murder (the 'final solution' being another euphemism), the code-word used was 'Operation Reinhard.' By the end of March 1942 the mass extermination of Poland's Jewish population was underway in camps like Belzec, Sobibor and Treblinka. The most notorious extermination camp of all, Auschwitz-Birkenau, began its systematic mass gassings of Jews in June 1942. The process of 'cumulative radicalisation' which started with intimidation and persecution culminated in a network of extermination camps (all outside Germany in occupied Poland) and the slaughter of 6 million Jews (and over a quarter of a million gypsies) during the Second World War. Similarly, Hitler's obsessive anti-Bolshevism culminating in his 'war of annihilation' led to some 3 million Russian POWs dying – mostly of disease and starvation.

Is it possible that the implementation of mass extermination on a European scale could have been undertaken without the knowledge or approval of Hitler? Hitler's precise role in the Holocaust continues to divide historians. Interpretations are invariably shaped by the fundamental differences that exist over the nature of the Nazi state. This brings us back to the 'Hitlerist' or 'intentionalist' explanations versus the 'structuralist' or 'functionalist' ones. Was it a monolithic structure subservient to the all-embracing will of Hitler – or was it a shapeless and fragmented collection of competing individuals and institutions that included Hitler? The debate centres less on Hitler's knowledge and responsibility – few historians would absolve Hitler from complicity – but on whether or not Hitler had a clear plan and timetable for extermination. Furthermore, did Hitler personally order the 'Final Solution'? These questions are outside the scope of this work which is concerned to explain the rationalisations used to 'legitimise' the Holocaust.[54]

At precisely the time that Jewish persecution was being intensified and final details of the 'solution' arrived at (i.e., the summer and autumn of 1941), the SD reports were noting either boredom with or massive indifference to the Jewish Question.[55] Such indifference proved fatal. Interest in the fate of Jews had in fact rapidly evaporated after the *Reichskristallnacht*. Ian Kershaw has written that the 'road to Auschwitz was built by hate, but paved with indifference'.[56] It was no longer necessary after 1941 to 'publicise' the threats posed by Jews, and as a result the Jewish Question became of no more than marginal importance in the formation of popular opinion within the Third Reich. Propaganda had helped to create such apathy and indifference by persuading people that they could retreat into the safety of their depoliticised private lives and leave the 'solutions' to such 'problems' to others. Tragically, the 'moral ambiguity' that characterised the public's response to the well-publicised plans to exterminate Jews and other 'inferior' races encouraged the regime to 'realise the unthinkable'.[57]

CHARISMATIC LEADERSHIP AND THE 'HITLER MYTH'

Just as National Socialism needed its enemies, so it also required its heroes. For their concept of the heroic leader the Nazis turned once again to *völkisch* thought and the notion of *Führerprinzip*, a mystical figure embodying and guiding the nation's destiny. In practical terms this meant that decisions came down from above instead of being worked out by discussion and choice from below. The roots and antecedents of such a concept are complex and derive from many sources: the Messianic principle of Christianity, the thaumaturgic kings of the Middle Ages, the Nietzschean 'superman' of *völkisch* mythology, and rightist circles in Germany before the First World War. However, the Nazi belief in the *Führerprinzip*, as it found expression in Germany after 1933, stemmed partly from the distaste which Germans felt towards the nineteenth century for the determining of policy by the counting of votes, and partly from the way in which Nazi philosophers such as Alfred Bäumler had reinterpreted Nietzsche's concept of the 'triumph of the will' through individual genius. The *Führerprinzip* was to be based on a very special personality which had the will and power to actualise the *Volksstaat*. This would be achieved by the man of destiny – resolute, uncompromising, dynamic and radical – who would destroy the old privileged and class-ridden society and replace it by the ethnically pure and socially harmonious 'national community'. By implication it would be the antithesis of democracy. The extreme fragmentation of Weimar politics, which were increasingly seen in terms of a failure to govern, served only to make such leadership qualities appear all the more attractive.

The cult of the leader, which surpassed any normal level of trust in political leadership, is central to an understanding of the appeal of National Socialism, and undoubtedly the most important theme cementing Nazi propaganda together. In his study *Behemoth*, which was published in 1942,

Franz Neumann pointed out that the Third Reich was no totalitarian dictatorship in the sense of a 'monolithic, authoritarian system inspired by a unified policy'.[58] Neumann argued that, despite all the revolutionary slogans, the old social order and traditional ruling class remained. Neumann attempted to show that the Nazi regime had created a form of direct rule over the suppressed masses which was without any rational legality and which was dependent upon four largely autonomous groups, each pressing its own administrative and legal powers. These were the Party, the army, the bureaucracy and industry. (Had he written the book when more information was available, he would surely have included the SS.) But towering above all the rival groups was the symbolic figure of the Führer, the head of State who was not subject to any constitutional checks and balances.

Following the 'seizure of power', the authority associated with charismatic leadership was transferred from the National Socialist Party to the German State and nation. On 19 August 1934, the law concerning the head of State of the German Reich merged the offices of Reich President and Reich Chancellor into the new office of 'Führer and Reich Chancellor', which became very quickly abbreviated to 'Führer'. Although Hitler's position was now defined in constitutional terms, the nature of charismatic leadership led to what has been called a 'polycratic' system of government where the traditional spheres of authority, like the State and the legal system, operated side-by-side with the more abstract notion of 'Führer power' (*Führergewalt*), which was exclusive and unlimited. Ernst Huber, the Nazi political theorist, defined such power as follows:

> The position of Führer combines in itself all sovereign power of the Reich; all public power in the State, as in the movement, is derived from the Führer power. If we wish to define political power in the *völkisch* Reich correctly, we must speak not of 'State power' but of 'Führer power'. For it is not the State as an impersonal entity that is the source of political power; rather, political power is given to the Führer as the executor of the nation's common will. Führer power is comprehensive and total; it unites within itself all means of creative political activity; it embraces all spheres of national life; it includes all national comrades who are bound to the Führer in loyalty and obedience. Führer power is not restricted by safeguards and controls, by autonomous protected spheres, and by vested individual rights; rather, it is free and independent, exclusive and unlimited.[59]

'Führer power' operated at a number of different levels. For disparate activists within the NSDAP, Hitler, as undisputed Führer, represented the unifying force of the movement. Embodied in the notion of the *Führerprinzip* was a recognition on the part of all the different interests within the Party of where power resided. As such the *Führerprinzip* governed the organisational structure of Nazism and provided it with its unique source of legitimacy. For the mass population who were not Party members, on the other hand, Hitler filled a vacuum caused by the sudden loss of the monarchy in 1918. Nazi propaganda presented him as a contemporary *Volkskaiser* who transcended party politics, but as a leader who demanded unconditional loyalty and obedience in order to bring about the *Volksgemeinschaft*. This mass recognition proved particularly important in persuading non-Nazi elites to accept Hitler's authority in the crucial transitional period immediately after the 'seizure of power'.

While in theory the Weimar Constitution was never abandoned, Hitler's position as Führer and exclusive representative of the nation's will was quickly consolidated. In order to achieve this position of unrestricted power, the Nazi State set up a judiciary which sanctioned what was happening and, by its total subservience to the 'will of the Führer', sacrificed its traditional function as an independent third force of the State.

Although few changes were made to civil law, the Nazis proved ruthlessly opportunistic in utilising the criminal law for their own ends. By gradually subverting legal norms to executive SS-police action acting under the guise of 'Führer-power', the Nazis could rely on the compliance of a national-conservative judiciary who had remained hostile to the liberal principles of the Weimar Republic which had protected individual rights against excesses of the State. Therefore, without necessarily being staunch Nazis, many judges and lawyers welcomed the Nazi regime in 1933 for their promise to restore a more authoritarion notion of 'law and order' and, by implication, the status of the judiciary.

Led by Reich Minister of Justice Franz Gürtner (who was not a Nazi), the erosion of legality began immediately after the Reichstag fire, when the Decree for the Protection of the People and the State retrospectively imposed the death penalty on van der Lubbe for allegedly setting fire to the Reichstag, even though the death penalty for arson had not existed at the time of the offence. In fact the 'Reichstag Fire Decree' (as it was popularly known) was used indiscriminately to arrest any political oppo--nent of Nazism who could not be interned without trial. Whereas 268 cases were tried for high treason in 1932, in 1933 the figure had risen to over 11,000. In March 1933, in order to deal with treason trials resulting from the 'Lex van der Lubbe', a new system of Special Courts, operating without juries, was introduced. It was Gürtner who also gave legal sanction to the massacre of the SA leadership in June 1934 ('Night of the Long Knives') by claiming that the State had 'anticipated' treasonable action and that the measures were justified on the grounds of 'self-defence'. The progressive erosion of the rule of law and the old *Rechtsstaat* was further undermined by the setting up in April 1934 of the so-called 'People's Court' (*Volksgerichtshof*) to deal with cases of treason. Many Party purists hoped that the People's Court would become the direct expression of a *völkisch* concept of the law. Staffed by five judges, only two of whom needed to be lawyers, and using juries made up only of Party officials, the People's Court denied defendants most of their rights, including that of appeal against a verdict. By 1937, however, the People's Court found itself increasingly supplanted by the massive expansion in the power of the merged police and SS who were operating outside the conventional framework of the law as a direct executive organ of the 'Führer's will'.

The basis for the interpretation of all laws was now the National Socialist philosophy, as expressed in the Party programme, and the speeches of the Führer. Carl Schmidt, a constitutional lawyer, defined the principles of Nazi law as simply 'a spontaneous emanation of the Führer's will'. This view was made quite explicit in a speech by Hans Frank, the head of the Nazi Association of Lawyers and of the Academy of German Law, in 1938:

1. At the head of the Reich stands the leader of the NSDAP as the leader of the German Reich for life.
2. He is, on the strength of being leader of the NSDAP, leader and chancellor of the Reich. As such he embodies simultaneously, as head of State, supreme State power and, as chief of the Government, the central functions of the whole Reich administration. He is head of State and chief of the Government in one person. He is commander-in-chief of all the armed forces of the Reich.
3. The Führer and Reich chancellor is the constituent delegate of the German people, who, without regard for formal preconditions, decides the outward form of the Reich, its structure and general policy.
4. The Führer is supreme judge of the nation. . . . There is no position in the area of constitutional law in the Third Reich independent of this elemental will of the Führer. . . . The Führer is backed not by constitutional clauses but by outstanding achievements which are based on the combination of a calling and of his devotion to the people. . . . Whether the Führer governs according to a formal written constitution is not a legal question. . . . The legal question is only whether through his activity the Führer guarantees the existence of his people.[60]

Thus Hitler's position of absolute power was justified not in legal–rational terms as that of chancellor and head of State but in charismatic terms as that of Führer of the German *Volk* – not a State, but a German nation as racially determined entity. As the custodian of the nation's will, constitutional limitations could not be imposed on his authority. The legal system and individual judges had no right to question the decisions of the Führer, which were increasingly disguised as laws or decrees, and thus given the façade of 'normality'. Such 'normality' could, however, be violated at any time by individuals or organisations, for example the Gestapo, who could claim to be operating within the sphere of 'Führer power'. In this way the constitutional State was delivered into the hands of the 'healthy feelings of the nation', which, it was claimed, would generate the strength and energy necessary for national revival and Germany's quest to become a dominant world power.

In 1941, at the height of Germany's military success, Goebbels informed his officials in the Ministry for Propaganda that his two notable propaganda achievements were, first, 'the style and technique of the Party's public ceremonies; the ceremonial of the mass demonstrations, the ritual of the great Party occasion', and, second, that through his 'creation of the Führer myth, Hitler had been given the halo of infallibility, with the result that many people who looked askance at the Party after 1933 had now complete confidence in Hitler'.[61] Ian Kershaw, who has subjected this relationship between Hitler and the German people to a systematic analysis, has demonstrated that Hitler was indeed the most vital legitimising force within the regime.[62]

By 1936 Nazi propaganda had proclaimed Hitler a leader of genius who had single-handedly restored Germany's international reputation, masterminded economic recovery and re-established law and order. These were not specifically 'Nazi achievements' rather they were achievements that any German politician or statesman would have been proud of. As such they transcended party politics and even sections of the community opposed to Nazism were forced into grudging admiration. Had the German people realised the nature of Hitler's haphazard style of leadership, his cavalier attitude to the day-to-day affairs of state and the ensuing administrative chaos, then public perception may have shifted. On the other hand when he was preparing for an important speech he would often resort to a frenzy of activity. Kershaw noted that the public image was vital: 'He remained, above all, the propagandist *par excellence*.'[62] Hitler now viewed himself, no doubt, encouraged by his own propaganda, as irreplaceable.

From 1933 the personality cult surrounding Hitler was burgeoning. Poems were written in his honour, towns and cities conferred honorary citizenships and the commercial exploitation of the Führer cult created an entire industry of kitsch. Artists in particular felt duty-bound to capture the magnitude of Hitler's genius and his achievements. Carl Protzen painted the grandiose building schemes in *The Führer's Roads* (see Plate 19) while Georg Poppe depicted Hitler as a messiah-like figure blessing a sick child surrounded by representative 'disciples' from the *Volksgemeinschaft* at the Frankfurt Physicians' Corporation (see Plate 20). Portraits of Hitler dominated the artistic landscape (see Plate 5). The SS weekly *Das schwarze Korps* summed up the significance of such representation:

> The Führer is the highest gift to the nation. He is the German fulfilment. An artist who wants to render the Führer must be more than an artist. The entire German people and German eternity will stand silently in front of this work, filled with emotions to gain strength from

Plate 19 Carl Protzen (1940), *The Führer's Roads.*

Plate 20 Georg Poppe (1940), *Portrait of the Führer.*

it today and for all time. Holy is the art and the call to serve the people. Only the best may dare to render the Führer.[64]

Although Goebbels was quick to exploit such hero-worship there was nonetheless a genuine outpouring of adulation that took on all the characteristics of a pseudo-religious movement. No amount of propaganda could have manufactured what one writer has referred to as the 'politics of faith'. For a brief period in the mid-1930s Hitler's standing as a *national* leader was unmatched by any previous German leader.

By appearing to stand above the day-to-day realities of the regime, Hitler acted like a kind of medieval monarch, as a positive symbol, a focus of loyalty and of national unity. Hitler was presented not just as another party leader, but as the leader for whom Germany had been waiting – a leader who would place the nation before any particularist cause. The nature of Hitler's position as charismatic leader, as the Führer of the German people, rested on his continuing ability to detach himself from day-to-day politics, with the result that he was never personally associated with the worst extremes of the regime. Different social groupings, ranging from the industrial working class to church leaders continued to perceive Hitler as a 'moderate', opposed to the radical and extreme elements within the movement. One of the most significant achievements of the propaganda construction of the 'Führer myth' was success in separating Hitler from the growing unpopularity of the Nazi Party itself. The Sopade reports, for example, show that the Führer myth was a genuinely integratory force in society after 1933, penetrating even into sections of the working class who opposed the Nazi Party itself, and eliciting an extraordinary degree of loyalty to Hitler.[65] According to the SD, this loyalty only began to disintegrate after Stalingrad and the refusal of Hitler to address the nation.[66] Even as late as 1944, Goebbels achieved a short-lived revival of trust in the Führer following the failure of the 20 July plot against him. The abortive attempt on Hitler's life was widely greeted with shock and horror and enabled Goebbels to exploit the attempted assassination to show that the hand of providence was guiding Hitler by coining the slogan 'Hitler is victory' (*Hitler ist der Sieg*).[67]

The ritual of the mass meeting was an important element in the projection of the Führer cult. Uniforms, bands, flags and symbols were all part of Goebbels' propaganda machine, to increase the impact of Hitler's strong words with strong deeds. This is the fundamental rationale behind the constant display of Nazi symbols in posters and in films like *Triumph of the Will* (*Triumph des Willens*, 1935) and the weekly German newsreels (*Deutsche Wochenschauen*). Leni Riefenstahl's *Triumph of the Will*, the documentary film, commissioned by Hitler, of the 1934 *Reichsparteitag*, opens with a slow fade-up of the German eagle and the title *Triumph des Willens*, with the caption:

> Twenty years after the outbreak of the First World War, sixteen years after the beginning of Germany's time' of trial, nineteen months after the beginning of the rebirth of Germany, Adolf Hitler flew to Nuremberg to muster his faithful followers.[68]

In projecting the image of the strong leader to an audience that had come to associate the Weimar Republic and the Treaty of Versailles with national ignominy, *Triumph des Willens* portrayed Hitler as a statesman of genius who had single-handedly rebuilt the nation and staunchly defended Germany's territorial rights over the hegemony imposed by foreigners. However, the determination to feel and be united was not enough; the Nazis had to give public testimony to this 'unity'. The Nuremberg Rallies were carefully staged theatrical pieces devised to create such an effect. This also explains why the Nazis repeatedly staged 'national moments' (*Stunden der Nation*), when Hitler's speeches would be broadcast simultaneously throughout the Reich. On such occasions life would come to a standstill, demonstrating the sense of national community where the individual participant in the ritual, moved by Hitler's rhetoric and swayed by the crowd, underwent a metamorphosis, in Goebbels' famous phrase, 'from a little worm into part of a large dragon'.[69]

Nonetheless, Goebbels' manipulatory skill alone could not have created the quasi-religious faith in Hitler demonstrated by large sections of the German population. Without concrete achievements Hitler could not have sustained his positive image as Führer. By the spring of 1939 Sopade was identifying the reduction in unemployment and a series of foreign-policy successes as the two major achievements consolidating Hitler's position. In domestic politics, Hitler was recognised for having won the 'battle for work', building the autobahns, and generally revamping the economy. Although industrial workers continued to view the 'economic miracle' in terms of longer hours and low wages, nevertheless they welcomed the restoration of full employment and the social-welfare schemes for the poorer sections of the community. The middle class, which had benefited from the rearmament boom of the mid-1930s, remained devoted to Hitler, whom it saw as the father-figure of the regime.

Much of Hitler's popularity after he came to power rested on his achievements in foreign policy. A recurring theme in Nazi propaganda before 1939 was that Hitler was a man of peace but one who was determined to recover German territories 'lost' as a result of the Treaty of Versailles. Providing foreign-policy propaganda could show the achievements of revisionism without German bloodshed, then it was relatively easy to feast upon the consensus that favoured overthrowing the humiliation of the post-war peace settlements. From the moment in 1936 when Hitler ordered German troops to re-occupy the demilitarised Rhineland, until the Munich agreement in 1938 which gave the Sudetenland to Germany, Hitler had successfully carried out a series of audacious foreign policy coups which won him support from all sections of the community. He was now widely acclaimed, enjoying unparalleled popularity and prestige. However, there was a basic contradiction between propaganda that presented the Führer as a 'man of peace' and an ideology that was inexorably linked to struggle and war. Obsessed by territorial expansion in the east, Hitler confirmed to his military leaders at the Hossbach Conference in November 1937 that 'Germany's problems can only be solved by means of force'. A year later, after he had sent troops into Austria to secure the *Anschluss* and had acquired the Sudetenland at the Munich Settlement, Hitler summoned 400 of the regime's leading journalists and media experts to Munich and instructed them in their future role in the coming war: 'It is absolutely necessary gradually to prepare the German people psychologically for the coming war and to make it clear to them that there are some things which only force, not peaceful means, must decide.'[70] Goebbels now switched track and claimed that war was unavoidable and was being forced upon Germany. Anticipating Germany's expansion as a major world power, propaganda set out to prepare psychologically and to mobilise the nation into a 'fighting community' for war. An ominous slogan of the period proclaimed: 'Today Germany, tomorrow the world.'

When the war came, Hitler's astonishing run of *Blitzkrieg* victories, culminating in the fall of France, confirmed Goebbels' propaganda presentation of him as a military strategist of genius who even confounded his own generals. When the war started to turn against him in the winter of 1941–2, it would take some time before military reverses had any noticeable effect on his popularity. Although the standing of his Party dropped considerably, Hitler's personal standing remained remarkably high. However, following the catastrophe of Stalingrad, a defeat for which Hitler was held responsible, his popularity began noticeably to decline (see chapter 5). With no new military victories to talk of, Hitler retreated into his bunker and refused to address the German people. In the final year of the war Goebbels attempted to resurrect the *Führer* cult by depicting Hitler as a latter-day Frederick the Great, ultimately triumphant in the face of adversity. This absurd image, in the face of the gathering Russian occupation of Germany, represented an alarming flight from reality which no amount of propaganda could sustain. The 'Hitler myth' and 'charismatic leadership' could not survive such lack of success and were on the verge of extinction.

5

NAZI PROPAGANDA AT WAR, 1939–45

INTRODUCTION

In any state involved in war, propaganda must be constantly adjusted to the changing military situation. To some extent, this is easier in a 'closed' society, where the means of communication are more tightly controlled. In the case of Nazi Germany the propaganda machine had been planning to meet the exigencies of war some eighteen months before war was declared in September 1939. However, while Hitler was preparing to launch his war, Goebbels was among the few Party leaders who sought to avert it. Albert Speer relates that 'we who were members of Hitler's personal circle considered him [Goebbels], as well as Göring, who also counselled peace, as weaklings who had degenerated in the luxury of power and did not want to risk the privileges they had acquired'. Goebbels' disapproval stemmed from his belief that the war would affect his own position. He is reported to have remarked that Hitler would 'soon listen to his generals only, and it will be very difficult for me'. Goebbels' fears were justified, for in the early years of the war the Ministry for Propaganda would be forced to share its responsibilities with the OKW and the Section for Wehrmacht Propaganda and this included censorship powers over the media.

The war imposed considerable strains on the political, social and economic structure set up by the Nazi regime. The difficulties for propaganda were exacerbated by the distinct lack of enthusiasm for the announcement of war, compared to the kind of enthusiasm that had apparently gripped the masses in 1914. The trust in leadership which had been so carefully nurtured in the years leading up to war had now to be preserved at all costs. In the course of maintaining an effective link with the regime's leadership, propaganda had to convince the German people of the justness of their own cause and German invincibility. It was important to persuade the German people that the war could and would be won. But abroad it also had to win over neutral nations and at the same time undermine the enemy's spirit of resistance. Therefore the exigencies of war demanded of Goebbels a more intense concern with the tactics of propaganda and, moreover, a flexibility that could respond to changing military situations. His directive 'Guidelines for the Execution of NSDAP Propaganda', issued at the outbreak of war, outlined the means he expected his staff to employ in disseminating propaganda. The means included the radio and newspapers, films, posters, mass meetings, illustrated lectures and 'whisper' or person-to-person propaganda (*Mundpropaganda*). Preparations for war had been set in motion before 1939. For some years a regular daily meeting had taken place in the Propaganda Ministry on the Wilhelmplatz in Berlin, attended by Goebbels, senior officials of the RMVP and liaison and media staff from other ministries, the Party Chancellery and the Wehrmacht. These press conferences would normally begin at 11.am (although the time could vary from 10.00 am to noon) and lasted for half an hour to forty-five minutes. Goebbels dominated proceedings and the only other regular speaker was the OKW liaison officer who would give a brief account of developments at the front(s). The ministerial conference was very much a platform for Goebbels to perform. The Minister would use the 'conference' to provide guidelines and detailed instructions for the implementation of German propaganda. It was not intended to offer a dialogue with journalists. As Goebbels widened the scope of his brief during the war the conference expanded from twenty in attendance gradually increasing after the invasion of Russia to fifty or sixty persons.

Although propaganda was the responsibility of the RMVP, Goebbels never retained complete control of all aspects of propaganda. As we have seen, one of the limitations on his authority was that he had to share responsibility for war reporting with the Wehrmacht who prepared the daily military communiqué. The communiqué contained a summary of the military situation and was subject to final approval by Hitler who tended to meddle with the wording. Since the military communiqué was often delayed, in large part due to Hitler's alterations, Goebbels had to content himself for most of the war with a draft communiqué. Moreover as Hitler tended to use the Wehrmacht (as opposed to the Propaganda Ministry) communiqué for foreign purposes, this exacerbated another problem, namely the Wehrmacht's tendency to put an excessively optimistic 'spin' on the military situation, which in turn could often lead to popular disappointment and consequent disillusionment with the media.

Goebbels' other problem was Dr Otto Dietrich, Reich Press Chief and State Secretary in the Propaganda Ministry. Dietrich was in the anomalous position of being, on the one hand, a member of Hitler's immediate entourage and in principle autonomous, and, on the other hand, of being theoretically subordinate to Goebbels. In addition, Dietrich, like Goebbels, was a *Reichsleiter* of the Nazi Party, which gave him the rank of a cabinet member. Dietrich, not Goebbels, issued the 'Daily Directives of the Reich Press Chief', which contained Hitler's detailed directives to the newspaper editors. Dietrich remained a thorn in Goebbels side and the personal rivalry between the two was symptomatic of the chaotic nature of the Nazi political system that Hitler encouraged. Goebbels plotted to have him replaced claiming that he 'was an inveterate weakling' and 'a foreign body in my Ministry'. For most of the war, however, Dietrich sheltered behind Hitler largely ignoring Goebbels' orders. Finally on 30 March 1945 he was replaced. Goebbels joyfully recorded in his diary: 'I hear from *Reichsleiter* Bormann that the Führer had a three minute interview with Dr Dietrich at which Dietrich and Sündermann [Dietrich's deputy] were sent packing in short order. I shall take full advantage of the opportunity and create *faits accomplis* in the press which it will be impossible to countermand later.'[1] Goebbels would never fulfil this task and this was to be one of the last entries that he ever wrote.

During the course of the war four major propaganda campaigns emerged – all of which were dictated by changing military fortunes. They were (1) *Blitzkrieg*; (2) the Russian campaign; (3) total war and the need for strengthening morale; and (4) promises of retaliation or 'revenge' (*Vergeltung*). Of the following case studies the first two deal with the military campaigns abroad and their effect on public opinion at home; the last two analyse the response of the regime to Germany's changing military fortunes and the prospect of imminent defeat.

BLITZKRIEG AND VICTORY

Goebbels' immediate task once war had been declared was to counteract the negative opinions held by the population at home. In the first years of the war, propaganda had a relatively easy task capitalising on the *Blitzkrieg* victories. But in many respects war circumscribed the independence of the RMVP, in that it was made to serve military objectives like any other branch of the armed forces. Propaganda still had to be thought out and disseminated, but for a while Goebbels ceased to force the pace and instead was carried along with the tide.

As the Wehrmacht launched its campaigns with astonishing success, the dominant theme became the futility of resistance to German military might. The broad theme of *Blitzkrieg* was applied in a variety of ways, depending on the target, but it was invariably accompanied by intimidation and fear. Goebbels believed that propaganda must not only be supported by force but should itself incite violent action. In his diary he argued that 'a sharp sword must always stand behind propaganda, if it is to be really effective'. It is not surprising, then, to discover that from the outset of every campaign the accent was on terror. Propaganda was able to advertise military victories and indirectly help to prepare an atmosphere, or expectation, of new ones. In this way the propagandist served to support military campaigns by creating a confident and aggressive spirit at home and by challenging enemy leaders to reveal their military prowess in the arena of combat. Thus during the period of lightning victories in Poland, Scandinavia, the Low Countries and France, German belief in an early termination of the war was strengthened by a concerted propaganda campaign which recognised the lack of any widespread enthusiasm for the war and the desire of the population for an early peace.

In these first crucial years of the war Goebbels made considerable use of newsreels and feature-length war documentaries. Not only were they employed to illustrate Germany's military superiority and the futility of resistance, but more importantly they served to reinforce a feeling of security and reassurance on the part of a reluctant German audience. Until the outbreak of war there were four newsreels operating in Germany: *Ufa-Tonwoche*, *Deulig-Woche*, *Tobis Wochenschau*, and *Fox tönende Wochenschau*, which was American-owned. A fifth newsreel, *UfaAuslandswoche*, distributed German home news abroad. It was the Ministry for Propaganda's task to coordinate all newsreel reports into one 'official' version of contemporary Germany. They were assisted in this by legislation, notably the so-called 'Newsreel Law' ('*Wochenschaugesetz*'), which was introduced on 30 April 1936 in order to ease the problems of distribution and copyright. In October 1938 further legislation reduced the number of editions from fifteen to eight and made the showing of a newsreel compulsory at every film programme. Throughout the 1930s the newsreels had attempted to create a consensus among the German people on the projected deeds of the regime in both domestic and foreign affairs. As a result, a special style emerged in both structure and documentary sequences which bore little relation to objective reporting. Not surprisingly, a propaganda weapon as important as the newsreel was subject to strict military and governmental control before being distributed. Censorship was exercised by the *Wochenschauzentrale*, which was directly subordinate to the RMVP. Its main responsibility was to liaise between the four newsreel companies, ensuring that their film reports represented the political and cultural views of the National Socialist community.

In the months leading up to the announcement of war, newsreels stressed Germany's military preparedness for war against an attack from the West. Newsreels were used to convince the people that Hitler's revisionist foreign policy was justified and that Germany was once again being encircled by her old enemies. In this respect the newsreels echoed the sentiment of the time expressed in the propaganda slogan 'He who wants peace must also prepare for war.' Throughout 1939 the newsreels continued in this fashion, attempting to prepare the people for the coming war by concentrating on military subjects. Indeed, in August the newsreels were already giving the impression of a Germany at war, provoked by alleged Polish atrocities inflicted on the German community in Poland. The need to manufacture such a barbaric image of the Polish enemy clearly reflected the regime's desire to dispel popular anxiety over the prospect of war.

After the outbreak of war the Ministry for Propaganda merged the four newsreels into a single war newsreel. This was achieved with a minimum of disruption, owing largely to the measures that had been taken by the ministry since 1936. On 21 November 1940, the Deutsche Wochenschau GmbH was founded and all other newsreel companies dissolved. Goebbels ordered that in future the war newsreel should simply be referred to as *Deutsche Wochenschau*. By concentrating such vast resources, the new company was intended not only to establish a European newsreel monopoly but also to pose a serious challenge to America's supremacy in this field.[2] Until this time the public were largely unaware that the newsreels were State-controlled, as very little was known about the Wochenschauzentrale. From Goebbels' point of view, such a revelation would have reduced their effectiveness and therefore no information had been given of his ministry's role in this field. However, he confided in his diary:

> Discuss the re-organisation of the newsreels with Hippler [president of the Reich Film Chamber]. We have established a new company including Ufa, Tobis and Bavaria, I intend to keep personal control of it. After the war there will be three different newsreels again. Now, in the middle of a war, this is not a practical proposition.[3]

War invariably produces an excess of good propagandist material, and Goebbels was determined to control the cameramen whose responsibility it was to capture it. Such a concentration of resources permitted swift and economic reporting of events both at home and abroad. Reporting the war was the responsibility of the Propaganda Kompanie Einheiten (PK units) which were established in 1938. They were appointed by the RMVP, but at the front they operated under the command of the Oberkommando der Wehrmacht (OKW). However, all film shot was at the exclusive disposal of the Ministry for Propaganda. The material shot by the PK units was also used in the prestigious *Blitzkrieg* documentaries: *Feldzug in Polen* (*Campaign in Poland*, 1939), *Feuertaufe* (*Baptism of Fire*, 1940), *Sieg im Westen* (*Victory in the West*, 1941). By 1940 cinema attendances had almost doubled within two years. The documentaries proved particularly successful in the rural areas where peasants were not regular cinema-goers. Goebbels responded to this by providing 1,000 mobile cinemas which travelled continuously around the countryside, ensuring that Germans saw a film-show (with a newsreel) at least once a month. Goebbels also ordered that special newsreel shows be established in the spring of 1940. Initially these were for Saturdays only, when past and present newsreels would be screened continuously. The admission charge was 30–40Pf.; soldiers and children payed half-price, but the theatre owners were expected to contribute 20 per cent of the costs. After 1940, newsreels were also incorporated into the schools and HJ programmes with great success. An extended extract from the SD report on the reception of the fifth war *Wochenschau* in June 1940 indicates the undoubted success of newsreels at this time in presenting military victories and also provides a revealing insight into how the 'Hitler myth' was being received:

> Allenstein, Münster, Halle, Breslau, Stuttgart, Lüneburg – just some of the areas that have confirmed an enormous success. Many reports state that this is the best *Wochenschau* yet – a peak has been reached with cinemas reporting overflowing auditoriums. . . . The conquering of Dunkirk made an overpowering impression and was followed breathlessly by spectators. . . . Reports from Brunswick: spectators want to wreak destruction above all on England in order to gain revenge for the crimes she has committed against Germany. Shots of the Führer . . . according to reports from all over the Reich, people applauded and there were shouts of 'Heil'. Applause, however, died to a pregnant silence when these shots were followed by pictures of Hitler moving to the map table with his generals. Every move of the Führer was followed with rapt attention. The people discussed, above all, the tired and serious features of his face. Reports from Aachen speak of relief in the auditorium when 'Adolf' laughed – the people are very concerned for his health and safety.[4]

There can be little doubt that stylistically the newsreels were impressive examples of Nazi film propaganda. They also proved an initial success with German audiences. One explanation for their popularity and the increase in cinema attendances during this period was that after 1939 the war in the West was presented in such an immediate way that the public was fascinated by these reports. But as the war dragged on they suffered, as did all Nazi propaganda, through their close association with German military success. However, this came later. During the first year of the war, Geobbels' main concern was to convince the nation of the magnitude of Hitler's *Blitzkrieg* success. To this end, the newsreels were supplemented by the feature-length war documentaries, which now figured prominently in Geobbels' film schedules. *Feldzug in Polen* was released in February 1940 and concentrated on the part played by the Wehrmacht in the Polish campaign. Two months later, *Feuertaufe* depicted the annihilation of Poland and her capital, Warsaw, by the Luftwaffe. Nine months after the fall of France, the relentless advance of the German army across Europe was meticulously chronicled by the PK cameramen in the third of the series, *Sieg im Westen*.

One of the main functions of the campaign films, which were compiled from newsreel footage, was to illustrate the lightning speed and devastating power of the German armed forces. Goebbels was fully aware of the potential psychological effects that these newsreels and documentaries could achieve when they were shown by German embassies to audiences in neutral countries. Thus in 1940 *Feuertaufe* was shown by many German embassies in neutral countries with a view to intimidating foreign diplomats. In celebrating the Nazi 'fighter stereotype', whether the Luftwaffe in *Feuertaufe* or the Wehrmacht in *Feldzug in Polen*, the campaign films invoked almost every aspect of the Nazi mythology of war and generally set the tone for a whole series of military education feature-films (*Wehrerziehungsfilme*) directed specifically at the youth audience. During the first half of the war such films would include *Jakko* (1941), *Kadetten* (1941), *Kampfgeschwader Lutzow* (*Battle Squadron Lutzow*, 1941), *Kopf hoch Johannes!* (*Chin Up, John!*, 1941), *Blutsbruderschaft* (*Blood-Brotherhood*, 1941), *Himmelhunde* (*Sky Dogs*, 1942). Interestingly enough, these early war films were the only film genre that the Nazis felt confident enough to present in a contemporary context.

Feuertaufe, which is arguably the most impressive of all the propaganda films depicting the magnitude of Hitler's *Blitzkrieg* success, was drawn from over 230,000 feet of newsreel material. The final scenes of the film deal with the capitulation of Poland and the preparations for the forthcoming attack on Britain. After the surrender of Warsaw on 18 September 1939, the Luftwaffe inspects the extent of the damage. The camera zooms in to take close-range shots of the wrecked city:

Narrator: What have you to say now, Mr Chamberlain? Here you can see the catastrophe for yourself . . . the ruin into which you plunged the Polish capital. Aren't you afraid of the curse of the nation you betrayed? . . .
Remember, this is what happens when the German Luftwaffe strikes.

(*The capitulation document is signed and 130,000 prisoners are marched out of the city. A victory fanfare follows, culminating in a Luftwaffe parade.*)

Hermann Göring: [speaking into the camera]: It is mainly to the Luftwaffe's contribution that we owe this annihilation of the enemy. When this great weapon was taken away from us [at Versailles], no one suspected that under the leadership of Adolf Hitler, this force would rise up again, mightier and more impregnable than before. . . .
What the Luftwaffe has shown in Poland it will fulfil in the coming battles in England and France. . . .

Luftwaffe Song: Thus our youngest weapon has been baptised and tempered in the flames. Now the winged host reaches out to the sea, we are ready for battle. Forward against the British lion, for the last, decisive blow. . . .

Comrade, comrade, all the girls must wait. Comrade, the order is clear, we're on our way. Comrade, the slogan you know: forward at the foe, forward at the enemy. . . . Bombs, bombs, bombs on England!

Despite the rapid victory over Poland, the German population still remained to be convinced of the efficacy of such a war, especially as Britain and France had now entered the conflict. This cautious mood was somewhat offset, however, by the astonishing advance of the Wehrmacht through the Low Countries, culminating in the surrender of France in May and June 1940. These campaigns serve to illustrate the extent to which Nazi radio propaganda in particular had been integrated into Germany's military operations. From the beginning of the war German radio had managed to build up large audiences in Europe who had grown suspicious of the statements of their home sources of information. The 'radio *Blitzkrieg*' that was launched on Holland, Belgium and France in 1940 was timed to create maximum fear and terror in order to undermine resistance. It depended for its success on the splits within the Allies and on the timing and the ability of the German armed forces to reinforce the propaganda claims made by Nazi broadcasts.

The pattern was invariably the same. Radio propaganda would first of all attempt further to divide the Allies. In the case of Holland the Germans appealed directly to the Dutch army: 'Soldiers, why are you fighting? Why are you allowing yourselves to be butchered? For the capitalists in France and England?' They would then try to divide the country under attack. In Belgium for example, they broadcast to one-half of the nation in Flemish: 'Flemings, you have always been treated as second-class citizens. We Germans will give you back your self-respect.' And, broadcasting in French to the Walloons: 'Belgium doesn't care about you, she only expects you to die for her. We will help develop your country.' Linked to this kind of onslaught was a further attempt to undermine the credibility of a government. As the Wehrmacht was rapidly advancing on Paris in June 1940, Nazi propaganda claimed: 'Your Government no longer deserves your respect. Despite its claim to defend the city to the end, it has left the capital and its people to their own fate. Why expose Paris to such senseless destruction and slaughter?' Nazi radio propaganda during this period has been compared with the praying mantis which, by separating its hind parts from its legs, so terrifies its prey that it meets with no resistance. However, recent research has suggested that the success of the propaganda campaign was more apparent than real. While 'radio *Blitzkrieg*' was a technique that undoubtedly helped sow the seeds of defeatism in the countries that were about to be attacked by Germany, nonetheless such a campaign depended heavily for its ultimate success on the ability of the armed forces to validate their propaganda claims.

The first reactions in Germany to the victories in the West were ecstatic. Hitler's standing amongst the population reached its highest point with the signing of the armistice with France on 22 June 1940. If ever there was widespread enthusiasm for the war in Germany, then this was probably the period when it existed. It even overshadowed the general discontent felt about the coal shortages and the workings of the rationing system. The SD claimed that the military victories had united the population behind Hitler's war aims:

as a consequence of the military victories, an unprecedented solidarity has developed between the front and the domestic population, as well as an unprecedented solidarity amongst the whole population. The basis of any effective oppositional activity has been completely removed.[5]

The victory over France marked the high point of Nazi propaganda but was to prove the last great military success the Germans would celebrate. Nevertheless, the special *Deutsche Wochenschau* of Hitler's 'Triumphant Return to Berlin', released to celebrate the fall of France, testifies to the remarkable nature of the cult of the Führer. The train journey back to Germany from France, and particularly his arrival in Berlin, where he is greeted by *Bund deutscher Mädel* girls and adoring women, is a powerful emotional reminder of the manner in which the Hitler myth was presented. The final scene culminates in Hitler receiving the ecstatic crowd's adulation from the balcony at the Reich Chancellory. Such triumphalism was captured in the poetry of SA *Sturmführer* Heinrich Anacker. His hugely popular 'Frankreichlied' became the official song of the battle of France when it was put to music by the prominent bandleader Herms Niel:

> Comrades, we're marching in the West,
> Together with our bomb squadrons –
> And though many of our best will die,
> We will strike down the enemy!
> Forward! To the fore! To the fore!
> Over the Meuse, over Scheldt and Rhine
> We march victoriously through France –
> We march, we march
> Through France![6]

The campaign in France presented Anacker with the opportunity to celebrate Hitler as the 'greatest military commander of all times'. In the poem entitled 'The Grey Coat' ('*Der graue Rock*'), Hitler is presented as the first soldier of the Reich, sharing the dangers of the battle with his men:

> Now as Commander of Greater Germany's army he leads
> It to victory from the Argonne Forest to the sea.
> Motors thunder and roar –
> Announcing the triumph of German arms
> In the forest of Compiègne.[7]

According to Anacker, Hitler's very presence appeared to guarantee victory:

> Unseen the eagle of eternal glory circled. . . .
> Everything that happened was conceived by Hitler
> Who, weighed down with care, leads us to the dawn!⁸

Seduced by military conquest supported by propaganda, German public opinion appears to have been convinced that Hitler was in command of the situation and that final victory seemed assured. But once again it is perhaps too easy to make sweeping generalisations. Although there was a feeling of euphoria within Germany, the SD reports reveal that there was still a strong desire for an end to the war.[9] Fuelled by a 'united Europe' theme that rationalised *Blitzkrieg* as 'liberating' Europe from the Jewish–Bolshevik threat, the population was still able to be persuaded that all Hitler wanted from the war was a 'just and lasting peace and living space for Germans'.

With the defeat of France sealed by the signing of the armistice on 22 June 1940 the focus of German propaganda switched back to Britain. Nazi propaganda reached a new crescendo in the summer and autumn of 1940 when the overwhelming majority of the German people fully expected the British to capitulate. In May 1940 Goebbels introduced *Das Reich*, a weekly newspaper for the more discerning Nazi readership which reached over 1½ million homes. Throughout the early part of the summer *Das Reich* continued to reflect the stance of the press in general by postulating that it was only a matter of time before England's fate was sealed. Propaganda emphasised British hypocrisy and British 'plutocracy'. Churchill in particular was targeted and mercilessly mocked and lampooned. One famous poster depicted him as a American-style gangster ('The Sniper') brandishing a machine gun! (see Plate 21). Incited by incessant propaganda, hatred of Britain was now widespread. Interestingly enough, in June Goebbels had ordered the media to tone down anti-British statements: 'In treating our future policy towards England, it is important to emphasize that our struggle does not aim at the destruction of the British Empire, but rather at smashing British hegemony on the continent.' To some extent Goebbels' caution reflected Hitler's own ambivalence regarding the British: 'Despite everything, the Führer still has a very positive attitude towards England,' Goebbels wrote in his diary. Having laid preparations for the invasion of Britain ('Operation Sealion') on 16 July, Hitler made his 'peace offer' speech in the Reichstag on 19 July which was promptly rejected by the British. Some days before General Franz Halder noted: 'the Führer is greatly puzzled by England's persistent unwillingness to make peace.' An SD report of 7 October 1941 indicated that the German population was also becoming frustrated about the failure to defeat Britain and disillusioned by over-optimistic reports and forecasts in the press and on the radio of German military successes. 'Grudgingly and reluctantly the population is getting used to the thought of a second winter of war, and daily worries, particularly about fuel, have come to the surface.'

In 1941 the *Reichsjugendführung* (Reich Youth Leadership) released an anti-British documentary film entitled *Soldaten von Morgen* (*Soldiers of Tomorrow*). The film takes the form of a Hitler Youth theatrical skit on the

Plate 21 A 1941 poster of Churchill, 'The Sniper'.

Plate 22 An anti-Bolshevik poster that claims: 'Europe's Victory is your Prosperity'.
Having destroyed Great Britain (depicted as one graveyard with Churchill's grave
symbolically prominent – the mailed fist of Germany now turns its attention to the
East and provides a knock-out blow for Stalin and the Soviet Union.

English public school system and the resultant effete degeneracy through this type of education, of Britain's youth. The film cites Winston Churchill, Lord Halifax and Anthony Eden as examples. British youth are ridiculed quite savagely. The first half of the film ends with dishevelled British troops being captured at Dunkirk. The moral of the story is clear: effete young English schoolboys turn into easily captured British troops. The second half of the film compares the virile and athletic qualities and activities of the Hitler Youth who are seen fencing, gliding, parachute jumping, horse riding, participating in 'mock' battles and a final parade. The film ends with shots of the German Wehrmacht as if to emphasise the fruition of such an educational and cultural process. *Soldaten von Morgen* reflects the euphoric nature of Nazi propaganda in general during this period; it is brash, confident, one might almost say arrogant. This began to change after the Battle of Britain.

The Battle of Britain turned out to be a failure not only for the Luftwaffe, but also for Nazi propaganda which was not prepared to admit a victory of British defence in the air. Goebbels' anti-British propaganda suffered a further setback in May 1941, when Rudolf Hess flew to Scotland in a desperate attempt to bring the British to their senses. The momentous event to come a few months later was not the invasion of Britain, which had been postponed indefinitely, but the invasion of the Soviet Union ('Operation Barbarossa').

THE RUSSIAN CAMPAIGN

After the failure to invade Britain in 1940, with Göring's Luftwaffe decisively checked in the Battle of Britain, Hitler switched his attack in the following April and ordered his troops into Greece, Yugoslavia and then Egypt. On 22 June 1941, the Nazis unleashed 153 divisions on Russia. In less than a month, they were two-thirds of the way to Moscow. But by the beginning of 1942 Hitler had begun to lose control of the military situation. Despite hopelessly premature announcements of an early victory in the East, the Russians held Moscow, the Americans were now in the war and, having committed the fundamental error of waging war on two fronts, Hitler's shortcomings as a strategist were exposed. In February 1943 General Paulus surrendered at Stalingrad. The relentless thrust of the German armed forces had come to an end.

The anti-Bolshevik concept was central to the Nazi *Weltanschauung*. The movement had developed and finally emerged from a struggle in which the Communist together with the Jew formed the main target of Nazi propaganda and violence. By 1924 anti-Communism was firmly established as one of the major themes of Nazi propaganda, as Hitler increasingly began to regard himself as the crusader against Jews and Marxists. It was a belief which remained with Hitler, even when all was lost in 1945.[10] Russia, therefore, figured not only as the centre of world Communism, but also as the repository of international Jewry. As *Gauleiter* of Berlin, Goebbels directed his propaganda during the Third Reich's last days in a manner that rationalised the regime's existence and lent coherence and credibility to Hitler's ideological posture. The Führer's death was broadcast on the evening of 1 May 1945 to the solemn accompaniment of Wagner and Bruckner, followed by the *Horst Wessel Lied*: although Hitler took his own life, cursing the German people for their weakness, the impression left by Goebbels' propaganda was that of a hero's death, of a fight to the last against Bolshevism.

Stereotypes invariably come ready-made, having evolved, whether consciously or subconsciously, over a considerable period of time. This was particularly the case with the anti-Bolshevik motif in Nazi propaganda. In 1933 the National Socialists were fully aware of the sources of their strength. By discovering the Jewish–Bolshevik conspiracy the Nazis not only found a scapegoat for the defeat of 1918 and the Versailles *Diktat* but also managed to appeal to long-standing fears of the German middle classes by portraying the Bolshevik as the barbarian *Untermensch* (sub-human). With this in mind, Antikomintern was founded under Goebbels' patronage in 1933, with the express intention of undermining the Communist International. The year 1936 saw an increase in the anti-Communist campaign; indeed, the *Reichsparteitag* in September was devoted to it. Two treaties were signed in late 1936 in quick succession. Germany and Italy signed a treaty (the Rome/Berlin Axis), and, with Japan, both signed the Anti-Comintern Agreement. These treaties were intended by Hitler to rally other powers to resist the spread of world Communism. The Spanish Civil War also provided Goebbels with a further opportunity to exploit this theme by dividing international opinion into the desired polarity: the evil forces of Jewish Bolshevism on the one hand, resisted by the champions of Western civilisation on the other.

In the light of this long history of antagonism towards the Soviet Union, the Nazi-Soviet Non-Aggression Pact, signed on 23 August 1939, came as something of a surprise. Goebbels was confronted with the serious problem of interpreting this treaty and of maintaining a façade of friendly relations with Russia. Public-opinion reports suggest that he was never able to convince the people that the pact was anything more than a delaying tactic which in time would be reversed. The German public was not so naïve as the Nazi leadership supposed, and the SD reports were confirming that the vast majority of the population expected war with the Soviet Union to come sooner or later. Within a year the situation was reversed: though the declaration of war against Russia was not greeted with enthusiasm, the German people accepted the decision as inevitable, while the initial victories of the Wehrmacht served to still any open dissent.

Very little propaganda preparation had been made for the invasion of the Soviet Union on 22 June 1941. However, once the offensive had been launched it provided Goebbels with the ideological cohesion that had been absent in Nazi propaganda since the signing of the Nazi-Soviet pact in 1939. Goebbels referred to the invasion as a 'settling of accounts with Moscow'. In his message to the German people explaining the reasons for the invasion, Hitler described the war as a great ideological struggle:

> German people! At this moment a movement of troops is taking place which in its scope and expanse is the greatest that the world has ever seen . . . the German eastern front stretches from East Prussia to the Carpathians. . . . The task of this front is no longer to protect single countries but to ensure the security of Europe and thereby save them all.[11]

In a campaign that added a new dimension to the 'united Europe' drive, Nazi propaganda claimed that there existed two distinct European civilisations: the vastly superior instincts and culture of Western Europe, compared to the primitive Asiatic and Slavic 'sub-humans' from the East. It was this arrogant conviction that all eastern nationalities were sub-human that prevented the Nazis from fully appreciating the opportunities with which they were presented. Owing to the ruthlessness of Stalin's regime, many social groups and national minorities within the USSR might have been prepared to help the Nazis in return for ending Stalin's reign of terror. The Soviet Union, therefore, was an ideal target for psychological warfare. Indeed, in areas such as Latvia, Lithuania and Estonia the advancing Wehrmacht was greeted as a liberator.

Thus in the summer of 1941, Nazi propagandists were faced with two options: they could identify the entire nation with the Soviet regime; or they could establish a series of alliances with, for example, the peasants who were disaffected by the brutal collectivisation of the farms programme, national minorities like the Ukrainians and the Cossacks, who resented Greater Russian oppression, and the officer corps of the Red Army, where morale was low after the purges of the late 1930s. In fact what is so interesting about Nazi propaganda during the Russian campaign is its inconsistency. Hitler's position is well documented and he never wavered from his belief that all the Eastern nationalities were inferior races. Accordingly, Hitler intended to gain control of the rich agricultural and mineral resources of Russia and to colonise the people. Goebbels also appears initially to have taken this view. However, a month after the invasion of Russia he did set up a secret radio station which specialised in broadcasting to the Soviet Union and which was far more sophisticated than the run-of-the-mill Nazi propaganda. These broadcasts took the form of different opposition arguments to Stalin's policies. By claiming that Stalin was a slave of the capitalists who had 'sold the Socialist fatherland to the plutocrats', it intended to undermine further the cohesion of the

Communist Party ranks.[12] In general, though, the Nazis were quick to revive their traditional anti-Bolshevik propaganda, and in the summer of 1941 their reporting of Europe's crusade against Bolshevism became progressively more strident. Typical was the poster which was widely distributed and showed a wolf-like figure against a background of destruction and snarling above a drowning person, with the title: 'The aim of Bolshevism: to drown the world in blood' (see Plate 23).

Bolshevism offered the Nazis certain advantages as a bogey. Initially they were able to rationalise the invasion of Russia as a defence measure against an imminent attack from barbaric Slavs from the East. Later it proved to be a telling argument in favour of continued resistance. In this way they were able to link the fear and salvation motives intrinsic to the crusade against Bolshevik 'sub-human' beings. On 10 July 1941 the Ministry for Propaganda received a message from the Führerhauptquartier: 'The Führer wants shots of Russian cruelty towards German prisoners to be incorporated in the newsreels so that Germans know exactly what the enemy is like.' Later during the same month the SD were reporting that the propaganda campaign waged in all the media against the racial inferiority of the Slav and the 'cruel deeds of the GPU and the Bolshevik soldier towards the civilian population' was having some success. Cinema audiences in particular were 'outraged by the pictures of these criminal types with their barbaric features'.[13]

Although the German media trumpeted variations of the 'Russian–Jew–sub-human' stance, it was never able to convince the nation that the war against the USSR was unavoidable. This was of little consequence at first, as the German people was able to celebrate further Wehrmacht victories, culminating in the taking of Kiev in September 1941. A month later Hitler went so far as to claim publicly that the war against the Soviet Union was already won: 'Our opponent has already been broken and will never rise again!' Nevertheless Goebbels was already shifting his ground, having concluded that Hitler's *Ostpolitik* was ill-advised. Despite the highly emotional reporting of these victories in the German press, the Minister for Propaganda was aware of the extent to which the invasion of Russia had lowered the expectations of the population of an early end to the war. These fears were fully justified when the SD reports noted the damaging effect on civilian morale of the hastily arranged collection of winter clothing for the unfortunate German troops stranded in Russia in December 1941. In contrast to the grossly exaggerated propaganda claims of an early victory, the Wehrmacht were dug in outside Moscow experiencing the worst winter for fifty years. The Nazi leadership had not anticipated this; so confident were they, that the troops were still in summer uniforms. Goebbels, who had been misled himself into believing that the winter needs of the Wehrmacht had been taken care of, confided to his staff that as a result of these revelations the people would turn accusingly and say: 'Look, we can see how Goebbels lies!'[14]

Plate 23 An anti-Bolshevik poster. 'The aim of Bolshevism: to drown the world in blood.'

The *Winterhilfesspende* ('the Christmas gift of the German people to the eastern front'), inaugurated by Goebbels in a radio appeal on 22 December, drew an immediate response from all sections of the population. His appeal for warm clothing, which figured prominently in the newsreels and the press in the first few months of 1942, greatly strengthened the links between the home and the fighting fronts. On 14 January 1942, Goebbels claimed in a radio address that the total number of items of clothing received had reached over 67,232,000, and hailed the response as 'convincing evidence of the determination with which the German nation is ready to carry this war through to victory'.[15] Although the *Winterhilfesspende* was useful in diverting and strengthening the flagging community spirit, it could not be maintained indefinitely. What underpinned *Winterhilfesspende* was the tacit recognition that *Blitzkrieg* had come to an end and this was going to be a prolonged and costly war in which the home front would have to dig deep into their own resources. The fact that the winter clothing did not reach the eastern front until March 1942 is irrelevant to the limited success enjoyed by the propaganda; its 'success' lay in keeping the population busy and persuading them that they could make a personal contribution to help relieve the suffering of German troops freezing in Russia. However, the set-back of December 1941 had clearly shaken the confidence of the population in the leadership. The public's lukewarm response to Hitler's speeches of 30 January and 26 April 1942 show that, for the first time, the Führer's own standing and credibility were also being questioned. As Ian Kershaw has argued, a subtle reading of the regime's public-opinion reports indicates that the 'Hitler myth' had already been considerably undermined before the catastrophe of Stalingrad.[16]

Goebbels now realised that he could no longer continue the line of Nazi infallibility. The change in the strategy of propaganda is reflected in a revealing entry in Goebbels' diary for 24 February 1942:

> We shall have to change our propaganda and our policies in the east as already arranged with the Führer. These were hitherto based on the assumption that we would take possession of the East very quickly. This hope, however, has not been realised. We must therefore envisage operations of longer duration and are accordingly compelled to change our slogans and our policies fundamentally.[17]

Russian resistance had proved tougher than the Nazis had expected. Furthermore, Goebbels would have to put an end to the *Untermensch* propaganda which treated all the Russian peoples as inferiors. Not only did the 'sub-human' propaganda theme alienate various Russian national groups, but attempts to maintain racial–national stereotypes were encountering difficulties as a result of the personal contact with Polish and Russian workers, and because German soldiers on leave from the Eastern front were returning with different opinions about the Red Army. Clearly, the German people were questioning previously held opinions of the bestial and primitive Russian that had been portrayed in Nazi propaganda and concluding (according to the SD) that it 'did not correspond to reality'.

In rejecting the *Untermensch* theme Goebbels was returning to his original mission of safeguarding Europe from the 'Jewish–Bolshevik conspiracy'. He could now dramatise the war as a fight against Bolshevism rather than the Russian people. In a series of articles in his paper *Das Reich* (a more 'up-market' version of the Party's *Völkischer Beobachter*), Goebbels proclaimed that Nazi Germany was the defender of all that was sacred and traditional in Europe. In 1942 an exhibition entitled *Europa gegen den Bolshewismus* (*Europe against Bolshevism*) toured Nazi-occupied Europe, while in Germany Goebbels staged an exhibition called *Das Sowjetparadies* (*Soviet Paradise*), which stressed the horrors of daily life under Bolshevism and revealed the alleged inhumanity of the Soviets to their own people. The exhibition, which was premièred in Berlin, featured 'original' Bolshevik housing conditions, torture chambers and corpses. In his diary Goebbels claimed that the exhibition was a 'classic example of effective propaganda' and ordered that it should tour the provinces. A popular joke in Berlin, however, told of people complaining to Goebbels about sending the exhibition on tour because 'they wanted their furniture back!'.[18]

German press and radio reports of the military situation in Russia were now confined to local events, while anti-Bolshevik feature films like *Dorf im roten Sturm* (*Red Storm over the Village*, previously released in 1935 under the title *Friesennot*) and *GPU* (1942) continued to stress the brutality of such a political system. Writing in *Das Reich*, Goebbels evoked for the first time the fear of a Russian victory, but he remained confident that final victory was assured providing the war effort at home was intensified. To this end he ordered that there was to be no talk of easy victories. In a speech on the Hero Memorial Day of 15 March 1942 Hitler assured the population that 'whatever fate holds for us, it can only be easier than what is behind us'. He also predicted that Bolshevism would finally be destroyed in the coming summer. Indeed, in the summer and autumn of 1942 Nazi troops advanced as far as the Caucasus and Stalingrad, and in North Africa Rommel briefly raised the morale of the German population when he captured Tobruk in June. Nevertheless Goebbels continued to insist on caution. The order of the day was 'No propaganda of illusion'. Staff at the RMVP were instructed that no over-optimism should be allowed to emerge in the German people. The people, according to Goebbels' Ministry for Propaganda briefings, must be firmly supported by 'the corset of realism'. There was even a special 'Song of the Eastern Campaign': 'We have been standing guard for Germany, keeping the eternal watch. Now the sun is rising in the East, calling millions into battle.' Its solemn rhythm epitomised the increasing pessimism of the German people, particularly working-class morale, which had sunk even further during 1942 as a result of more stringent rationing and the heavy Allied air offensive on West German towns. In October came news of Rommel's defeat at El Alamein, immediately followed by the Anglo-American landings in North Africa. But above all there was still the prospect of another grim winter in Russia with no end of the war in sight.

The next few months were to witness some of the most bitterly fought battles of the war. By the end of October it appeared that Stalingrad was about to fall as the German Sixth Army under General Paulus seized four-fifths of the city. However, having learned a lesson the previous year, the press and radio were ordered to exercise restraint to avoid raising unwarranted hopes on the part of the German people. The battle for Stalingrad was to be depicted as a fortress which needed to be stormed. This did not prevent Hitler from ordering the press to prepare special editions on the eventual fall of Stalingrad. In a major speech on 30 September 1942, in which he stressed the great strategic importance of Stalingrad, Hitler confidently predicted: 'The capture of Stalingrad will be completed, and you may be sure that no one will drive us out of this place again.'

The victory was never to be. Goebbels in fact had not been happy with the bragging type of propaganda put out by the Führer HQ during the Stalingrad campaign. He feared that such 'official' optimism was out of touch with the pessimism felt by the majority of Germans about the eventual outcome of the war. Goebbels' dissatisfaction proved well founded when, on 19 November, the Russians launched their counter-offensive. For the next month, as the Sixth Army was being destroyed, Hitler was reluctant to release the news of the Soviet breakthrough. Goebbels attempted to reassure the population. In his New Year message to the nation he spoke of 'a light in the distance'. However, he could not counter the cynicism and suspicion that were spreading throughout Germany as a result of the failure of propaganda to keep the people informed of the progress of the campaign. On 22 January 1943 Hitler refused a suggestion from Paulus that, as there was no longer any possibility of stopping the Russian advance, he should be allowed to enter into surrender negotiations. Fearing the psychological effect of such a defeat, Hitler replied that there was to be no surrender. But time was running out for the severly battered German divisions. When they finally surrendered on 2 February, some 124,000 German soldiers had been killed in the course of the battle. German propaganda tried to explain away Stalingrad by creating the impression that the Sixth Army had fallen nobly to the last man. This propaganda line of 'heroic death' (*Heldentod*) was also pursued when Goebbels addressed a rally on 30 January, the tenth anniversary of the regime. Reaffirming the nation's trust in Hitler in the final stages of the war against 'Jewish–Bolshevism', Goebbels concluded a defiant speech by declaring: 'There is no such word as capitulation in our vocabulary.'

A month earlier (27 December 1942) in a major article published in *Das Reich* entitled 'The Fulfilled', Goebbels had linked the theme of *Heldentod* to Greek heroism and Germany's mission of 'Gross-deutschland'. Goebbels compared Germany's struggle to climbing a towering mountain – a daunting, but not an impossible, task. According to the Minister for Propaganda, those who had fallen had not made their heroic sacrifice in vain. The German people was now so firmly united in its destiny (*Schicksalsgemeinschaft*) that all considerations of class conflict had been replaced by a community based on social unity and equal sacrifice. Goebbels distinguished Germany's current struggle from the *Fronterlebnis* of the Great War, and pointed out that theirs truly was an 'experience of equals' in which workers and farmers died side-by-side with the former aristocracy. Goebbels concluded: 'The dead have earned more than our tears . . . they form the national conscience and urge us to demonstrate the same zeal and endeavours in both work and battle that they themselves have shown.'[19]

On the whole, Nazi anti-Bolshevik propaganda was inconsistent and unconvincing. First of all, the German people had not been prepared for a drawn-out war in Russia. Second, by stressing the *Untermensch* line and the superiority of the Aryan race, Goebbels was unable to reconcile the regime's ideological position that the Bolshevik system was reactionary and bankrupt with the failure of the Wehrmacht to defeat the Red Army on the battlefield. The bankruptcy of Nazi propaganda was highlighted by its inability to respond to the military setbacks with a flexible contingency plan. Finally, the SD reports were pointing out that, whereas propaganda had depicted the Russians as bestial and primitive, actual contact with Russian 'foreign workers' did not accord with the stereotype Bolshevik monster. Moreover, these reports also noted that the new respect for the Russians was leading to a reappraisal of anti-Bolshevik propaganda. One such report concluded: 'Propaganda is finding it increasingly difficult, especially among the workers, to disseminate with positively convincing arguments that Bolshevism really is the danger that it has always been painted.'[20] Although Goebbels fought against the excessive optimism of the reporting of the Russian war and the short-sightedness of the 'subhuman' propaganda, he was never able to overcome the basic contradictions intrinsic to anti-Bolshevik propaganda. Stalingrad represented not only a major military defeat but also a propaganda fiasco of the first magnitude. As a result of the wholly misleading campaign that was conducted throughout 1942, Goebbels' propaganda was in serious danger of losing all credibility with his own people.

TOTAL WAR AND THE NEED FOR STRENGTHENING MORALE

The impact of Stalingrad on the morale of the German people cannot be over-estimated. It affected their attitude towards the war and created a crisis of confidence in the regime amongst broad sections of the population. Hitherto Nazi propaganda had always tried to give the impression that the Third Reich was waging one war with an unbending consistency. With its armies now on the defensive on three fronts, it was obvious that it was in fact fighting several wars and sometimes with contradictory objectives. The capture of the Sixth Army at Stalingrad did, however, bring Goebbels back into the forefront of German politics, and he, of course, did his best to give meaning to the catastrophe. In an attempt to sustain the myth of the heroic sacrifice of the Sixth Army, he claimed that their 'heroic epic' was not in vain since it had served as the 'bulwark of the historic European mission'.

The Nazis refused to admit that the Sixth Army had surrendered; instead they claimed that the entire army had fought to the last man. The press was directed to report 'this stirring event, which outshines every feat of heroism known to history, in such a manner that this sublime example of heroism, this ultimate, self-sacrificing dedication to Germany's final victory, will blaze forth like a sacred flame'. In an effective piece of stage management, the Special Announcement over the radio on 3 February 1943 opened with slow marches, followed by muffled drum rolls and by three stanzas of the German war song 'Ich hatt' einen Kameraden'. Then came news of the fall of Stalingrad. After the playing of the German, Italian and Croatian national anthems there was a silence of three minutes broken by martial music and Beethoven's Fifth Symphony. A three-day period of mourning was then declared and all theatres and cinemas were ordered to close. In subsequent broadcasts and press statements these clichés of heroism and sacrifice continued unabated. The myth of Stalingrad, then, was an attempt to evade the reality of defeat by turning it into an emotional Wagnerian celebration of a nation's unbending will to continue the battle against Bolshevism. What it failed to reveal was that General Paulus and 90,000 men of the Sixth Army had surrendered to the Russians and were now in captivity.

Stalingrad marked a turning-point in Nazi war propaganda, as it allowed Goebbels finally to implement his drive for the total mobilisation of all Germany's human resources for the war effort. The fate of the Sixth Army gave impetus to the radical idea he had been proposing for some time – the proclamation of 'total war'. Goebbels was one of the few Nazi leaders who had realised as early as 1942 that final victory could only be achieved by a full mobilisation of German resources incorporating every citizen. The Minister for Propaganda envisaged a radical departure from the measures that other leaders like Bormann had established for civil defence. For Goebbels, success could only be achieved by the complete mobilisation of the home front in order that Germany should become one fighting body, united under a powerful leader. This entailed shifting propaganda strategy from the optimistic, almost arrogant claims of the previous three years. In particular, Goebbels attempted to create toughness in the civilian population by resorting to one of the oldest techniques of persuasion – the indoctrination of fear. Fear of the sub-human Bolshevik 'beast-man' endangering Western civilisation ('strength through fear'), together with 'total war', became the leitmotiv of his propaganda during 1943.

Hitler's decline as the Party's leading speaker left a gap which Goebbels began to fill. By 1943 Goebbels had become the principal spokesman for the regime. It is interesting to note that in his speeches he adopted a posture similar to that of Winston Churchill: he made no secret of the difficulties ahead, admitted that a German defeat was possible, and called for total involvement in the war effort. It is somewhat ironic to see the master of the 'lie indirect' suddenly discovering and openly proclaiming the tactical advantages of 'absolute truth'! Proud of what he believed were his close contacts with the people, he adopted a pose of frankness and realism. However, after the catastrophe of Stalingrad he was convinced of the need for some mass demonstration of national resistance. Strangely enough, the Allied demand for 'unconditional surrender' conceived at the Casablanca Conference in January 1943 would provide just the impetus he needed. He could now use this to conjure up terrifying images of a nation fighting for its very existence. Total war, he could argue, was the only alternative to total destruction. Writing in his diary on 4 March 1943, Goebbels declared: 'Our slogan should be, now more than ever: "Total War Is the Imperative Need of the Hour".'

Thus in the aftermath of military disaster the Minister for Propaganda achieved a remarkable personal victory. The huge rally at the Sportspalast in Berlin on 18 February 1943 was the setting for his notorious 'total war' address. It was a masterpiece of mass propaganda, carefully orchestrated for the benefit of radio and the newsreel. Rudolf Semmler, one of Goebbels' aids at the RMVP, recorded the Minister for Propaganda's preparations for the event:

> Goebbels is brooding over a daring plan. He will try to bring pressure on Hitler by putting forward radical demands in a speech at the Sports Palace. The crowd will applaud wildly. In this way he may be able to force Hitler to put an end to half-measures. If his demands are not met, then the Government will be compromised. The Führer could not afford this at the moment.[21]

The audience of reliable Party functionaries had been meticulously rehearsed beforehand and knew exactly what was expected of them. Goebbels started his speech by saying that the situation reminded him of the *Kampfzeit*, the period of struggle before 1933. He said he now demanded even more effort and sacrifices from the German people for the sake of final victory. Above the speaker's platform there hung an immense draped banner with the words *Totaler Krieg – Kürzester Krieg* (Total War – Shortest War). It was claimed that the audience represented all sections of the community. The frenzied reactions of this 'representative' audience to Goebbels' speech were broadcast to the rest of the nation. A special newsreel also recorded the event. At the climax of the speech, the Minister for Propaganda posed ten questions touted as a 'plebiscite for total war', all of which illicited the appropriate chorus of 'spontaneous' assent. The following extract shows how it was presented to German cinema audiences in the *Deutsche Wochenschau* released on 27 February 1943:

Commentator: The mighty demonstration in the Berlin Sportspalace. Reich Minister Goebbels speaks. He declares: 'In this winter, the storm over our ancient continent has broken out with the full force which surpasses all human and historical imagination. The Wehrmacht with its allies forms the only possible protective wall. (*Applause*). Not a single person in Germany today thinks of hollow compromise. The whole nation thinks only of a hard war. The danger before which we stand is gigantic. Gigantic, therefore, must be the efforts with which we meet it. (*Shouts of 'Sieg Heil'*). When my audience spontaneously declared its support for the demands I made on 30 January, the English press claimed that this was a piece of theatrical propaganda. I have therefore invited to this meeting a cross-section of the German people. . . .'

Goebbels: The English claim that the German people are resisting Government measures for total war.

Crowd: Lies! Lies!

Goebbels: It doesn't want total war, say the English, but capitulation.

Crowd: Sieg Heil! Sieg Heil!

Goebbels: Do you want total war?

Crowd: Yes. (*Enthusiastic applause*)

Goebbels: Do you want it more total, more radical, than we could ever have imagined?

Crowd: Yes! Yes! (*Loud applause*)

Goebbels: Are you ready to stand with the Führer as the phalanx of the homeland behind the fighting Wehrmacht? Are you ready to continue the struggle unshaken and with savage determination, through all the vicissitudes of fate until victory is in our hands?

Crowd: Yes!

Goebbels: I ask you: are you determined to follow the Führer through thick and thin in the struggle for victory and to accept even the harshest personal sacrifices?

Crowd: Yes! Sieg Heil! (*A chant of 'The Führer commands, we follow'*)

Goebbels: You have shown our enemies what they need to know, so that they will no longer indulge in illusions. The mightiest ally in the world – the people themselves – has shown that they stand behind us in our determined fight for victory, regardless of the costs.

Crowd: Yes! Yes! (*Loud applause*)

Goebbels: Therefore let the slogan be from now on: 'People arise, and storm break loose!' (*Extended applause*)
Crowd: Deutschland, Deutschland über alles, über alles in der Welt.[22]

In his 'total war' speech outlined above Goebbels pulled out all the stops; total sacrifices and participation are put forward by Goebbels as the alternatives to the type of total destruction that only the Wehrmacht was preventing. Partly this was to convince foreign governments that there was full accord between the rulers and the ruled in Germany, but it was also intended to persuade Hitler to mobilise the homefront completely to facilitate a concentrated war effort. On 19 February Goebbels wrote in his diary:

> Many people are of the opinion that this mass meeting is really a type of *coup d'état*. But we are simply straddling the many hurdles which the bureaucracy has placed in our path. Total war is no longer just a question on the minds of a few perceptive men, but the whole nation is concerned with it.

Albert Speer, who attended the rally and was Hitler's Armaments Minister, recorded its impact and the cynicism that shaped Goebbels' methods:

> On February 18, 1943, Goebbels delivered his speech at the Sportspalast on 'total war'. It was not only directed to the population; it was obliquely addressed to the leadership which had ignored all our proposals for a radical commitment of domestic reserves. . . . Except for Hitler's most powerful public meetings, I had never seen an audience so effectively roused to fanaticism. Back in his home, Goebbels astonished me by analysing what had seemed to be a purely emotional outburst in terms of its psychological effects – much as an experienced actor might have done. He was also satisfied with his audience that evening. 'Did you notice? They reacted to the smallest nuance and applauded at just the right moments. It was the politically best-trained audience you can find in Germany.' This particular crowd had been rounded up out of the party organisations; among those present were popular intellectuals and actors like Heinrich George, whose applause was caught by the newsreel cameras for the benefit of the wider public.[23]

Although Hitler personally congratulated Goebbels on his address and referred to it as a 'psychological and propaganda masterpiece', he would, however, never agree to complete mobilisation, despite repeated requests from his Minister for Propaganda.[24] Nevertheless, in the short term at least, Goebbels enjoyed considerable success with this campaign. Its immediate effect was to strengthen morale. The SD reports noted that the newsreel of the rally 'made a deep impression and subsequently dissipated any feelings of scepticism which have prevailed up until now. Even rather reticent sections of the population were aroused when they saw the ecstatic effect of the speech.' But once this intoxication had worn off, people began soberly to question the nature and implications of the threat coming from the East. Towards the end of May 1943 the SD was referring to 'the beginnings of a crisis of confidence' in the regime and concluding that 'Party comrades no longer dare think about the military situation for fear that they would lose all heart'.[25] The working class in particular appeared to be suspicious of some of the injustices brought about by the 'total war' economy. For many workers the most visibly symbolic change was the increasing mobilisation of the female population into the workforce. Thus, for the first time, women began to appear regularly in the weekly newsreels. In line with the ideological chauvinism that pervaded all aspects of National Socialism, the newsreels had previously confined the coverage of women's activities to domestic scenes. Now, because of their new role within the home front, they were shown enthusiastically contributing to the war effort. Despite the image that was presented in the media, working-class discontent was fuelled by the not entirely erroneous belief that many middle-class women were placed in less arduous employment or were able to avoid industrial work altogether.[26] Moreover, the closure of 'inessential' shops and businesses which accompanied the regime's attempts to mobilise Germany's reserves for 'total war' appeared to hit the 'little man', whilst the middle and upper classes seemed to have been successful in 'avoiding the strictures of the total war economy'.[27] The failure of the regime to implement the total mobilisation of German society until the summer of 1944, with the creation of the *Volkssturm*, only fuelled the belief in the eyes of some sections of the working population that the Third Reich 'remained a class society to the very end'.[28]

But paradoxically the growing feeling of pessimism actually served Goebbels' short-term aims, for he was about to launch a new propaganda campaign based on 'strength through fear' and aiming to persuade the German people and the West that a Bolshevik victory would be more dangerous than a compromise peace with the Third Reich. From 1943 onwards Nazi propaganda continued to insist that final victory was assured, however great the difficulties. By invoking the *Untergangsmotif* and declaring that the war was 'an ideological fight to the death', Goebbels was once again appealing to German fears of the barbaric Bolshevik that he had employed so successfully in 1933. Wall posters throughout the Reich proclaimed the threat of impending doom should the nation fail to rise to the challenge: 'Hard Times, Hard Work, Hard Hearts', 'Victory or Bolshevism', 'Total War – the Shortest War'. In a ministerial conference on 12 February 1943, Goebbels instructed that: 'From now onwards, every radio talk, every press report, every speech and every weekly slogan must end with the stereotypical comment that the struggle against Bolshevism is our great task'. Interestingly enough, in the same directive Goebbels drew a sharp distinction between Bolshevism and Communism; 'which has a different resonance to it and may remind people of past times'.[29] The Post Office also contributed to the war effort with the letter stamp 'Our Führer Will Banish Bolshevism'. Curiously enough, it was a German military victory that posed a major problem for Goebbels. This was the recapture of Kharkov in March 1943. Goebbels chose to play this success down in case it aroused a false sense of security. Clearly it was difficult to explain Kharkov at the height of his anti-Bolshevik campaign. As a result of the limited success of the 'new realism' of Goebbels' 'total war' speech, emphasis was placed on minimising the public's expectations by stressing the orderly nature of Germany's new defensive war. This allowed the accumulating military defeats to be rationalised as 'strategic withdrawals'. Fear was to be the major component of home propaganda, and this meant painting an extremely bleak picture of the military situation in the East, avoiding all mention that the Wehrmacht might be launching a grand offensive. The fear of 'Mongol hordes from the East', which was exaggerated by Goebbels' propaganda, was intended to produce a galvanising rather than a paralysing effect and to spur the population on to even greater sacrifices and efforts.

Both the anti-Bolshevik campaign and the propaganda line of exaggerated pessimism were greatly enhanced by the news of the discovery of the Katyn massacres in April 1943. Its repercussions led to the breaking-off of diplomatic relations between the Soviet Union and the Polish Government in exile in London. On 13 April German radio announced the discovery of a mass grave in the Katyn Forest near Smolensk, where Polish officers had been methodically killed. Goebbels regarded the incident as first-class material with which to undermine Russia's prestige in the eyes of her allies. He commented in his diary:

> we are now using the discovery of 12,000 Polish officers, murdered by the GPU, for anti-Bolshevik propaganda in a grand style. We sent neutral journalists and Polish intellectuals to the spot where they were found. Their reports now reaching us from abroad are gruesome. The Führer has also given permission for us to hand out a dramatic news item to the German press. I gave instructions to make the widest possible use of this propaganda material. We shall be able to live on it for a couple of weeks.[30]

And they did. Both the press and the newsreels carried lurid accounts of the manner in which the Poles were slain, charging that Jewish officers of the Red Army were responsible for the murders. A documentary film entitled *Im Wald von Katyn* (*In the Forest of Katyn*) was also compiled, and shown in all the major cinemas. On 16 April, after previewing the newsreels on Katyn, Goebbels wrote:

These shots are terribly gruesome. One hardly dares to imagine what would happen to Germany and Europe if this Asiatic-Jewish flood were to inundate our country and our continent. All hands must be set to work to the last breath to prevent such a misfortune.[31]

The discovery of the Katyn massacres provided Goebbels with an opportunity to fuse his deep-seated anti-Semitism with the anti-Bolshevik campaign. In May 1943 a press circular from the Reichs Propaganda Office illustrated how this joint campaign was to be orchestrated:

Further to previous instructions on the Jewish question, you are requested to devote more attention to this question in the future and to make the Jewish question a permanent feature . . . Jews are to blame; Jew wanted the war; the Jews are making the war worse . . . etc. . . . The possibilities for exposing the true character of the Jews are endless. . . . For example, the Jewish-Bolshevist murder at Katyn is a model example for the German press of how one can use such a topic to bring out the Jews' initiating role and their guilt. . . .[32]

Goebbels was hardly exaggerating (for once) when he claimed that 'a complete triumph of German propaganda' had been achieved. Not only had he raised morale and strengthened the nation's resolve to resist Bolshevism, but the break between Moscow and the Polish Government in exile was seen as a major success in the international arena. By the beginning of June 1943 Goebbels' confidence was so high that he declared that the crisis he had highlighted in his 'total war' speech at the beginning of the year was now officially over. The 'total war' campaign, the *Untergangsmotif* and the Katyn massacres, all served in their different ways to lift morale at a time of widespread war-weariness and gave the false impression of a people at one with its leadership. In fact, the intelligence reports suggest that the 'success' of these campaigns was short-lived and raised expectations not of final victory, but of a swift end to the war by means of a negotiated peace.

RETREAT INTO MYTHOLOGY AND PROMISES OF RETALIATION

The military setbacks following Stalingrad were accompanied by an alarming increase in the intensity of Allied bombing of Germany. These raids began in the second half of May 1943, with the RAF attacking during the night and the US Eighth Air Force by day. Virtually all attempts by Nazi propagandists to offset this clear evidence of enemy superiority failed miserably. Between 1942 and 1944, the tonnage of bombs dropped over Germany increased 25-fold and, by the end of the war, in the worst-affected areas like north-west Germany some 40 per cent of housing had been destroyed. In many respects the defeat of the German offensive in the USSR signalled by July the beginning of the end for the German war effort.

The effects of the Allied bombing on the German civilian population have been a matter of intense debate. Hans Rumpf, for example, considered the Allied air attacks as a 'factor which welded the people together to the end' and welded them, moreover, 'to a state for which they no longer felt any enthusiasm'.[33] More recently, Marlis Steinert has argued that the intensification of the Allied onslaught at the beginning of 1943 'stimulated and strengthened the population's will to fight', but the inability of the regime to prevent aerial attacks meant that by the autumn of 1944 it had itself lost credibility.[34] The SD reports covering Germany as a whole tend to confirm that by the beginning of 1944 there was a massive loss of confidence in the regime, particularly after Allied bombers had demonstrated that they could reach as far south as Bavaria. This manifestation of the enemy's superiority in the air was a topic the propagandists would have preferred to ignore. But for some time Goebbels had been aware of the danger of remaining silent about the devastation that was affecting large sections of the urban population. In order to underline the fortitude of the civilian population and draw a parallel between the inhabitants of the stricken towns and the soldiers at the front, phrases such as the 'battle for the home front' were coined. The press was forbidden to describe the extent of the destruction, except to churches, hospitals and cultural monuments, but instructed instead to concentrate on the 'heroic fortitude of the population of the bombed cities'.

However, such propaganda did not square with the experiences of many evacuees seeking refuge from the bomb-damaged cities. Complaints sent by refugee wives to their husbands serving on the fighting front revealed that, when it came to offering food and shelter to air-raid victims, many members of the so-called 'national community' simply turned their backs, wishing not to be inconvenienced. Some areas of the Reich were so incensed by the stream of refugee 'intruders' that they referred to the evacuees as 'gypsies'.[35] When Hitler heard of this, he insisted that *Gauleiter* should impress upon all loyal *Volksgenossen* that refusing to take in the homeless was an offence punishable by imprisonment. Nevertheless numerous Party members continued to refuse to shelter homeless refugees in their own homes. Responding to widespread complaints that the leadership had failed to set an example, the Party was forced in December 1943 to issue a warning to all Party members, including those in senior positions, warning them to be more 'accommodating'.

The spirit of discontent with the Nazi leadership for its inability to protect German cities was further exacerbated by regional feelings which threatened to split the Reich into two parts – the bombed and the undamaged areas. Areas that were experiencing the brunt of the Allied attacks in the north-west (Cologne to Hamburg) were demanding official recognition for the ordeal they were undergoing nightly. In the Rhineland, for example, many people were intensely irritated by the prominence given to the relatively few raids at this time on Berlin. On more than one occasion, the SD noted satisfaction in north-west Germany that 'loud-mouthed Berliners have at last copped it'. The Allied air attacks also tested the sensitivity of Nazi propaganda to the response of its audience. Radio broadcasts often failed to consider the sensibilities of an unbombed and a bombed population to whom it was broadcasting at the same time. Intelligence reports wearily pointed out the insensitivity of broadcasting frivolous, popular contemporary melodies such as 'Dancing with you into Heaven' and 'For a Night of Bliss' to an audience that had recently suffered an air attack![36]

One suggestion for improving morale was for the Führer to be given a higher profile in German propaganda. According to the SD in April 1943, the German public wanted to see and hear the Führer more often 'in order to keep alive the contact between leader and nation'. There was a widespread belief that he had become too reclusive. There had also been much speculation about the (poor) condition of his health. In fact on 21 March 1943 on the occasion of Heroes' Memorial Day Hitler had spoken to the nation in a radio broadcast for the first time since Stalingrad. Hitler had confided in Goebbels that he felt like an 'old propagandist' and wanted to use the speech for a fierce attack upon Bolshevism.[37] The routine attack on Jewry and Bolshevism which was delivered in a dreary monotone made little impression with the people and prompted further rumours about Hitler's poor health. The anticipated excitement and resultant disappointment were profound.[38] The lacklustre reaction to the speech was further evidence that Hitler's popularity was in decline and that this decline had been markedly accelerated by Stalingrad. In April, the Reich Chancellery reported that *Gau* headquarters had noticed a sharp increase in the number of political jokes involving Hitler. Two in particular, are worth citing:

> What's the difference between the sun and Hitler? The sun rises in the East, Hitler goes down in the East.

> Zarah Leander (popular film actress) is summoned to the Führer's headquarters. Why? She has to sing 'I know there'll be a miracle one day, every day.'[39]

The overriding impression that one gains from the propaganda during this final period is one of a 'fortress Germany' preparing for Hitler's last stand. The Ministry for Propaganda did its best to bolster civilian morale, but clearly Nazi propaganda had been forced on to the defensive. This was confirmed by Goebbels in an address to his *Gauleiter* in February 1944, when he stressed the need to reassure the population by emphasising the merits of fighting a defensive war within Germany's borders. The German newsreels in particular bear unwitting testimony to the changing reality of the military situation. Almost every newsreel report of this period ends by referring to the disciplined retreat and high morale of German troops. 'Digging in' became synonymous with the *Deutsche Wochenschauen*; little wonder that they were no longer received rapturously by war-weary cinema audiences. Unable to conceal that the tide of the war had taken a turn for the worse, the Nazi leadership began to allude to some forthcoming retaliation by means of a secret 'miracle' weapon.

Goebbels had launched the campaign way back in June 1943, when he assured an audience in the Berlin Sportspalast: 'One day the hour of revenge will come.' In his speech the Minister for Propaganda stressed the development of new, secret weapons which would avenge the country for its suffering. The SD reports noted at the time that the country generally welcomed his announcement of counter-terror – particularly the inhabitants of bombed cities. It also served to set off a wave of rumours about the nature of the revolutionary weapons that were being tested at Peenumunde. Realising that the idea of retaliation was popular with the masses, Hitler had insisted on the term *Vergeltung* (retaliation or revenge), against the advice of the military.[40] But the success of *Vergeltung* depended on its realisation.

By the summer of 1943, the RMVP had come to realise that *Vergeltung* was such a sensitive issue that they would have to move cautiously to prevent a 'boomerang effect'. As the intensity of Allied bombing continued to increase, so did the demand for retribution. Indeed, for many town-dwellers *Vergeltung* was rapidly becoming a question of individual survival. Allied propaganda began to point to the discrepancy between Nazi promises and deeds. The SD reports also confirmed that the Nazi leadership would lose all credibility if the promised retaliation did not begin soon. Even more worrying for Goebbels was the growing belief that these 'miracle weapons' were now the only means left of winning the war. This was the reason why in a speech on Harvest Thanksgiving Day (3 October) Goebbels declared:

> As regards the question of *Vergeltung* discussed by the entire German people with such heated passion, I can only say that the English commit an exceedingly fatal error if they believe that this is a mere rhetorical or propagandist slogan with no reality behind it. England will one day make acquaintance with this reality.

Throughout the autumn and winter of 1943–4, German morale continued to deteriorate. Goebbels responded by instigating his '30 War Articles for the German Nation', which he outlined on 26 September 1943 (see Document 9). Insisting that the *Volksgemeinschaft* should maintain its discipline ('the most important of all virtues'), Goebbels concluded by reminding the nation of its 'racial background' and demanding that the people remain loyal to the leadership: 'Believe faithfully and firmly in the Führer and final victory.' Hitler, whose absence from the bombed cities was widely commented on in the intelligence reports, repeated the call for heroism in a rare speech he made in Munich on 9 November, when he promised that the Reich would never capitulate and warned that 'slackers' at the home front would be executed. *Gauleiter* were informed by the Führer HQ that it was their responsibility to take action at the first sign of any dissent or pessimism; 'complainers' and 'troublemakers' were now branded as 'enemies of the State' and were in real danger of their lives. However, despite such intimidation (or perhaps *because of* such intimidation), the morale reports taken in the autumn of 1943 continued to register widespread pessimism and a new mood of defeatism (*Untergangsstimmung*) (see Document 10). In addition to what the SD referred to as the 'air-raid psychosis', the other factor shaping morale during this period was the deterioration of the food supply to the civilian population. Throughout 1942 and 1943 seasonal shortages of particular foodstuffs had been offset by the exploitation of occupied Europe. This had enabled the regime to provide an adequate level of nutrition, despite the need to introduce rationing. From the beginning of 1944, however, the failure of the rationing system had given rise to a flourishing black market. By the winter of 1944–5, the average daily intake of the population sank below the long-term nutritional survival minimum (1,800 calories per day). One regional opinion survey noted that 'the morale of the population is determined essentially by the following factors: hunger, the air terror and the military situation'.[41]

In the face of these factors, Nazi propagandists had little to offer in the way of assurance other than the promise of *Vergeltung*, which was widely seen as a panacea to all Germany's troubles. At the beginning of 1944 Goebbels issued a directive that the term 'retaliation' should for the time being not be used in the press, radio and newsreels. This was intended to play down the expectations of the population. However, the continuing delay in the appearance of the 'miracle weapon' served only to increase pessimism and bring about another crisis of confidence in the German leadership. It was decided, therefore, to resume a 'baby Blitz' of the United Kingdom, particularly London. In the months January–March the British capital was the target of thirteen major attacks by a makeshift Luftwaffe striking from northern France. Nazi propaganda portrayed the raids as bridging the gap to all-out *Vergeltung*. Goebbels did not hesitate to exploit them to the full. He confidently predicted that 'very soon every Anglo-American raid on a German town will be paid back in full by a German raid on an English town'. However, the renewal of the Blitz on London was insufficient to divert people's attention from the theme that was still believed by many to represent the only hope of final victory.

As the months passed without the weapon appearing, Goebbels' prestige fell lower and lower. The reticence of Nazi propagandists and the media in general did not go unnoticed. Many Germans were now convinced that

Vergeltung was an invention of Goebbels' ministry, to secure the fanaticism necessary to carry on a war that could not be won. When the V1 and V2 (*V* for *Vergeltung*) missiles were eventually deployed in mid-June 1944, they failed to live up to expectations. A Wehrmacht communiqué of 16 June announced that London had been blanketed 'with a new type of explosive projectile of the heaviest calibre'. These 'miracle weapons' made their first appearance in the *Deutsche Wochenschau* in early July, when the V1 rocket was officially announced and shown being launched on London. In a radio programme on 'The Question of Retaliation', broadcast on 21 July, Goebbels spoke of the 'paralysing feeling of horror' caused by the V1 and claimed that Britain could no longer defend itself against these pilotless guided missiles. A few weeks later Goebbels was seen in the newsreels telling a rally in Breslau that 'the Reich was now answering terror with counter-terror' and claiming: 'The Führer can rely on the loyalty of his people as they follow him. We deserve victory!' Although this was the retaliation that the nation had been expecting for months, Goebbels continued to pursue a restrained propaganda line on the impact of these weapons, for fear of building up hopes which might lead to more disappointment.

While there is evidence that Goebbels' exploitation of the *Vergeltung* theme did initially raise the morale of both the homefront and the German troops, this soon gave way to a spirit of dejection once it became apparent that the new weapons would not bring England to her knees or alter the course of the war. The promised retaliation had been so long coming and people had pinned such high hopes on miracle weapons that propaganda could do little to counter this feeling of having been let down. On the one hand, the concept of 'orderly retreat' of German forces had been designed to minimise the public's expectations, whereas, on the other hand, the whisper campaign of 'miracle' weapons had falsely raised them. After Stalingrad and the absence of military success, Goebbels had turned to 'total war' and *Vergeltung* to bolster German civilian morale. Total war attempted to mobilise the homefront and elicit a fanaticism to fight to the death against Bolshevism. *Vergeltung*, the promise of 'revenge', was the Nazis' last-ditch guarantee of future victory. It was a promise which could not be kept. Belief in retaliation and other propaganda clichés had worn thin some time ago (see Document 10). Criticism of Nazi propaganda often expressed itself in the form of political jokes. Typical is this anecdote reported by the SD towards the end of 1943:

> Goebbels is bombed out in Berlin. He has two suitcases, leaves them on the street and goes back into the building to rescue other things. When he re-emerges the suitcases have been stolen. Dr Goebbels is very unhappy. He shouts and moans. Someone asks him why the suitcases were so important and he replies: 'One had the revenge weapon in it and the other final victory.'[42]

In the last year of the war Goebbels continued his activities relentlessly. After the failure of the V1 and V2 secret weapons to realise his promises of revenge, Goebbels achieved a short-lived revival of trust in the Führer following the failure of the 20 July 1944 plot against him. He even exploited the attempted assassination to show that the hand of providence was guiding Hitler by coining the slogan '*Hitler ist der Sieg*' ('Hitler is Victory'). Goebbels had already embarked upon a major campaign to intensify personal commitment to the cult of the Führer before the abortive plot on Hitler's life. In April 1944 a special *Deutsche Wochenschau* was released to celebrate Hitler's fifty-fifth birthday. It was to be one of the last appearances Hitler made in the German newsreels. At an NSDAP concert on the eve of his birthday (where Beethoven's *Eroica* is played), Goebbels offers the Party's congratulations to Hitler and reaffirms the nation's faith in him: 'We want to assure him that he is able to rely on his people absolutely in this great struggle – that he is today as he always was – our Führer!' The scene in the concert hall is followed by shots of bomb-damaged Berlin recovering from an Allied sortie. In the background, just visible, slogans can be seen daubed on the ruins and on the banners hanging from windows. As the commentator says that this is the German people's gift to Hitler, the camera pans in to reveal the words: 'Our walls may break but our hearts do not.' A few months later, the August edition of the *Wochenschau* reported the attempt on Hitler's life in the following manner:

> Hitler visits the bomb-plot victims in hospital – Scherk, Wortmann, Assmann, Admiral von Puttkammer and General Buhle. Outside the hospital crowds and government officials wait to congratulate the Führer on his escape – Funk, Gauleiter Sauckel, Speer, Sauer, Lammers, Himmler, General Schörner, Göring, Goebbels, Guderian, Bormann and Jodl are all present. Major Remer, who suppressed the bomb plot insurrection, is promoted to colonel and inspects a guard of honour. In his speech he thanks God that they have all become 'political soldiers following political orders, dedicated to the defence of the Fatherland and the National Socialist ideal until final victory is assured'.

By portraying the Officers' Plot of 20 July as a cowardly, unpatriotic act, Goebbels attempted to diminish their status in the eyes of the people. The intelligence reports confirmed that after the initial shock there was indeed a short-lived revival of trust in Hitler. But optimism was soon dissipated by the harsh realities of the war and the failure of Hitler to address the nation. The 'Hitler myth' was on the verge of disintegration.

However, the final two years of the war were in general a period of decreasing propaganda effectiveness and increasing dependence on the substitution of myth for reality. During this period the credibility of the press declined rapidly, despite the fact that the public was eager for news from the Eastern front. Newspapers had been badly affected by the war. They had to overcome problems caused by severe paper rationing, reduced staffs, wartime taxation and insurance, and transport difficulties. As early as May 1941, the Reich Press Chamber had suspended over 500 news-papers, and this number increased still further in the next few years. Moreover, radio programmes which had proved so popular in the early part of the war were now openly derided. Instead, the civilian population turned increasingly to foreign broadcasts for their information, despite the heavy penalties if discovered. Nazi propaganda encountered growing criticism, not simply on account of war weariness but because the press and radio announcements failed to measure up to the sacrifices and the common experiences of ordinary Germans.

By 1943 this disillusionment was clearly reflected in the reception given to the war newsreels which had been so eagerly followed during the *Blitzkrieg* campaigns. Not only were cinema audiences questioning previous assumptions and the banality and lies they were witnessing in the weekly newsreels, but they were actually lingering outside the cinemas until the newsreels were over. Goebbels responded by closing all cinemas during the showing of the newsreel, so that if an individual wanted to see the feature film he was forced to sit through the newsreel as well! The response of the film industry to the military setbacks which threatened the fighting morale of the people is of particular interest. Goebbels no longer felt confident enough to commission the aggressive militarist films (*Wehrerziehungsfilme*) which celebrated the Nazi 'fighter hero'. Admittedly, there were a few political works which portrayed various themes that had been important in previous years. *Germanin* (1943) attacked British colonialism; *Paracelsus* (1943) was a thinly disguised exposition of the *Führerprinzip*; *Immensee* (1943) and *Opfergang* (*Sacrifice*, 1944) dealt with aspects of the doctrine of 'blood and soil': *Junge Adler* (*Young Eagles*, 1944) addressed itself to the German army of the future and stressed the need for obedience and discipline. But on the whole the film industry abandoned political and military subjects in favour of love stories and operettas – a combination which may well have had an important propaganda function in that it gave the people what they wanted, but one which manifestly failed to capture contemporary experiences of the people undergoing total war. Goebbels rationalised this switch (given his desire to 'revolutionise' the German cinema) by arguing that as both front-line soldiers and home-front civilians would be 'living' National Socialism there would be less need to express the ideology in films. Entertainment films, well made, would enhance the regime's cause by providing relaxation and escapism.

In a desperate attempt to raise morale and to intensify the war effort, Goebbels stepped up his propaganda of hate and fear against the Bolsheviks. There could be no mention of surrender, for life under the bestial and primitive *Untermenschen* did not bear contemplating. Evidence of Bolshevik atrocities had figured prominently in the newsreels for months, and the press regularly listed the horrors which retreating Wehrmacht officers had witnessed. The German people were left in no doubt as to what they could expect.

Goebbels now urged everyone, including women and children, to join in the struggle, and to set an example by their heroism and sacrifice. The popular rising which Goebbels had been demanding since his 'total war' speech in February 1943 culminated in the formation of the new home defence force, the *Volkssturm*. Every man between the ages of sixteen and sixty, regardless of class or occupation, was ordered to join the *Volkssturm* and defend the homeland. The announcement of the *Volkssturm* had been given a big build-up in the November 1944 edition of the *Deutsche Wochenschau*, where Himmler was seen proclaiming the Führer's instructions for the new home guard. At this stage Goebbels was continually looking for a sign that would persuade the people to believe in final victory. With the military situation becoming increasingly desperate, Goebbels somehow had to link his fear campaign with the need for endurance in the face of overwhelming odds. Since the future was uncertain and the present unbearable, Goebbels turned to history for the reassurance he needed to offer, particularly the hagiography of Frederick the Great. The Prussian king had always been a significant symbol in German history, but it was only towards the second half of the war that this figure came to epitomise the indomitable spirit who refused to accept defeat. One of Goebbels' aids at the RMVP, observing the exceedingly large number of portraits of Frederick the Great scattered throughout the Ministry for Propaganda remarked sardonically: 'It would appear that old Fritz is the protector of Goebbels' intellectual world altogether.'[43] In 1942 the film industry had produced *Der grosse König* (*The Great King*), one of the most expensive films made during the Third Reich, and also one of the most popular with wartime audiences. The film stressed the superiority of Frederick's judgement over that of his generals and also emphasised the sufferings of the Prussian people during the Seven Years' War and the faith they kept with their leader. A slogan that is repeated throughout is 'Prussia will never be lost as long as the King lives.' In the last year of the war, Goebbels launched into another of his discourses on Frederick the Great. It was the same message as is found in *Der grosse König*: if only Germans would fight as the Prussians had done during the Seven Years' War. He even quoted a letter from Frederick to his sister Amalia written in 1757, in which the king commented that 'victory and death were the only alternatives'. Goebbels promised that if the German people kept faith with the Führer, Hitler would produce a 'similar victory'.[44]

Consumed by the lure of historical parallels, Goebbels likened the adolescent and ageing *Volkssturm* to the *Landsturm*'s resistance to Napoleon in the previous century. New recruits to the *Volkssturm* recruiting stations were greeted with the slogan: 'Believe, Fight, Victory'. Late in 1944, when it was clear that the war was lost, Goebbels made one last attempt to raise civilian morale by producing *Kolberg* (1945), a lavish film about the Napoleonic Wars, in which the besieged Prussian city of Kolberg fought to the last and was saved by a miraculous military victory. Prior to commissioning the film, Goebbels had informed his staff: 'It ought to be the mission of all German propaganda to create a myth from the heroism of Stalingrad, a myth which can become a precious ornament in German history.'[45] Goebbels wanted to show that resistance to Napoleon came from the people and not from the military. However, the overriding problem in producing *Kolberg* was that, despite the Kolbergers' courageous resistance, they were eventually overwhelmed by the French. It is a measure of how far Nazi propaganda had become entrenched in a mythical world that the film chose to disregard historical fact, even when it revealed such heroism. The thrust of his message was that if only the German people stood firm, a miracle might yet save them. But there were no 'miracles' to offer in 1945, only the *Volkssturm* and the fear of terror and reprisal from the Werwolf organisation. In his diary Goebbels lamented: 'We need a military victory now as much as our daily bread.'[46] 'From the gloomy reports of defeatist behaviour coming in from all over the Reich, the people, it would seem, would gladly have settled for the bread!'[47]

The expense lavished on *Kolberg* testifies to the importance of the project and the extent to which Goebbels' propaganda had lost touch with the military situation. A budget of RM 8.5 million was allocated (twice the normal budget for a film of this importance). And at a time when Soviet forces were crossing the East Prussian border Goebbels withdrew 187,000 soldiers and 4,000 sailors from active duty in order that the film could be completed on time. The director, Veit Harlan, has stated that both Hitler and Goebbels were 'convinced that such a film was more useful than a military victory'.[48] The explanation for this extraordinary behaviour lies in Goebbels' continual obsession with dramatic effects. As Joachim Fest observed, 'to the end, he was what he always had been: the propagandist for himself'.[49] On 17 April 1945 Goebbels summoned his staff in the RMVP together. Some fifty of them were there, many demanding to be released in order to escape from encircled Berlin. Goebbels spoke to them about *Kolberg* and its message of heroic resistance. Then he mentioned another, even more splendid film which would be shown 100 years hence. It would be a film of the 'Twilight of the Gods' in Berlin in 1945:

> Gentlemen, in a hundred years' time they will be showing another fine colour film describing the terrible days we are living through. Don't you want to play a part in this film, to be brought back to life in a hundred years' time? Everybody now has a chance to choose the part

which he will play in the film a hundred years hence. I can assure you that it will be a fine and elevating picture. And for the sake of this prospect it is worth standing fast. Hold out now, so that a hundred years hence the audience does not hoot and whistle when you appear on the screen.[50]

Clearly, Goebbels was happy to accept *Kolberg* as his testament to future generations and to preserve a niche for himself in history by his Führer's side. His staff, however, were not so impressed by these heroic gestures. They looked at him incredulously and concluded that he had gone mad! Kolberg itself is now Kolobrzeg, on the Baltic coast of Poland. It is perhaps ironic that a society which placed so much emphasis on the cult of the young, highly trained warrior should have as its testament a film glorifying the heroic resistance of an ageing civilian militia. It would not be an over-simplification to suggest that such a parallel could be extended to the history of the Third Reich.

Nevertheless it took a prodigious effort to keep the propaganda machinery functioning during the last months of the war. The lines of communication between the RMVP and the local propaganda offices were often broken, resulting in chaos and disorganisation. Not surprisingly, with several German cities on the verge of capitulation, the 'activity reports' of the RMVP (one of the few sources left on public opinion and morale) reflected the general sentiment of resignation in the face of imminent military defeat. One such report, towards the end of February, explicitly stated that German morale could sink no lower.[51]

On 5 February 1945 Goebbels had issued a directive to all *Gau* propaganda chiefs, declaring: 'The great hour has arrived for German propaganda.' In fact it marked the beginning of the end for Nazi propaganda. Myth need not necessarily be reconcilable with truth, but if such propaganda is to prove effective it must survive the battlefield. Under such adverse military conditions, a 'propaganda success' in the spring of 1945 was hardly feasible. The meeting of the Allied leaders in Yalta, 7–12 February, did present Goebbels with the opportunity to draw a historical parallel with the 'Wilsonian swindle' of 1918–19 and reveal that the true meaning of Yalta was to destroy Germany. The press (such of it as was still printing) made great capital out of the gains made by the Russians at Yalta and outlined in stark terms what lay in store for Germany (and Europe). For many Germans the greatest fear at this stage was falling into the hands of the Russians. The penultimate *Deutsche Wochenschau* was released in March and contained the last appearances of Hitler and Goebbels, acting out roles that had changed little over twelve years. While Hitler is seen simply meeting officers and driving off in a car, Goebbels' speech to a mass rally in Görlitz is worth quoting in full, for it reveals the extent to which the Minister for Propaganda had lost touch with reality:

When our soldiers shoulder their guns and climb into their tanks they will have only their slaughtered children and dishonoured wives before their eyes, and a cry of rage will rise from their breasts (*among the crowd, the camera focuses on a nun in habit*), that will make the enemy turn pale. (*Loud applause*) As the Führer achieved victories in the past, so he will in the future. Of this I am firmly convinced; only the other day he said to me: 'I believe so much that we will overcome this crisis. By placing our forces on to new offences we will beat the enemy and push him back. And I believe as I have never believed in anything in my life that one day we will hoist our flags in victory.' (*Applause*)

In the final year of the war 'heroic death' (*Heldentod*) and 'sacrifice' figured predominantly in Nazi propaganda; there was no mention or suggestion of surrender. And yet a few days before Hitler and Goebbels were both to commit suicide the Führer's presence in Berlin was still apparently delaying the end of the war. Slogans such as 'Where the Führer is – victory is!' were a continuing expression of defiance. In April 1945, with the Russians encircling Berlin, the Ministry for Popular Enlightenment and Propaganda, like other Government departments, was disbanded. Hitler and Goebbels retreated to the *Führerbunker*, abandoning the German people to their fate, accusing the nation of weakness in the 'life-and-death' struggle against 'Jewish–Bolshevism'. It must be said, however, that the reasons why so many Germans fought to the bitter end in 1945 were only partly due to propaganda. When all other methods of persuasion had failed the Nazis had, for some time, resorted to terror as an antidote to cowardice. On Easter Sunday 1945, for example, broadcasting from its own radio station, the Werwolf issued a 'Proclamation to the German People' declaring that this was now a people's war and that every German citizen was to form part of a new 'German Freedom Movement' to repel the invaders. As a postcript, the Werwolf warned that those who refused to fight would be hunted down and dealt with mercilessly. The worse the military situation became, the more unrestrained the threats. On 19 April, the Werwolf was still warning that 'death awaited the cowardly'. Indeed, it has been suggested that the escalation of terror denoted the collapse of any form of consensus in Germany. This is probably going too far; such terror associated with the Werwolf really only played a significant part in the last months of the war. A more likely explanation for the limited success enjoyed by Goebbels during this final period of fighting lies in a traditional German patriotism and respect for authority, together with a fear of Bolshevism, which led people to defend their country intuitively. This sense of resignation has been described most aptly by the historian Helmut Krausnick, as one of 'reluctant loyalty'.[52]

Such defiance to the bitter end, which allowed the Russians to enter the German capital, would have profound consequences for the future of

Germany. In his final appeal to his troops and the nation just before the Battle for Berlin, Hitler once again alluded to 'Jewish–Bolshevik hordes intent on exterminating our people'. Declaring that whoever does not do his duty at this moment 'is a traitor to our people', Hitler concluded: 'Berlin will remain German.' The further the Russians advanced on Berlin, the more intense German propaganda and resistance became. Fear of what awaited Germans at the hands of the Russians ensured that everyone joined the 'life-and-death' struggle. This 'reluctant loyalty', shaped to no small degree by twelve years of an all-embracing manipulation of the mass-media and education system, resulted in a legacy that would take forty-five years to resolve, before Berlin would become truly German again.

CONCLUSION

The history of Nazi propaganda during the war is one of declining effectiveness. This is hardly surprising. War imposes considerable strains on political systems, even a so-called 'textbook police state' like Nazi Germany. The difficulties for propaganda were exacerbated by the distinct lack of enthusiasm for the announcement of war. This lack of enthusiasm reflected the basic contradiction between propaganda that presented Hitler as a 'man of peace' who had successfully 'revised' the Treaty of Versailles without German bloodshed, and an ideology and economy that were inexorably linked to struggle and war. However, as we have seen, the SD noted that propaganda quickly persuaded the population that war was unavoidable and had been forced upon them, and the success of *Blitzkrieg* only served to increase the people's faith in Hitler's protean ability. The dissemination of the core themes in the Party's ideology that I outlined in Chapter 4 did not suddenly stop in 1939, but the exigencies of war demanded that propaganda should respond to military developments. The débâcle of Stalingrad undoubtedly affected the morale of the German people. It forced them to question Nazi war aims and led to a crisis of confidence in the regime amongst broad sections of the population. Nazi propaganda had become so intrinsically linked to German military success that defeat after Stalingrad found propaganda in a difficult position. The leadership's inability to prevent the Allied bombing campaigns and its failure to hit back by means of the much-heralded 'revenge' weapon, further undermined its credibility, particularly in the urban centres. In the final two years of the war Goebbels was still capable of achieving some propaganda successes, but the overriding conclusion must be that propaganda failed to compensate for the worsening military situation. The complexity of German society, from which emerged a range of attitudes and responses shaped by geographical, class and religious affiliations as well as by propaganda, repression and terror, ensured that the civilian population held out until 1945 in an increasingly hopeless struggle. We should be wary, however, of drawing conclusions similar to that of Robert Herzstein, who has interpreted this willingness to fight on as proof of a Goebbels 'victory'.[1]

157

This need not, however, lead us automatically to revise our attitude to 'resistance' in the Third Reich, or to suppose that popular support for National Socialism was not as widespread as previously assumed. It is too simplistic to explain away the appeal of the Nazis in crude emotional terms, although undoubtedly their monopoly of the mass-media and the projection of the Führer myth were major contributory factors. Was National Socialism an aberration, a unique but short-lived consensus artificially manufactured by manipulatory propaganda techniques? I think not. The Nazi 'achievement' was not simply in mobilising support but in maintaining it over a period of twelve years. Of course there was dissent (mainly the result of cleavages that existed before 1933), but this occurs in one form or another in any political system during such a prolonged period in power. Such 'opposition' as existed in Nazi Germany ('White Rose', the 1944 bomb plot on Hitler's life) remained isolated and was largely confined to grumblings about material conditions. In fact a remarkable degree of consensus was achieved during a period of European crisis and only began to break down after a series of unrelieved military disasters. The *petit bourgeoisie* continued to identify with the values of the regime while complaining about food shortages; the workers welcomed the restoration of full employment while complaining about low wages and poor working conditions; and all groups respected Hitler as an 'economic miracle-worker' and as the symbolic father-figure of the regime.[2]

Terror was always at the back of such a 'consensus' and represented a real fear, but Nazi terrorism could not, of itself, ensure quiescence. By persuading people that the Party's policies were either right or, at worst, a necessary evil, Nazi propaganda was normally sufficient to achieve at least passive support for the regime. The fact that protest could and did take place – and over such controversial humanitarian issues as in the 'euthanasia question' – undermines the argument put forward by some 'apologists' that terroristic repression alone deterred any dissent. While accepting that dictatorship gradually corrupts the moral fibre of its citizens and that resistance became increasingly difficult as the authority of the Nazi State became more firmly established, nevertheless one is still left with the legitimate question: why was there so little resistance (particularly at the beginning)? The reasons for the lack of coordinated protest against the worst excesses of the regime are, as I have tried to show, many and complex.

As Germans now look back after more than fifty years, they cannot, of course, be consumed by collective guilt. Different interpretations of Nazism are matter of continuous debate and have come to play an important role in shaping Germany's political identity, and no doubt they will continue to do so long after unification. Nevertheless there are dangers that by overstating 'resistance' at the expense of the social bases of 'consent', historians may be guilty of under-estimating the widespread acceptance of Nazism, or what one distinguished historian has referred to as the 'vulnerability of Germans to National Socialism'.[3]

The idea that propaganda was all-pervasive and totally successful needs to be challenged, as does the belief that Hitler's power was unlimited. But one must be careful not to assume that simply because Germany lost the war propaganda had 'failed'. In one of his first speeches as Minister for Propaganda Goebbels informed representatives of the press that the overriding purpose of the Nazi movement was 'to mobilise people, to organise people and to win them over to the idea of the National Revolution'. Goebbels claimed that the Nazi electoral success in 1933 was public confirmation and a 'positive verdict that the people had passed on our propaganda methods'. Goebbels went on to outline the broad role that the RMVP would play in consolidating the Party in government:

> The new ministry has no other purpose than to place the nation firmly behind the idea of the National Revolution. If that end is achieved, people can condemn me: that would make absolutely no difference if the ministry and its workers had achieved their purpose. If that end is not achieved, then I could prove that my propaganda methods have satisfied all the laws of aesthetics, but in that case I ought to have been a theatre director or the director of an academy of art rather than the Minister for Propaganda and Popular Enlightenment.[4]

It is tempting to speculate what course German history might have taken had Goebbels become a theatre director or a director of an academy of art rather than Reich Minister for Propaganda. I have attempted to demonstrate that propaganda played an important role not only in the rise of National Socialism but also in maintaining its ideology and totalitarian visions and creating a largely acquiescent public. According to Goebbels, one of the great achievements of Nazi propaganda was to have rescued Germany from the nadir to which it had sunk during the Weimar Republic. 'Had it not been for the National Revolution', Goebbels argued, 'Germany would have become completely Swissified, a nation of hotel porters and bowing waiters, a nation having no political sense whatsoever, that had lost any idea of its own historical significance.'[5] Within twelve years of his making this claim, Germany would lie in ruins. In the light of such statements (and numerous similar expressions of faith in Hitler and the Party), proclaimed with such fanaticism at the time, it is a supreme irony that amidst the rubble and debris of the collapsed Reich two very different Germanys would emerge: in the west, the Federal Republic, embracing liberal democracy in determined pursuit of its own *Wirtschaftswunder*; in the east, the German Democratic Republic, which until the Gorbachev era proved to be one of the Soviet Union's most trustworthy supporters and allies.

POSTSCRIPT: GERMANY'S SEARCH FOR A BEARABLE PAST

I began this book by stating that the recent controversy surrounding the so-called 'Historikerstreit' and the totally unexpected unification of Germany persuaded me to reappraise the popular base of Nazism. It is important, I feel, to return to these questions by means of a brief postscript in order to bring the story up to date.

Once the initial euphoria over events in Eastern Europe died down, fears were aroused immediately by talk of a united Germany and the evocation of the 'Fourth Reich' as a fearsome monster to be avoided at all cost. Much of the subsequent debate has been irresponsible, resulting in predictions of the future extrapolated from the past and wilfully ignoring developments in Germany and Europe since the end of the Second World War. There are many who instinctively recoil from any prospect of a unified Germany. Nevertheless the intensity and bitterness of much of the debate raises a number of legitimate questions about Germany's recent past. Why did millions of Germans vote for the Nazi Party, and how could such a repugnant regime maintain its totalitarian visions over such an extended period of time?

In November 1988 the speaker of the Bundestag, Philipp Jenninger, resigned after delivering a commemorative speech to a parliamentary session on the fiftieth anniversary of the *Kristallnacht* ('Crystal Night'). The controversy was subsequently further fuelled when Michael Fürst resigned as deputy leader of the Central Council of Jews in Germany. Fürst pronounced the contents of Jenninger's speech 'correct' and defended him against criticism from the Council's chairman, Heinz Galinski. The speech also highlighted the confusion among German Liberals too. The Liberal flagship, *Die Zeit*, devoted five pages to the affair but was unable to deliver a united verdict. Jenninger's rather clumsy attempts to explain how and why the German people identified themselves with Hitler and his policies – and the ensuing outcry – confirmed, not for the first time, that Germany had once again stumbled in Hitler's shadows. Jenninger is one of the more recent casualties among those who, without adequate precaution, have tried to relate the German present to the German past.

A similar controversy was sparked off when the German Chancellor Helmut Kohl announced that his Conservative coalition was proposing to build a national historical museum in the old imperial capital of Berlin. This again raised fundamental questions in the light of Germany's past. Should there be a national museum? If so, what form should it take? Should it celebrate or simply record the past? Moreover, would such a museum, as the Green Party claimed, 'discard and lock away the memory and horrors and the crimes of National Socialism . . . and absolve Germans from guilt'?[1] One of Chancellor Kohl's advisers was the historian Michael Stürmer, who, in a series of essays, advanced the need for a more active role for historians in creating a positive sense of identity with a German past. Stürmer has spoken about a 'land without memory' in which 'everything is possible'. Citing former Chancellor Helmut Schmidt's dictum that no people can exist in the long run without historical identity, Stürmer argued that the role of the historian and a future national museum was to create meaning from the past; this, he claimed, would consolidate the present and ensure the future through building national identity in a society self-destructively preoccupied with its own guilt.[2]

Stürmer's writings prompted widespread controversy. Why should Germany be ashamed of her past? Nazism, it was claimed, should be seen and explained in terms of the context of her past. This would allow the Third Reich to be set in a historical perspective that emphasised its 'singularity' in an otherwise proud history. The debate continues unabated, and nothing better illustrates the intensity associated with attempting to explain the place of the Third Reich in German history than the passionate debate which was conducted in the public arena and has become known as the *Historikerstreit* (the 'historians' dispute'). The unification of the two Germanys in 1990, far from taking the sting out of the debate, has in fact sharpened its importance for the future of a politically stable Germany. Reports since unification of a rise in neofascist activities and attacks upon ethnic groups have once again pitched the German past into the forefront of analysis and debate.

THE *HISTORIKERSTREIT*

The recent debate among German historians and others about the uniqueness and comparability of the Holocaust has aroused much international interest, and raises once again the question of how Germans come to terms with the past. For German historians this is not just an intellectual exercise about the quest for a bearable historical identity: it carries intense emotional connotations as well. The debate erupted in *Die Zeit* and other West German newspapers and magazines, in the months leading up to the January 1987 election, about the place of the Third Reich in modern German history. The controversy was sparked off by historians such as Ernst Nolte and Andreas Hillgruber, both of whom attempted to relativise Auschwitz by placing it in a wider international context. The roots and antecedents of this debate can be traced back to 1963, when, in *The Three Faces of Fascism*, Ernst Nolte argued that the rise of the fascist movements, including National Socialism, should be understood as a counter-revolution against the threat of Soviet Bolshevism. In Nolte's view, Bolshevism itself was an illegitimate child of Liberalism, and was able to flourish only because Liberalism had undermined the religious and conservative traditions which restricted the attempt to rebuild modern society according to the ideological blue-prints of totalitarian philosophies.[3]

This most original interpretation brought Ernst Nolte widespread acclaim, even from those who did not share his conservative views. Without actually renouncing the basic insights of totalitarian theory, Nolte began to move in a new direction; as well as looking at what differentiated fascism and Marxism, he began to examine their respective priorities. In this sense he went further than the classical theories of totalitarianism, which had concentrated on what they had in common.[4] From this, Nolte developed his thesis that in the gulag archipelago lay the origins of Auschwitz, and that anti-Bolshevism was a far more compelling motive for Hitler than anti-Semitism. Nolte thus moved from the parallel version of the totalitarian theory to a historic–genetic concept. In his most recent book, *The European Civil War, 1917–1945*, Nolte attempts to justify his views. He argues that National Socialism was 'a justified reaction' against the Bolshevik threat of world revolution, abeit a reaction which in time far surpassed the Russian example in terms of brutality and totalitarian mass mobilisation. To put it in its crudest form, Nolte argues that genocide has to be seen in the comparative context of the twentieth century (whether it be the victims of Stalin, Hitler, Pol Pot or Idi Amin) – and the gulags came first![5]

In 1986, in the run-up to the West German election, Nolte repeated his claim that the policies of the Holocaust had been merely a copy of the mass murders committed by Stalin. Nolte continues to maintain that the National Socialists embarked upon a policy of annihilating European Jewry because they were afraid of the threat of Bolshevism to the German people and because they identified Judaism with Bolshevism. Critics of Nolte (and there were many German historians who responded in the German press) pointed out that this would simply not do, since the historical roots of Hitler's anti-Semitism pre-date Bolshevism and are located in nineteenth-century German nationalist (*völkisch*) radical thought. Many of these critics went even further and suggested that, by deliberately underplaying the *singularity* of National Socialism, Nolte's intention was to show the Nazi atrocities in a milder light. By implying that National Socialism was not so bad after all, Nolte was accused of being an apologist for using Bolshevism as a scapegoat.[6]

Similarly, Nolte's repeated references to the 1939 declaration by Chaim Weizmann (President of the Jewish Agency) that the Jews were in a state of war with Nazi Germany has allowed him to revive David Irving's theory that Hitler was entitled to segregate Jews in concentration camps.[7] Against this, critics have pointed out that the Nazis never justified their anti-Semitic policies on such grounds. Furthermore, there can be little doubt that even after the Nuremberg Laws of 1935, most Jews who remained in Germany considered themselves loyal to the German national cause even during the earlier phases of the Second World War.

In the debate that followed it became clear that the unique nature of Nazi extermination policies could not effectively be denied. Nevertheless the controversy failed to raise any new points or provide new evidence. By comparison to the earlier 'Fischer debate', centring on whether or not Germany bore sole responsibility for the outbreak of the First World War, the scholarly content of the *Historikerstreit* was largely 'thin'. However, the controversy has raised important questions such as whether the 'Final Solution' can be compared with other historical examples of mass extermination, what historical, ethical, or moral implications this has, and whether after almost fifty years Germans can now discharge collective responsibility for their past (the death of Emperor Hirohito raised similar questions about the nature of Japanese war crimes). In view of this time-span, there is also the question of how the Third Reich should be seen in the wider context of German history. Was Nazism the inevitable culmination to which all previous developments pointed, or an accidental aberration in an otherwise 'proud' history that Germans can happily identify with?

As far as professional historians are concerned, the nature of the *Historikerstreit* has confronted them with the problems of how to reach and influence a wider audience, and the role they play in the political education of a nation. Historians have been criticised for failing to present their research for the benefit of the public, and instead writing in such a hermetic style that politicians have been able to justify their policies by distorted references to history. For German historians, the emotional (as well as intellectual) pressure has often forced them to elevate themselves to the position of guardians of the nation's collective memory. Different interpretations of National Socialism are a matter of continuous debate and in many ways have come to play an important role in shaping West Germany's political identity, and no doubt they will continue to do so in the future of a united Germany. What is perhaps so poignant about the *Historikerstreit*, is that in a period of 'revisionism' underpinned by conservative trends hardly anyone spoke up in favour of Ernst Nolte – either in Germany or outside it.

Germany's search for a bearable past is thus part of an ongoing *political* controversy. But because, as one critic has written, Hitler has 'boobytrapped' Germany's future, the arguments are invariably made obliquely. Much of the political debate is carried out in language full of references to Nazi times. The German past, it has become clear, can never be 'assimilated' or 'coped' with – or at least only with great difficulty. From their different perspectives, recent controversies surrounding the desirability (or otherwise) of a national history museum, the manner in which German history has been dramatised in film and television (whether it be the American series *Holocaust* televised in Germany in 1979, or Edgar Reitz's serialisation, *Heimat*) and the intensity of the *Historikerstreit* are all part of a national neurosis that has less to do with the history of politics than, more significantly, with the politics of history and who will control the German past.[8] In that respect, the painful experience of the 'German dilemma' is not likely to fade away with unification; indeed it is more likely to be intensified once the euphoria of the honeymoon period is over.

As a State, West Germany has assumed the moral responsibility for crimes carried out under Nazism and paid DM 31 billion (£10.3 billion) in compensation to victims and to Israel. While at the same time being the focus of anti-German feelings, the Federal Republic has repeatedly reminded its citizens that while they have inherited a burden of responsibility, they should not be consumed with collective guilt. Nevertheless for the past forty years West Germans have been perceived as the sole heirs of the Third Reich. The 16 million Germans in the German Democratic Republic, on the other hand, have largely been spared such guilt by association. East German leaders have blamed it all on 'the Nazis', from whom they 'liberated' the country. In a system anchored in Marxist–Leninist principles, fascism has been seen as a product of capitalist imperialism. Not only did 'anti-fascism' legitimise the German Democratic Republic, but furthermore it allowed its leaders to warn its citizens of the dangers intrinsic to capitalism. The spectacular collapse of Stalinist Communism in Eastern Europe will inevitably mean that many East Germans will be confronting their past for the first time, freed from ideological dogma. The painful internal process of recognition and penitence will undoubtedly result in demands for 'revised' approaches to the Nazi past. During such a transitional period it would not be surprising to witness an explosion of feeling similar to that which accompanied the *Historikerstreit*.

With German unification and all the transitional problems that this will bring, fundamental questions about interpreting and explaining Nazism will inevitably be re-examined in the light of changing political circumstances. Indeed, recent examples of intolerant behaviour, such as the anti-immigrant backlash against foreign *Aussiedler* (Poles and Russians who can claim German descent) and *Übersiedler* (East Germans who have moved to West Germany), have been viewed in some quarters as signs of latent fascist tendencies which can be traced back to the Third Reich. In 1993, the controversy flared up again over the inauguration of Germany's first memorial to those who died in the Second World War. The German Government had hoped that a memorial 'to the victims of war and tyranny' would serve both as a symbol of German unification and reconciliation.

In the end, a compromise was necessary whereby two plaques were added on which were listed the various victims of Nazism, including Jews, gypsies, homosexuals and soldiers on all sides. Others remain to be convinced that it is acceptable to commemorate the victims of Auschwitz at the same place as German officers who died in the war. As the *Historikerstreit* has clearly shown, conflicting interpretations of National Socialism will form part of a continuing reappraisal of Germany's political identity and future. Coming to grips with and learning from Germany's recent history (*Vergangenheitsbewältigung*) will, I believe, help to strengthen that identity. Although the German obsession with 'identity' must transcend the past, that does not mean that Germany should abandon and simply regret its 'uncomfortable' history and concentrate on its more acceptable 'good' history. Indeed, Helmut Schmidt has recently affirmed: 'we are morally bound to uphold the murderous and inextinguishable memory of Auschwitz'.[9] Interestingly enough, Germans have responded to this dilemma with considerable curiosity and enthusiasm. Thus in the late 1970s and early 1980s, at a time when some *Länder* were removing history from the school curriculum, sales of history books increased remarkably. It was during this period that alternative approaches to history began to attract widespread interest. By shifting the emphasis away from the pervasive general theories that had dominated the historical investigation of the Third Reich, these 'alternative' approaches focused instead on women, workers – the so-called 'victims' of history – allowing historians to redress what was seen as undue concentration on abstract speculation and to concentrate instead on 'the politics of everyday life' (*Alltagsgeschichte*).[10] Edgar Reitz's impressively detailed television series *Heimat* is an example of this approach reaching a wider audience.

New approaches to the Nazi past, including *Alltagsgeschichte*, with all its shortcomings, will serve to enrich our understanding of the German past. Following unification in 1990, many Germans, particularly Conservatives in Germany, hoped that there might now be a drawing of the line under the Nazi past. These hopes were dashed in 1996 with the publication of Daniel Goldhagen's book *Hitler's Willing Executioners. Ordinary Germans and the Holocaust*. The work was published to considerable media acclaim but to widespread hostility from historians of German history. In the process Goldhagen has become a rare phenomenon – a rich professional historian! To crudely oversimplify; Goldhagen claimed that Germans killed Jews in large numbers because they enjoyed doing it. And the reason for this was the pervasive anti-Semitism (what he terms 'genocidal anti-Semitism') that had, for Goldhagen, been a distinguishing feature of German history. According to Goldhagen, 'ordinary' Germans involved in the implementation of the Holocaust were not just obeying orders; there was no question of coercion and 'reluctance' in their involvement. The accusation then of Germans as *willing* 'executioners' was inflammatory and highly charged and amounted to nothing less than an indictment of a nation. *Der Spiegel* was moved to write a long discussion of the English language version of Goldhagen's book under the title: 'A Nation of Demons?'[11]

To substantiate his thesis (a new embellishment of the 'from Luther to Hitler' theory that had gained currency in the early 1950s) Goldhagen traces this pervasive anti-Semitism back to Luther and medieval times (he talks about the ingrained hatred felt to be Christian for the 'murderers of Christ'). It penetrated deep structures of German social mentality and became an indissoluble ingredient of the German 'national character' Thus a uniquely German brand of anti-Semitism took root, and this became so entrenched by the beginning of the nineteenth century that a genocidal or 'eliminationist' form of anti-Semitism developed which led *inevitably* towards repression, removal and ultimately 'extermination'.

Goldhagen's definition of anti-Semitism is all-embracing. It goes well beyond a 'conspiracy theory' held by some right-wing groups in Germany that Jews were intent on destroying Western civilization and needed to be 'prevented' (thus rationalising anti-Semitism in terms of a justified 'mission'). In other words, it was not the case that Hitler's state succeeded in gradually persuading sufficient numbers to participate in the Holocaust – far from it - the Nazis merely opened the floodgates – enabling the Germans to implement their 'eliminationist' anti-Semitism. Goldhagen's book provided a new demonising variation on the German *Sonderweg* ('special path' that is divergent from other Western cultures) thesis. As Hans-Ulrich Wehler noted in his detailed review of the book: 'it is a species of ethno-cultural determinism; fixated on a mono-causal "explanation", it is an elevation of dogmatic, ideological history into myth'.[12] Goldhagen's definition extends beyond Pan-German groups to include the mainstream of German liberalism. If this is the case, how was it that Jewish rights were guaranteed in legislation in the nineteenth century and that Jews played such an important role in the political life of the nineteenth and twentieth centuries?

That is not to suggest that anti-Semitism did not exist in Germany before the Third Reich. I have cited examples of this in my own work.[13] But this was not a peculiarly German phenomenon. One can refer to the anti-Semitism implicit in the Dreyfus affair in France in the late 1890s or the anti-Semitic pogroms in Tsarist Russia (under Nicholas II). Comparative studies of anti-Semitism across Europe before 1933 have been extensive enough to cast serious doubt on the alleged uniqueness of the German variant. Thus compared to Germany, France, Russia, Austria and some East European states were far more anti-Semitic – and without the rights guaranteed in Germany.

Goldhagen's book again raised questions of German complicity and the extent to which 'ordinary' Germans were aware of the Holocaust and their degree of participation in its implementation. How much ordinary

Germans knew about Nazi atrocities, and to what degree they supported them is the subject of a new book by Robert Gellately, *Backing Hitler*.[14] What was the reaction of 'ordinary' Germans to anti-Semitism? The simple answer is that it was 'mixed'. Notable examples of anti-Semitic behaviour range from the 1933 boycott of Jewish shops, the Nuremberg Laws in 1935 and the *Kristallnacht* in 1938. However, reports from within Germany reveal that public opinion was *not* homogeneous; reactions to the treatment of Jews were based on a number of factors – political, regional, class and religious affiliations. Many Germans, for example, were horror-stricken by the violence not just to Jewish property – but to Jews themselves. In many ways the *Kristallnacht* represented a watershed on the road to Auschwitz in that the largely negative responses of the German public persuaded the Nazi leadership that future anti-Semitic measures would have to be better coordinated and more furtive. Thus the measures taken after the Wannsee Conference (20 January 1942) when it was agreed to implement the final solution to the Jewish Question, were secret and largely undertaken outside Germany. Leading Nazi figures such as Goebbels feared that if an 'exterminationist' policy was widely known or implemented within Germany it would risk opposition. Therefore Goldhagen's claim that the lack of opposition is an indication of widespread anti-Semitism is in fact nothing of the kind. One also has to place this in the wider context of the fear and coercion that were intrinsic to the Nazi State. Political parties and opposition had been abolished within a remarkably short period of time (cf. the experience of the Bolsheviks) with little opposition to the loss of political, legal and trade union rights. Political opposition and avenues of protest in general had been successfully emasculated by the Nazis. The Episcopal protest at the 'euthanasia' programme was a rare exception.

Moreover it should also be recognised that there existed a large constituency of Germans that remained immune to anti-Semitic propaganda – both before and during the Third Reich (something Goldhagen ignores). For example, the SPD never tolerated anti-Semitism and different opinions within the Party never crystallised in openly racial terms. However, the Social Democrats and the Communists did tragically underestimate the strength of the anti-Semitism of the lower-middle class and the far right, and such anti-Semitism did play an important part in Nazi electoral successes (within these groups) in the early 1930s. There is evidence, furthermore, that many Jews in fact received signs of sympathy, particularly after they were forced to wear the Star of David (1 September 1941); Goebbels was so incensed that he complained to Speer that the German people 'haven't' grown up yet'.

How much did Germans know? About half a million were actually involved in the carrying out of the Final Solution (under 1 per cent of Greater Germany). Of course Germans would have noticed the disappearance of Jews from local neighbourhoods and there were few coordinated campaigns (both domestically and internationally) to prevent this. Mention must also be made of the enthusiastic denunciations by 'ordinary' citizens of Jews and other 'internal enemies' such as Communists, gypsies, homosexuals etc. Gellately has shown that by the end of the war Hitler was still receiving 1,000 private letters a week, many of them denunciations. But to say that they were 'enthusiastic' exterminators or willing executioners is surely going too far. As is shown in Chapter 4, at precisely the time that Jewish persecution was being intensified and final details of the 'solution' arrived at (summer and autumn of 1941) the SD reports were noting either boredom with or massive indifference to the Jewish Question. Such indifference proved fatal. It is worth recording once again Ian Kershaw's memorable point that the road to Auschwitz was 'built by hate but paved with indifference'.

One can state that a large minority of active anti-Semites was involved in the extermination programme. Beyond these groups the mass of society remained largely indifferent. This indifference may be termed 'passive anti-Semitism'. A situation created, I believe, by a combination of (1) Nazi propaganda that had skilfully presented a negative stereotypical image of Jews as the source of all Germany's troubles and as 'outsiders' in an exclusive, racial utopian community (the Nazis' much heralded *Volksgemeinschaft*); and (2) a series of laws and decrees that had *increasingly* marginalised Jews (a process, in other words, of 'incremental persecution'). By the early 1940s Germans had been convinced by an unrelenting propaganda machine that there was a 'Jewish problem' – a 'problem' that needed to be 'solved'. (Hans Mommsen has referred to the 'solution' as 'cumulative radicalisation' which started with intimidation and persecution and ended in a network of extermination camps.) Moreover, since 1933 Germans had become 'acclimatised' to the persecution of Jews and to murder. Although this is not offered as an excuse, one should not underestimate the insidious nature of familiarity with violence – particularly in war. Compare, for example, our own experience in Britain and our passive 'acceptance' of daily outrages, atrocities and murder in Northern Ireland that have been reported copiously in our media and over a considerable period of time.

Mention should also be made that there were minority groups outside Germany who actively participated in the murder of Jews. One only has to cite SS volunteers from the occupied countries of Europe – the Luxemburgers in Police Batalion 101, Latvians, Lithuanians, Ukranians and Romanians. Such evidence undermines Goldhagen's assumption of a uniquely German form of depravity. Finally, while not wishing to relativise the Holocaust in the manner of Ernst Nolte, it is nevertheless important to examine the whole edifice of National Socialist race and population policy. Hitler's 'willing executioners' did not murder only Jews. The first to be killed in fact were 'unhealthy' Germans in the 'euthanasia' programme which in turn was in direct line of succession from the compulsory sterilisation measures enacted in the first months of the regime. Millions of Slavic *Untermenschen*, gypsies, homosexuals and people with hereditary diseases or mental disabilities were also killed. The National Socialists pursued brutal programmes of eugenics, euthanasia, sterilisation and 'ethnic cleansing'. The 'advance planners of extermination' (to use Gotz Aly's phrase) had projected that more than 30 million Slavs would be killed in the event of the successful completion of *General Plan Ost* (General Plan East) – the war of annihilation against Russia would have been on a colossal scale had Hitler's march eastwards extended to the Urals.

Given the widespread hostility from the academic community one has to ask: why did Goldhagen's book cause such a stir and sell in such large numbers, particularly in Germany? Attacked by academics when it first appeared in English, it was not dismissed out of hand, but other works such as Christopher Browning's had already shown that anti-Semitism was a motive in the killing units and that the implementation of the Final Solution had drawn in wider elements in German society outside the SS – including some sections of the Wehrmacht.[15] German academics claimed that Goldhagen's mono-causal explanation went too far – and could not be substantiated. In fact many claimed that it undid much of the work generated by the *Historikerstreit* that had persuaded Germans to engage in a search for a bearable past. But when the German edition was published, the popular reaction was extraordinary. Thousands queued outside book-shops and attended his book signings. Many viewed Goldhagen as a 'prophet' telling them that they were 'guilty'. Indeed, he was often cheered in television debates whereas German historians who attempted to show that his book was simplistic and mono-causal were howled down. For historians who have been involved in this process over many years – of witnessing Germany's painful search for its past – this proved to be an almost inexplicable example of naked national self-examination that at times was painfully confessional. Goldhagen was seemingly able to profit from Germany's preoccupation with its own guilt.

What conclusions can be drawn from the shifting perspectives of the Nazi era? There are no easy or convenient conclusions that adequately draw these disparate but overlapping events together.[16] In the case of the *Historikerstreit* a mature and distinguished historian attempted to relativise the Holocaust and was widely condemned (I think rightly). The 'historian's dispute' that followed did at least raise important questions such as whether the 'Final Solution' can be compared with other historical examples of mass extermination, what historical, ethical, or moral implications this has, and whether after over 50 years Germans can now discharge collective responsibility for their past. In the aftermath of the *Historikerstreit* many Germans felt that by 1995 the past had been sufficiently discussed, or even 'overcome'. Few would disagree with Nolte when he described the Nazi era as 'a past that will not pass away'. Goldhagen's all-embracing condemnation that followed cannot simply be written off as the arrogant work of a young political scientist who believes he has made a brand new discovery. The intensity of the controversy following *Hitler's Willing Executioners* revealed once again a national neurosis that has less to do with the history of politics than, more significantly, with the politics of history and who will control the German past (it has to be said that it suits certain interests to remind Germans of this past – as it undermines their economic dominance). Whereas surely no one would argue that the genocide that took place under National Socialism should be forgotten – or indeed that we should not continue to examine its roots and antecedents, there is a danger that the huge commercial marketing drive that underpinned Goldhagen's book elevates this work into an undeserved *tour de force* at the expense of more balanced, scholarly accounts. In due course this may result in a generation of sixth-formers and undergraduates fervently believing that ordinary Germans in the Third Reich were 'willing executioners' – and that is a disturbing prospect.

Equally disturbing were the recent dramatic events that unfolded in the British High Court when the historian David Irving sued the American academic Deborah Lipstadt and her publisher, Penguin Books, for citing him as a 'Holocaust denier' in her book *Denying the Holocaust: The Growing Assault on Truth and Memory* (published in 1993). Irving contended that it was an 'unexplained tragedy' and denied that six million Jews perished as a result of systematic murder, or that Hitler was responsible, or that Jews were put to death in the gas chambers at Auschwitz on any significant scale.[17] Lipstadt offered to show that her allegations were true and she promptly did with the help of Richard Evans, Professor of Modern History at Cambridge, who performed a historian's 'clinical' autopsy on Irving's body of work. It was a rare example of historians placing their sources, methods and controversies into the public domain. It is no coincidence that on the occasions when historical controversies have attracted such public interest, the Third Reich is invariably the source of the controversy. The Irving trial (for in the end it was David Irving who was on trial) once more raised fundamental questions about the Holocaust, the respective role of Hitler and the nature and complexity of historical writing.[18]

What these shifting interpretations reveal – from the 'totalitarian' model of the 1950s (recently enjoying something of a renaissance), to the *Historikerstreit* of the 1980s, *Alltagsgeschichte*, and more recently the 'Goldhagen phenomenon' and 'Holocaust denial' – is the deep passion and moral outrage that the Third Reich arouses in the hearts of professional historians and the general public.[19] Nazi Germany has become something of a growth industry, particularly on television screens, where it is in danger of becoming uncomfortably voyeuristic. Yet, as Ian Kershaw has pointed out, 'moral denunciation in the long run will not suffice and can easily become the stuff of legend, not understanding'.[20]

In the area of public opinion and propaganda, with which this book is primarily concerned, the legacy left by National Socialism was a deep mistrust of how easily the mass media could be manipulated to serve the opportunist aims of a repugnant fascist regime. However, as with most aspects of politics, the relationship between propaganda and public opinion in the Third Reich was far more complex than the rather simplistic interpretations that continued to dominate historical investigation well into the 1980s. As the *Historikerstreit* and the 'Goldhagen phenomenon' have demonstrated, historians will continue to be placed under increasing pressure, not to condemn or justify, but to provide a greater awareness of the complexity of social and political reality in Nazi Germany. This book was written very much in this spirit and is offered as a contribution to that growing awareness.

SELECTED DOCUMENTS

DOCUMENT I

This speech by the Minister for Propaganda was not simply to explain the Government's intentions in setting up the new Ministry for Popular Enlightenment and Propaganda – the first of its kind in Germany. It also afforded Goebbels the opportunity to introduce himself to the German press as a fellow-journalist as well as a politician and to allay the fears of his audience. Not for the first time, Goebbels ingratiated himself by flattering his audience, referring to them as the 'seventh great power that is better suited than any other to shape and to influence public opinion'. By presenting himself as 'one of them' he hoped to gain a sympathetic understanding for some of the measures that he was about to outline. Bearing in mind that on 5 March 1933 the Nazis had made electoral gains but had failed to gain an overall majority, Goebbels begins by asserting the legitimacy of both the Government ('this Government is, in the truest sense of the word, a People's Government') and his ministry and its claim to represent the 'link between Government and people . . . the expression of the popular will'. According to Goebbels, propaganda would be the active force cementing the nation together.

Goebbels then returns to the specific functions of the press, which, he argues, should 'not merely inform but also instruct'. Quite clearly, however, greater emphasis would be placed on instruction and 'explaining Government policy to its readers in accordance with Government instructions'. By the autumn of 1933 journalists would have little doubt that Government directives were to be regarded as binding. Although Goebbels maintains in his speech that the press would have freedom to criticise, such freedom remained illusory.

Goebbels: the tasks of the Ministry for Propaganda[1]

(Speech to representatives of the press, 15 March 1933)

Gentlemen! First of all I should like to thank the previous speaker for the kind words of greeting with which he welcomed me here. I believe that I can present myself to you as a colleague, as it were, because I do not come to the press field as an innocent but am myself from the press. In addition, it has been my most heartfelt wish that the press above all might be drawn into this new Ministry for Popular Enlightenment and Propaganda that is being formed, because I know very well the very important role that the

172

press plays nowadays in public life. This instrument is the seventh great power that is better suited than any other to shape and to influence public opinion for or against a government.

There can no longer be any doubt that since 30 January a national revolution has been carried through in Germany, a revolution that in a single bound has moulded historical events in the course of six to eight weeks in a way that in normal times would require ten or twenty or even thirty years. No one can be in any doubt either that none of these events can be reversed or that, on the contrary, everyone, both in Germany and the world at large, must come to terms with the National Revolution and the events that it has brought about. Whether one supports or opposes this revolution and these consequences is in this context a matter of absolutely no importance. I see the establishment of this new Ministry for Popular Enlightenment and Propaganda as a revolutionary act of government because the new Government has no intention of abandoning the people to their own devices and locking them up in an airless room. This Government is, in the truest sense of the word, a People's Government. It derives from the people and it will always execute the people's will. I protest most passionately against the notion that this Government is the expression of some reactionary will and that we are reactionaries. We could reintroduce domestic service or the three-class franchise, for we have the power to do it. But we have no intention of doing so. There is nothing more alien to this Government than that sort of thing. We want to give the people what belongs to them, albeit in a different form from what has been the case under parliamentary democracy.

I see in the newly established Ministry for Popular Enlightenment and Propaganda a link between Government and people, the living contact between the national Government as the expression of the popular will and the people itself. In the past few weeks we have experienced a growing political coordination (*Gleichschaltung*) between the policy of the Reich and the policy of the *Länder* and I see the first task of this new ministry as establishing a coordination between the Government and the whole people. I do not believe that we have reached our goal when, if I may use one of those old-fashioned expressions, we have a 52 per cent majority in parliament. A government that faces the great and far-reaching tasks that the present Government faces could not survive for long and could not find the popular support it needs from these far-reaching measures if it were satisfied with this 52 per cent majority. It must, rather, see its task as making all the necessary propaganda preparations to win the whole people over to its side in the long term. If this Government is now resolved never to yield – never under any circumstances – then it has no need of the dead power of the bayonet: it will not be satisfied for long with the knowledge that it has 52 per cent behind it while terrorising the other 48 per cent, but will, by contrast, see its next task as winning over that other 48 per cent to its own cause.

That will not be done just by objective work. Rather, the objective work of the Government must also be made clear to the people. The task of the press cannot be merely to inform; rather, the press has above and beyond that the much greater task of instructing. It naturally has the task of making clear to the people what the Government is doing, but it must also explain why the Government is doing it, why the Government is forced to act in a certain way and no other. If we were to take over the legacy of the past fourteen years without explaining to the German people the causes of Germany's decline, I am convinced that our party-political opponents, with all the shrewdness that they possess in their sphere, would very soon succeed in holding the new Government responsible for the legacy that it has inherited without also inheriting the responsibility for it. But that cannot be the case: we shall have to make clear to the German people what we have inherited, how we have inherited it and what measures we have to take, and shall have to take, to reform this legacy.

The name of the new ministry tells us quite clearly what we mean by this. We have founded a Ministry for Popular Enlightenment and Propaganda. These two titles do not convey the same thing. Popular enlightenment is essentially something passive; propaganda, on the other hand, is something active. We cannot, therefore, be satisfied with just telling the people what we want and enlightening them as to how we are doing it. We must, rather, replace this enlightenment with an active Government propaganda, a propaganda that aims at winning people over. It is not enough to reconcile people more or less to our regime, to move them towards a position of neutrality towards us, we want rather to work on people until they are addicted to us, until they realise, in the ideological sense as well, that what is happening now in Germany not only must be allowed, but can be allowed. In this respect the National Socialist Movement has already done an enormous amount of preparatory work.

If we look at the work that lies behind us and at the unparalleled successes we have achieved even in the past few weeks, we must attribute this mainly to the fact that as a young revolutionary movement we gained a virtuoso mastery of all the means of modern mass influence, and that, rather than directing propaganda from a baize table, we as true popular leaders have come from the people and have never lost intimate contact with the people. I think that one of the most important advantages of the new Government propaganda consists in the fact that the activity of the men who have hitherto been responsible for National Socialist propaganda can now be made to bear fruit for the new State.

Propaganda – a much-maligned and often misunderstood word. The layman uses it to mean something inferior or even despicable. The word 'propaganda' always has a bitter after-taste. But, if you examine propaganda's most secret causes, you will come to different conclusions; then there will be no more doubting that the propagandist must be the man with the greatest knowledge of souls. I cannot convince a single person of the necessity of something unless I have got to know the soul of that person, unless I understand how to pluck the string in the harp of his soul that must be made to sound. It is not true that propaganda presents merely a rough blueprint; it is not true that the propagandist does no more than administer complex thought processes in rough form, in a raw state, to the masses. Rather, the propagandist must not just know the soul of the people in general but must also understand the secret swings of the popular soul from one side to another. The propagandist must understand how to speak not only to the people in their totality but also to individual sections of the population: to the worker, the peasant, the middle class; he must understand how to speak to both the south German and the north German; he must be able to speak to different professions and to different faiths. The propagandist must always be in a position to speak to people in the language that they understand. These capacities are the essential preconditions for success.

In the past people have done the National Socialist movement a great injustice by regarding what was expressed in it as propaganda as the sole form of expression for this revolutionary movement. That is wrong. In this regard the press has, in particular, made numerous accusations against me.

No aesthete can pass judgement on the methods of propaganda. A binding judgement can only be passed on the basis of success. For propaganda is not an end in itself but a means to an end. We are setting up here a Ministry for Propaganda which does not exist for its own sake and thus represent an end in itself, but which is a means to an end. If we achieve our end through this means, then the means is good; in any case, whether or not it meets strict aesthetic requirements is thus terribly irrelevant. But, if this end is not achieved, then this means will have been a bad one. The purpose of our movement was to mobilise people, to organise people and to win them over to the idea of the National Revolution. That end – and even the most ill-disposed person cannot argue with this – has been achieved, and so the verdict has been passed on our propaganda methods. The new ministry has no other purpose than to place the nation firmly behind the idea of the National Revolution. If that end is achieved, people can condemn me: that would make absolutely no difference if the ministry and its workers had achieved their purpose. If that end is not achieved, then I could prove that my propaganda methods have satisfied all the laws of aesthetics, but in that case I ought to have been a theatre director or the director of an academy of art rather than the Minister of a Ministry for Popular Enlightenment and Propaganda.

Coordination between the Revolutionary Government and the people will require tireless labour. I am absolutely certain that this coordination cannot be achieved in two weeks or so, or in two months or perhaps in two years, but I am convinced that our work will be directed so that this coordination is increasingly achieved. I am, however, also convinced that the methods that we employ must eventually convince even the most reserved and malevolent that the political course we have embarked on is the correct one.

Thus you see, gentlemen, that, unlike previous governments, we have no intention of calling on the bayonet, but we are quite serious about the slogan we shouted at governments when we were in opposition: 'The power that rests on the bayonet rests uneasily.' We have no intention of relying on the bayonet. We regard the Reichswehr not as an internal defence force but as a bulwark and a weapon for Germany's frontiers. We are conducting the internal political struggle from below through the popular movement that stands behind us and from above through the power of the State that we have at our disposal. Nobody will have any doubts that the struggle of our opponents against us is a hopeless one. It is quite pointless for anyone to indulge in either moderate or radical opposition. We are well aware of the methods of opposition: for too long we had to use them ourselves – and too well for us to be in any way misled by these methods. Our opponents have absolutely no prospect of achieving their aims in this way. This Government will not go away: it is resolved to stay. It will, however, also carry out its determination to find the necessary resonance in the broadest popular masses.

Now I should like to explain briefly the structure of the new ministry. You probably know as well as I do that the old system completely renounced the area of propaganda. That was partly because the propaganda organisations of the Reich and the *Länder* were completely scattered and divided between individual ministries so that they were working across, above and against one another. The second reason was that the methods of propaganda, insofar as it was officially conducted, were utterly outmoded. They had not kept pace with the tempo of today. They sometimes gave the impression that they had not changed at all since the time of Bismarck. In the meantime, however, there have been revolutionary upheavals in every field, and especially in technology. Today we live in the age of wireless, the age of large-scale mass demonstrations. Demonstrations of one, two or three hundred thousand people are no longer unattainable.

The most important tasks of this ministry must be as follows: first of all the propaganda organisations and educational institutions of the Reich and the *Länder* must be centralised and one person must hold the reins. Then it must be our task to breathe a modern impulse into these propaganda and educational institutions and tune them in to the present. Technology must not be allowed to run ahead of the Reich: the Reich must keep up with technology. The most modern is just not good enough. We are now living in an age where the masses will be brought over to a *single* policy. The National Socialist Movement and the Government of National Revolution that it leads have a claim to insist that both the movement and the Government it leads are based on the principle of the individual. The principle of the mass and the principle of the individual are not necessarily contradictory. On the contrary, the true individual will never submit to the mass but will rather subjugate the mass to him. This means that modern popular leaders must be popular kings. They must understand the mass, but they do not need to flatter the mass. They have a duty to tell the mass what they want and to make it so clear to the mass that the mass also understands. The concept of the limited intelligence of the subject must disappear once and for all from Germany, as must, for example, the evil notion that was once officially expressed in the Reichstag that the Young Plan could not be understood by the masses and that the masses therefore had no right to know all about the Young Plan. The mass was therefore expected to pay for treaties but did not need to understand them. The Government of National Revolution will not share this view. It is, rather, the task of State propaganda to simplify complicated trains of thought so that in the final analysis even the lowliest man in the street will understand them.

We proved that this is possible with the Young Plan. For years people in Germany thought that the policy of reparations was purely and simply a matter for the circles around the Wilhelmstrasse. Today no one can doubt that through our propaganda methods we have made the policy of reparations, its causes and its consequences, clear to the broad mass of the people. It can be the same with everything. You could not, for instance, pass an order relating to the compulsory blending of butter without explaining to the people why it is necessary. It would be unscrupulous for a government merely to inform the people that margarine has become more expensive without at the same time telling the people why it has to be more expensive. A government that behaves like that, that does one thing and not the other, must fall in the long term because the people themselves will not understand such a government. The people are not as unreasonable as is generally supposed. The people only become unreasonable if they do not understand something, and then they have a right to be unreasonable because they realise that they will have to bear the burden but that nobody will tell them why they must do it.

This is where our work will have to begin. We have inherited a terrible situation. There is complete disarray in every field of public life. It is a fearfully difficult and responsible task to rectify this situation. In clearing all this up we shall not be able to shrink from unpopular measures. The incisions, however painful they might be, will have to be made. The Government of National Revolution has no intention of misleading or swindling the people over certain situations but will give the people a clear and unvarnished picture of the state of affairs. That is where our work begins: we must explain to the people why the situation is as it is and why we must take steps to change it.

In this respect we shall lay claim to all the opportunities for, and methods of, mass influence. The new ministry will, seen as a whole, comprise five departments: Radio, Press, Active Propaganda, Film, and the Department for Theatre & Popular Education. Now I shall elaborate on the individual departments.

You need have no fear: we have no intention of making the *radio* boring or of depriving it of its modern tempo. On the contrary, we want to give the radio a modern tempo. I am of the opinion that the creation of a mood [*Gesinnung*] does not have to be boring. One has only to understand the art of creating a mood properly. Anyone who is really unbiased must concede that the radio propaganda conducted by the men of the Government of National Revolution in the weeks since 30 January has been exemplary. The consequences predicted by the know-alls, that listeners would switch off their sets, have not occurred. On the contrary, millions of new listeners have emerged, and this is because the Government produced its radio propaganda not in a vacuum, in the radio headquarters, but in the atmosphere-laden halls of mass gatherings. In this way every listener has become a direct participant in these events. I have visions of a new and topical radio, a radio that really takes account of the spirit of the time [*Zeitgeist*], a radio that we shall purge of all mustiness and hypocrisy, and a radio that is also aware of its great national responsibility. I have visions of a radio that really enables every individual listener to participate in great national events. I think it is an impossible situation if a national event, such as the opening of the new Reichstag or the Thanksgiving Service in the churches of Potsdam or a parade by a Potsdam regiment in front of the Reich President, has an audience numbering only 10,000 or 15,000. That is completely out of date. A government that permits that has no need to wonder why nobody above and beyond that 15,000 has any interest in the national event. On the contrary, I regard it as essential that the whole nation – for nowadays we have the technical means – must listen in to and play a direct part in these kinds of events. If television is one day developed, the whole nation should also be able to watch as these events take place. We have nothing to be ashamed of. If, in the old Reichstag, the broadcasting of proceedings was banned, that was a matter for others. *We* see no danger in it for ourselves. We shall ensure that these Reichstag sessions are held in a manner consonant with the honour and dignity of the German people. We shall ensure that the people know everything that the Government and the parties that support it are doing and that the people not only know that but also know why we are behaving in a certain way. Radio should not only offer the people the opportunity to participate directly in the great events of our time; it should at the same time also serve the conservation of German art, German science and German music – and not only objects from the past but also objects from the present when they have a future.

Now I come to a field that you yourselves represent: the *press*. I make no secret of it: I do not regard the banning of newspapers as a normal or an ideal state of affairs, although I was the first among us to have the right to ban certain sections of the press. If opposition papers complain today that their issues have been forbidden, they can talk to me as a fellow-sufferer. There is, I think, no representative of any newspaper who can claim to have had his newspaper banned fifteen times, as mine was. Nonetheless, as I say, the banning of papers is neither a normal nor an ideal state of affairs. On the contrary, I am of the opinion that the press must help the Government. The press may also criticise the Government, but it should not do it in order to misrepresent the Government to the people. The Government will use all possible measures against such attempts. They simply will not arise. No one need be in any doubt that we should recognise them straightaway. We shall know the right time to act.

As I have already said, the press must not merely *inform*: it must also *instruct*. I turn first of all to the explicitly national press. Gentlemen! You too will consider ideal a situation in which the press is so finely tuned that it is, as it were, like a piano in the hands of the Government on which the Government can play, a situation in which it is an enormously important and significant instrument of mass influence that the Government can make use of in the work for which it is responsible. It is quite possible that the Government and the press can work with and through each other in mutual confidence. I see it as one of my principal tasks to achieve that aim. I recognise the importance of the press and I know what it means to a government to have a good or a bad press. I therefore look upon myself as the top link-man, as it were, between Government and press. I shall make it my business to ensure that this link is never severed. But then, gentlemen, I must also ask you for your support. If you find fault with the Government, you must express yourself in a manner and tone that do not provide the enemy of this Government either at home or abroad with the opportunity of quoting you and thus saying something that he could not otherwise say without risking being banned. Just in the past few weeks I have frequently remarked that papers that support the Government have expressed their criticism in a form that gave the enemies of the Government a welcome opportunity to quote these articles. That must not happen. You may of course criticise the Government, but in the process you should not lose sight of the Government's interest, and you must ensure that the one is properly weighed against the other. You must not merely ensure that the Government's measures are communicated to the people, because the Government has a thousand other means of doing that: you must also view it as your major task to make the Government's measures intelligible to the people. For this reason I view the purpose of the press conference that takes place here every day somewhat differently from what has gone on here before. You should obviously get your information here, but you should also get your instructions. You should know not only what is happening but also what the Government is thinking and how you can most usefully explain this to the people. We want to have a press that works with the Government, just as the Government wants to work with the press.

From this there now inevitably arises the third area that this new ministry has to deal with. That is the area of *active propaganda*. I am of the opinion that the active propaganda conducted by previous governments has sometimes harmed these governments more than it has helped them. In any event I can only say from my own experience during the time we were in opposition that we were always pleased when the Reichszentrale für Heimatdienst [Home Defence HQ] issued a new leaflet. These leaflets were enormously useful to us; indeed we were sometimes tempted to distribute them ourselves. A government that wishes to conduct propaganda must gather round it the most able brains in mass public influence and resort to the most modern methods to achieve this mass influence.

The essence of propaganda is simplicity: we must reject all forms of flourish and decoration in explaining to the people our ideas in all their primitiveness. But we must also drum these thoughts into the public mind with such force and punch that in the final analysis even the lowliest man in the street will know what it is all about. The task of propaganda is not to say as much as possible, but the art of propaganda is to gather completely confused, complex and composite ideas into a single catch slogan and then to instil this into the people as a whole. I must once more cite as proof a precedent from our own propaganda past, namely the Day of the Awakening Nation on 4 March. No one, either friend or foe, can have any doubts that this day was the greatest propaganda achievement realised in Germany within living memory. But this achievement was only made possible because for a whole week we abandoned all other work and focused the popular vision as if by hypnosis on this *one* event. In that case, of course, we had to record the whole great success. The essence of propaganda is simplicity, force and concentration.

When I speak of *theatre and film* I emphasise expressly that these matters, in so far as they were ever dealt with by the provincial authorities, remain untouched and that the new ministry will only have to deal with them in so far as the interests of the Reich are concerned. In this connection I am also of the opinion that one should not follow contemporary developments but lead them. For this reason I think it is in the long run intolerable that, for instance, in an era of enormous revolutionary changes, in an era when we are living through history every day, our theatres and a large part of our film industry have no opportunity to treat these revolutionary events in an artistic manner. Talk to a film producer today. He is crying out for material while outside on the streets the films of reality and the artistic dramas of politics are playing every day. If we lived in an era that was burdened with a fatal boredom, then this cry for material, for dramas, for example would be understandable. Here too the new ministry will play a pioneering role.

In the fifth area, *popular education*, we must endeavour to instil into the people that united national spirit that is, as it were, the basis of the new National Government, so that everyone understands what we want, so that the entire people will begin to react as one, and so that everyone will place themselves willingly at the disposal of the Government. As I have already indicated, everyone must reconcile themselves to us. We are there, we are not going to go away and we shall gradually win the people over in this way completely to our side. . . . We do want to do that not by banning newspapers but by gradually influencing the people while we shape and form public opinion. The National Revolution that we have experienced and participated in in recent weeks has been carried out with a discipline and inner determination that no previous revolution has seen. If people now condemn something that happened in the process and feel that they have to complain about it, then I can only reply: 'Be thankful that it stayed that way.' You must never forget that the men who now comprise the new Government and the new State were still marching naked on the street only a year ago because their brown shirts had been taken away from them! You must never forget that the men who now have the official authority to ban newspapers sometimes faced financial ruin only a year ago because their newspapers had been illegally suppressed. If you are impartial and weigh things up, you must come to the conclusion that we are animated by everything but a petty spirit of revenge, that we do not dream of venting our wrath on the defenceless, but that we have a duty and a responsibility to ensure that the people are not incited but are extensively involved in the true state of affairs. In this way the Government will in the end have the people in its hands.

As I stated once before, I am no stranger to these matters: on the contrary, I am at home in all the branches that constitute my ministry. I am at home with both press and film, with popular education and with theatre, and for this reason I do not come to this ministry as a contemporary rubber-stamped by the Party. You, gentlemen, must therefore reconcile yourselves to these events and decide one way or the other. You can be certain that a government that has in the last fortnight in Germany solved the problem of reforming the Reich will not in the end capitulate to the press but will find the necessary ways and means of finishing with the press. But we do not wish for a state of daily war, a state of constantly repeated bans; we should much prefer Government and press to work hand in hand in mutual confidence. You do not need to fear a single word of tendentiousness. There is nothing on earth that is not tendentious. Things that are not tendentious are sexless and therefore worthless. Everything is tendentious, whether overtly or covertly. I already believe that it is better if we admit to an overt rather than a covert tendentiousness. In addition, there is no such thing as absolute objectivity. Everyone living at this time and everyone who helps to shape this epoch bears an enormously heavy responsibility in so far as he is not merely forming his own opinion, because an article by him in the press sometimes gives hundreds and thousands their opinion too.

If you will cooperate with us in trust, I promise you that the Government will cooperate with you in trust. I also promise you that I shall stand up for the rights of the press everywhere and at all times but on one condition: that the press stands up not just for the rights of the Government but also for the rights of the German people. If you do that, we shall do our bit. You may be impartial towards everyone, including the Government, if they make mistakes. You should criticise them; but I shall conclude with a sentence which Klopstock uttered to the German people more than 120 years ago and in which he touched upon something that even then was a cornerstone of the German nation:

'Do not be too impartial: you do not think nobly
enough to see how beautiful your error is!'
(*Loud applause*).

DOCUMENT 2

As with his speech to representatives of the press (Document 1), Goebbels flatters those working in radio and goes so far as to suggest that 'in the long term radio will replace newspapers'. Again, this was intended to reassure his audience. Partly this was because Goebbels was realistic enough to appreciate that in the early stages of the 'National Revolution' the Nazis did need the support of the media. Moreover, following the elections of 5 March, the reorganisation of German radio that was to reflect this 'revolution' went hand-in-hand with a dramatic purge of its personnel. Indeed, in the period following the elections, hundreds of senior broadcasting staff were dismissed, including all but one (in Stuttgart) of the controllers of the State radio stations. This speech, then, is specifically addressed to the new Controllers of German radio and, like so many of Goebbels' speeches during this period, is a combination of *both* the carrot and the stick. Goebbels was extremely eager to establish what was called 'Rundfunkeinheit', complete unity in all radio matters. So, as with the press, radio 'must subordinate itself to the goals which the Government of the National Revolution has set itself'. Goebbels also confided that he had visions of a radio that would allow listeners to participate in great national events, 'where the individual would be replaced by the community of the nation'. To this end, 'National Moments' such as the opening of the Reichstag, the Service of Thanksgiving in Potsdam, or the *Führer's* speeches would be broadcast simultaneously throughout the Reich so that the whole nation could listen together in order to bring the people closer to the new community. However, the most important principle, according to Goebbels, was not to be boring ('at all costs, avoid being boring'). One of the features of German radio, particularly during the war years, was the continued emphasis placed on light entertainment.

Goebbels' address to representatives of radio, 25 March 1933[2]

On 30 January the age of individualism was finally destroyed and replaced by an age of national community feeling. The individual was replaced by the community of the nation. From now on the people will be at the centre of public, private, spiritual and political activity. The ideological break-through of a quite unimagined extent will not be abated.

The radio will also need to be brought into the new 'national movement'. The notion that the work of radio can remain an end in itself cannot be refuted enough. The National Revolution will also 'conquer' the radio stations. Those who have flown the flag for the past fourteen years cannot today represent future generations. Radio should not live by mere theories which have been cultivated in the past. Only with the help of ardent ideals can one win over the people. Radio is a thing which should delight spiritually; technically it must be of a standard worthy of the desire for renewal which marks this Government of national improvement. Had it not been for the National Revolution, Germany would have become completely Swissified, a nation of hotel porters and bowing waiters, a nation having no political sense whatsoever, that had lost any idea of its own historical significance.

We make no bones about the fact that the radio belongs to us and to no one else. And we will place the radio in the service of our ideology, and no other ideology will find expression here . . . The radio must subordinate itself to the goals which the Government of the National Revolution has set itself. The Government will give the necessary instructions. I do not consider it an ideal situation that twenty parties have existed in Germany: one is quite enough. . . . There is nothing at all that is not tendentious. The discovery of the principle of absolute objectivity is the privilege of German university professors – and I do not believe that university professors make history. . . .

The Ministry for Propaganda has the task of effecting a spiritual mobilisation in Germany. It is, therefore, in the spiritual field the same as the Defence Ministry is in the field of military protection. Thus the ministry will require finance, and it will receive finance because of a fact that everybody in the Government now realises: namely, that the mobilisation of the mind is as necessary as, possibly even more important than, the material mobilisation of the nation. The proof is that in 1914 we had been mobilised in material terms as no other nation had – what we lacked was the mobilisation of the mind within the country and in other countries which provided the basis for the material mobilisation. We did not lose the war because our artillery gave out but because the weapons of our minds did not fire; because people believed that any old privy councillor could do it, without his having any contact with everyday life. No, this is a task for men who have come from the people and understand the people. . . .

I hold radio to be the most modern and the most important instrument of mass influence that exists anywhere. I am also of the opinion – and one shouldn't say this out loud – I am of the opinion that in the long term radio will replace newspapers. . . .

First principle: At all costs avoid being boring. I put that above everything. . . . So do not think that you have the task of creating the correct attitudes, of indulging in patriotism, of blasting out military music and declaiming patriotic verse – no, that is not what this new orientation is about. Rather, you must help to foster a nationalist art and culture truly appropriate to the pace of modern life and to the mood of the times. The correct attitudes must be conveyed, but that does not mean that they must be boring. And simply because you have the task of taking part in this national enterprise you do not have *carte blanche* to be boring. You must use your imagination, an imagination which is based on sure foundations and which employs all means and methods to bring to the ears of the masses the new attitude in a way which is modern, up to date, interesting and appealing; instructive but not schoolmasterish. Radio must never go down with the proverbial disease – the intention is clear and it puts you off.

I am placing a major responsibility in your hands, for you have in your possession the most modern instrument in existence for influencing the masses. By means of this instrument you are the creators of public opinion. If you carry this out well, we shall win over the people; if you do it badly, in the end the people will once more desert us. . . .

As the piano is to the pianist, so the transmitter is to you, the instrument that you play on as sovereign masters of public opinion.

DOCUMENT 3

This speech is Goebbels' introduction to the German film world at a time when the film industry had recently undertaken considerable expenditure in transferring from silent to sound cinema and was also greatly weakened by the exodus of Jewish artists, producers, directors, etc. The film industry, therefore, had expressed fears about an uncertain future. In attempting to reassure the industry, Goebbels chose to stress continuity with the past but also that there was to be a revolutionary break with *some* aspects of the past. He talks about the attitude of the Government to films and the industry which produced them. Films, he says, are to have an important place in the culture of the new Germany. Goebbels then mentions four films that have made a lasting impression on him: *Battleship Potemkin*, *Anna Karenina*, *Die Nibelungen* and *Der Rebell*. He refers to *Battleship Potemkin* as being 'without equal in the cinema. The reason is its power of conviction. Anyone who had no firm political conviction could become a Bolshevik as a result of this film.' All films, Goebbels argues, have a potential power to influence people's beliefs and hence their behaviour. However, the cinema is in a state of spiritual crisis which will 'continue until we are courageous enough radically to reform German films'. However, Goebbels warns film-makers that if they wish to produce National Socialist films 'they must capture the spirit of the time'. Ominously, there is a passing reference to the failure of Jewish directors to understand public taste . . .

SELECTED DOCUMENTS

'One must have one's own roots firmly embedded in the German soil. One must be a child of this nation' – this is a clear reference to the discriminatory, anti-Semitic moves that were forcing Jews to leave the country.

The full text of the speech was not published until 1936, although a carefully censored version was published in the *Völkischer Beobachter*. Nothing illustrates more vividly the cynical opportunism with which Goebbels exercised his authority: on the one hand, the published speech would appease the more radical elements in the Party, who were calling for wholesale changes in the film industry; and yet he managed at the same time to comfort the film industry and lure it into a false sense of security by confidentially imparting his 'true' intentions, which he could not afford to make public.

Dr Goebbels' speech at the Kaiserhof on 28 March 1933[3]

After introductory speeches by Carl Froelich, the President of Dacho, by Ludwig Kitsch, Chairman of Spio and by Adolf Engel, Chairman of the Reich Union of cinema-owners, the Minister spoke on this historic occasion as follows:

'I am grateful for this opportunity to discuss the state of the film in Germany and the probable tasks of the German film industry in the future. I speak as someone who has never lost contact with the film in Germany: in fact, I am a passionate devotee of the cinematographic art. For many years I have seen what great heights the German film can attain as a result of the power and ingenuity of the German mind.

We must rid ourselves of the idea that the present crisis is a material one: it is more of a spiritual crisis, and it will go on until we are courageous enough to reform radically German films. For the last fourteen days, I have been having discussions with representatives from every branch of the German film industry, with very amusing results. These film gentlemen have the same picture of National Socialism as that given in the press hostile to us. These people have no real idea of the National Socialist movement and its supporters, even in their own minds.

In every discussion, fears of an uncertain future were expressed again and again. They thought that the future for film production was insecure. In fact, the exact opposite should be the case. At the time of Brüning and Müller, producers had every reason to feel insecure, since the concept of what was modern changed every four weeks or so.

But now we have arrived. Even the doubting will be convinced that we are going to stay in power for at least four years. That which is here remains – we shall not leave!

With this fact as a basis, the film industry has every reason to feel secure. But at the same time you can be sure that the National Socialist movement will assume an active role in the economy and in general cultural affairs, and therefore in the film industry as well. With the aid of a few examples, I want to illustrate what in films is artistically good and what is dangerous. A few films have made a lasting impression on me.

185

First of all, *Battleship Potemkin*: this is a marvellous film without equal in the cinema. The reason for this is its power of conviction. Anyone who had no firm political conviction could become a Bolshevik as a result of this film. This shows very clearly that a work of art can be tendentious, and even the worst kind of ideas can be propagated, if this is being done by an outstanding work of art.

Then comes *Anna Karenina*. Greta Garbo has proved that there is such a thing as cinematic art. This film is not substitute theatre, but art in its own right as a film.

The Nibelungen is a film which has not been removed from our own epoch; it is so modern, so close to our own age and so topical that even the old warriors of the National Socialist movement were deeply moved by it. It is not the themes themselves that are important. Themes from Greek mythology can have just as modern an effect as themes taken from the present day. The important thing is the way in which these themes are treated.

With the advent of the new era in Germany, certain attempts were made to produce so-called National Socialist films, but they were so out of touch with the spirit of the time that one shuddered inwardly on seeing them. This kind of National Socialism is simply a veneer. The new movement does not exhaust itself with parade-ground marching and blowing trumpets.

Finally there is a film which could even convert a National Socialist, called *The Rebel*. This example shows that it is not only a film's convictions that make it good, but also the abilities of the people making it.

The ability to make a film is not the only important thing. The inner greatness of the ideas must coincide with the external means. When this happens, German films can become a force in the world, with limitless opportunities for development. Vague, formless films are not capable of making this kind of impact on the world. The more closely a film reflects national contours, the greater are its chances of conquering the world.

If the film industry starts to exercise a dangerous influence, then it is the duty of the State to step in and exercise control.

Again and again I hear the complaint that we have no subject-matter. This is simply not true! What is lacking is the courage to come to grips with this subject-matter. The film-producer has forgotten that he should be a pioneer of his age. Films should not take such a superior view of the experiences of the common German people at the present time. If films do not treat popular themes, then they will no longer be able to fill the cinemas. It is possible to say that the people are better than the film-directors. Public taste should not be under-estimated, and if it is in need of improvement, then we young people in the new movement are not too old to set about a regeneration of public taste and gradually improve it, instead of lowering it by making bad films for materialistic reasons.

The crisis in Germany has left the film industry completely unaffected: while the German nation, full of worries and desires, was going through the greatest period of suffering in history, the gentlemen of the film industry were completely ignoring the whole affair. They did not come to grips with the interesting aspects of life but remained shallow and vague.

Whoever understands our present age is aware of what dramatic situations are at the disposal of films. They occur every night, outside on our streets. German films are estranged from reality, without any contact with the actual situations of everyday life. It is indeed appalling that all the creative work in films was done in the pre-war era. Time and again the argument is heard that the kind of films which we demand would not fill the cinemas. I was told the same thing in 1926, when I began discussing this. What is needed is imagination to bring to life the inner meaning and form of a new world. Many film-makers still regard the seizure of power of the 30th as a phenomenon to which the only possible reaction is a shake of the head.

One cannot understand the spirit of the new age by means of a sudden reversal of one's own position. Only the man who lives in the mainstream of his age can mould it; the man who lives on the side-lines can never do this. So this crisis is also a personal one.

Many people today must understand, then, that if the flag falls then the bearer must fall with it. Anyone who has not understood the age properly has neither a political nor a cultural nor a moral right to hoist another flag. The general mood in films is characterised by a lack of personal conviction and courage. 'Scold me, but don't try and change me' is what the film people say, and they are just content with hoisting a new flag which is wherever possible similar to the old one. That intellectual liberalism, which resulted in reality in intellectual anarchy, is dead and buried. The objection that all art is without bias is stupid, naive and illogical.

Where does this absolute objectivity exist, then? The real danger lies in a complete lack of bias, and we must examine more closely those who support this idea. In reality they want to prevent the root-and-branch reformation of the German people. But this reformation represents the common denominator of all public life.

Indeed, art is only possible if it has its roots firmly embedded in the National Socialist soil. I must strongly warn films against taking such a low view of the German people as the other branches of the arts unfortunately did before the advent of films.

We have no intention at all of allowing those ideas, which are being destroyed lock, stock and barrel in the new Germany, to reappear in films, whether in a camouflaged or an open form. Of course, this represents interference in the production of films.

The new age does not want to inhibit the art of films; it wishes, rather, to take measures to encourage it. This does not necessarily mean just financial encouragement. The German Government is also capable of promoting ideas, and I believe that soon it will occupy such a distinguished position in this respect that it will be regarded as the highest of honours to be honoured by the Government. The artists and producers must draw their own conclusions from this situation. They must profess their desire to create anew; the courageous approach of the new age is a precondition for this. There must not be only new ideas, but new people must also emerge.

The creative artist must lead the way with a profession of faith in the new age. There is no more wonderful feeling than to be completely involved in one's age, and to be able to say for one's own modest part, 'We were there!'

In any case, public taste is not as it is conceived in the mind of a Jewish director. It is impossible to gain an idea of the German people while living in a vacuum. One must take an honest look at the German people, and for this one must have one's own roots firmly embedded in the German soil. One must be a child of this nation.

It is said that the film industry lacks money! When I see some films and hear how much they have cost, I would like to say to the producer: 'Get the money back that you paid out on your training!' If a government, which in its heart of hearts is kindly disposed towards the film industry, then people should be grateful to this Government, since it is not our intention to put the film industry in a strait-jacket. We reject authoritarian doctrinairism, but we do require that people should be ready to work in close contact with the new ideas and aspirations. Art is worth nothing without this direction of will or this partisan intent.

At the same time, we do not want to suppress the creation of a daily ration of small amusements, designed to combat the boredom and troubles of daily life. We do not want to concentrate attention the whole time on political attitudes. Our temperament is itself too gay and artistic for this. Art is free and should remain so, but, of course, it must accustom itself to certain norms. In any other country than Germany it would be superfluous to have to emphasise this. But in the last few years every mode of normal political thinking has been destroyed.

From the point where censorship must intervene, right up to the film which is a model of all artistic creation, there is an ample amount of scope for all kinds of artistic talent to roam freely.

Below this point, no allowance can be made. It is here that dangerous experiments begin, which all too often can only be treated as the excesses of a sick brain. Our film-producers will have to get used to the fact that gradually new standard-bearers will arrive on the scene.

If the Government picks out from the production of a whole year one film which is in complete accordance with its aims, wishes and tasks, then the whole film industry will as a result be given a push forwards which it would not have been possible to achieve by means of purely financial encouragement.

We have no intention of laming the film industry, or of allowing a state of insecurity to develop. In this time of great changes, films must draw closer to the genuine experiences of the people. Also, we do not want to hinder private enterprise; on the contrary, it will receive great encouragement from the national movements as a result of the firm foundation which these events have created for a new Germany.

It is not the intention of the Government to interfere in the affairs of the professional organisations. These organisations will, in fact, be given greater rights. The Government wants to proceed in full cooperation with the creative film world and to tread a common path with it. For this it is not necessary for the artist to be tied to the Party, but he must clearly acknowledge the new basis of society, raise himself fully to the general spiritual level of the nation and acknowledge the demands of its views on life.

You must not believe that we feel ourselves compelled to make life difficult for you. The young men who are now in the Government feel very sympathetic to the problems of the German film artist. I myself on many evenings recently have sat in a cinema with the Reich Chancellor, and have found relaxation after the trying battles of the day. Believe me that we are grateful to you for this.

What we want is that you should find pleasure again in your work. It must be a great feeling for a creative artist to feel totally involved in his age and to be able to say that he has also played a modest part in events. I believe that with this new sense of conviction in films a new moral ethos will arise.

I ask for trustworthy cooperation, so that it will be possible to say of German films, as in other fields, Germany leads the world.

DOCUMENT 4

The task set for the new Reich Chamber of Culture in Berlin was remarkably ambitious. It took upon itself the responsibility for furthering German culture on behalf of the people and the Reich. It attempted to encourage and supervise everything relating to what was referred to at the time as *Kulturgüter* (cultural goods), by setting up these seven chambers for literature, theatre, music, films, fine arts, the press and broadcasting. Only members of these chambers would be allowed to produce, distribute or interpret such 'cultural goods'. Interestingly enough, a provisional Chamber of Film had been set up in the July before Goebbels had decided to extend the idea to the whole of German life and form the Reich Chamber of Culture in September. Inevitably, its organisation and power became all-embracing in the field of cultural policy. On the one hand this meant encouraging a certain amount of cooperation between the various chambers; but more sinisterly, it involved regulating individuals and groups in a rather crude attempt to encourage conformity. The law of 22 September 1933 is signed by Hitler and

Goebbels and represents a triumph for the new Minister for Propaganda over Alfred Rosenberg, who had claimed a special position as arbiter of National Socialist culture. Nevertheless Goebbels felt the need to reinforce this law in November 1933 by issuing a further decree, which stated even more explicitly the extent to which the Chamber of Culture would regulate membership of the various chambers. In addition to the creative artists, the new decree set out a wide range of categories of people employed in the industries that now had to belong to a relevant chamber if they wished to continue to work.

The law setting up the Reich Chamber of Culture, 22 September 1933[4]

§1 The Reich Minister for Popular Enlightenment and Propaganda is ordered and authorised to organise the members of those branches of activity which affect his sphere of competence into public corporations.

§2 Pursuant of §1 the following chambers are established:

1. a Reich Chamber of Literature;
2. a Reich Press Chamber;
3. a Reich Radio Chamber;
4. a Reich Theatre Chamber;
5. a Reich Music Chamber;
6. a Reich Chamber of the Creative Arts.

§3 The regulations and supplementary regulations which have already been issued for the film industry by the 'Law concerning the Establishment of a Provisional Film Chamber' of 14 July 1933 are to be applied for the establishment of the chambers referred to in §2. . . .[5]

§4 The establishment of the chambers is to keep within the directives decided for the setting-up of the workings of the Reich Government.

§5 The corporate bodies in §2, together with the Provisional Film Chamber, referred to as the Reich Film Chamber, are combined in a Reich Chamber of Culture. The Reich Chamber of Culture is under the supervision of the Reich Minister for Popular Enlightenment and Propaganda.

§6 The Reich Minister for Popular Enlightenment and Propaganda and the Reich Minister of Economics are authorised through a joint decree to bring the trade regulations into line with the regulations of the law.

§7 The Reich Minister for Popular Enlightenment and Propaganda is authorised to decree laws and general administrative regulations as well as amendments for the purpose of enforcing this law. The laws and general administrative regulations affecting the financial or trade interests of the Reich require the consent of the Reich Minister of Finance, in agreement with the Reich Minister of Economics.

Signed
Adolf Hitler (Reich Chancellor)
Joseph Goebbels (Reich Minister for Popular Enlightenment and Propaganda)

DOCUMENT 5

From March 1933 the press department of the Ministry for Propaganda took control of the daily press conference, which was attended by several hundred journalists. Each of the large newspapers was allowed one representative. Admission was strictly controlled and Jewish journalists were unofficially barred. The Editors' Law of 4 October 1933 reinforced this measure by discriminating against non-Aryans, who could no longer become journalists. The real significance of this law is that it represented a victory for Goebbels and the RMVP over the publishers. Under this legislation the responsibility for editorial content now rested squarely with the editors, who were protected from dismissal by publishers, who now became simply business managers. The freedom of editors, however, had also been severely circumscribed; editors were now held personally responsible for any infringement of Government directives. Failure to publish such directives could lead to dismissal by the Minister for Propaganda and/or a fine.

Editors' Law, 4 October 1933[6]

§1 Participation in the shaping of the intellectual content of the newspapers or political periodicals published within the area of the Reich, whether by written word or by dissemination of news and pictures, and whether carried out as a main employment or based on an appointment to the position of editor-in-chief, is a public task, of which the professional duties and rights are regulated by the State through this law.

§2 1. Newspapers and periodicals are printed matter, appearing in regular sequence at intervals of at most three months, not limited in circulation to a certain group of persons.
   2. All reproductions of writings or illustrations destined for dissemination which are produced by means of a massreproduction process, are to be considered as printed matter.

§3 1. The provisions of this law relating to newspapers are also valid for political periodicals.
   2. This law does not apply to newspapers and periodicals published by official order.
   3. The Reich Minister for Popular Enlightenment and Propaganda will determine which periodicals are to be considered as political within the meaning of the law. In case the periodical affects a specific

vocational field, he will make the decision in consultation with the highest Reich or State agency concerned.

§4 Participation in the shaping of the intellectual content of the German newspapers is also considered as such, even if it does not take place in the management of a newspaper, but in an establishment which is to supply newspapers with intellectual content (the written word, news or pictures).

§5 Only those persons can be editors who:

1. possess German citizenship;
2. have not lost their civic rights and the qualification for the tenure of public office;
3. are of Aryan descent, and are not married to a person of non-Aryan descent;
4. have completed their twenty-first year;
5. are competent in business;
6. have been trained in the profession;
7. have the qualities which the task of exerting intellectual influence on the public requires. . . .

§14 Editors are especially obliged to keep out of the newspapers everything:

1. that confuses the public between individually useful aims and aims of common use;
2. that is calculated to weaken the strength of the German Reich abroad or at home, the community will of the German people, German defence, culture or the economy; or to injure the religious sensibilities of others;
3. that is offensive to the honour or dignity of a German;
4. that harms the honour or welfare of another, that injures his reputation, or makes him an object of mirth or scorn;
5. that for other reasons is immoral.

§20 1. Editors of a newspaper bear the professional responsibility and the responsibility before the criminal and civil law for its intellectual content in so far as they have composed it themselves or have accepted it for publication.
2. The chief editor is responsible for the general stance of the text.
3. It is the chief editor's duty to:

   (a) ensure that a newspaper only uses contributions which have been written by an editor or are designated to be used;
   (b) ensure that each edition of a newspaper carries the full

name and place of residence of the editor-in-chief and his representatives, as well as of each editor responsible for a particular section of the newspaper;

    (c) to give anyone who expresses a credible interest, information on which editor is responsible for a contribution, as long as this is not to be found in the details of (b).

§21 Editors who collaborate in forming the spiritual contents of a newspaper through their activity in an enterprise of the sort described in §4, are responsible for the contents, to the extent of their collaboration.

§22 The editorial group as a whole will watch over their individual professional colleagues' fulfilment of their duty and will look after their rights and their welfare.

§23 Editors are legally combined in the Reich Association of the German Press. Every editor belongs to it by virtue of his registration on the professional register. By virtue of this law the Reich Association becomes a public corporation. It has its headquarters in Berlin.

§24 The Reich Minister for Popular Enlightenment and Propaganda will be responsible for appointing the head of the Reich Association, who will issue a Charter for the Association which will need to be approved by the Minister. The head of the Reich Association will appoint an advisory council. . . .

§30 A publisher may only dismiss an editor because of his intellectual position if it undermines the public professional duties of an editor or the agreed guidelines. . . .

§35 Apart from the professional proceedings in the courts, the Reich Minister for Popular Enlightenment and Propaganda can order the removal of an editor from the professional register if he considers it essential for the public good.

§36 Whoever works as an editor without having his name on the professional register . . . will be punished with imprisonment of up to one year, or fined. . . .

DOCUMENT 6

The Reich 'Cinema Law' was the result of long and careful preparation. This decree attempted to create a new 'positive' censorship by which the State undertook to encourage 'good' films that it could approve instead of merely discouraging 'bad' ones. The new 'Cinema Law' saw three ways of achieving this positive censorship: a compulsory script censorship, an increase in the number of provisions under which the Censorship Office might ban a film, and a greatly enlarged system of distinction marks. The comprehensive nature of this piece of legislation reflected Goebbels' intense interest in all matters relating to film and the cinema industry.

Lichtspielgesetz of 16 February 1934 in its original form[7]

The Government of the Reich has decided on the following law, which is hereby announced.

Preliminary examination

1. Feature films produced in Germany must be handed in to the Reich film adviser in draft form together with the film script, so that they can be evaluated. Feature films in the terms of this law are films which present a continuous, fictional action, for the sake of which the films were made.
2. The functions of the Reich film adviser are as follows:

   (a) to assist the film industry in all dramaturgical questions;
   (b) to advise on the producing of films in draft form and in the adaptation of materials;
   (c) to give a preliminary examination to film material, manuscripts and film scripts which are submitted to him by the industry, to see whether the filming of these subjects is in accordance with the provisions of this law;
   (d) to advise the makers of films turned down in rewriting the material;
   (e) to prevent in time the treatment of themes contrary to the spirit of the times.

The film adviser keeps a register in which all the film titles submitted to him are entered.

3. The Reich film adviser keeps the film censorship office permanently informed of all the draft films and film scripts approved by him.

The examination of films

4. Films may only be publicly shown, or circulated for the purposes of public showing, if they have been licensed by the official censorship office. Performances in clubs, associations and other closed bodies are treated as public performances. No permission is needed for the showing of films in public, or those organised as public, or those recognised as public, educational or research institutes. Films which only consist of written texts, as well as foreign-language translations (versions) of films produced at home, are also subject to the provisions of this law.
5. Films turned down can also on application be given a licence for showing abroad. Exceptions to this are films which are refused a licence because they endanger the vital interests of the State or public order or

security, or because they offend against National Socialist, religious, moral or artistic feeling, or because they jeopardise German prestige or the relations of Germany with foreign countries.

6. The licence for a film is given upon application. In the case of home feature films, the Censorship Office must turn down the application, if the necessary evaluation applies according to 1.

7. The licence is refused if it transpires from the examination that showing the film is liable to endanger the interests of the State or public order or security, or to offend National Socialist, religious, moral or artistic feeling, or to have a brutalising or immoral effect, or to jeopardise German prestige or the relations of Germany with foreign countries.

A film is regarded as having jeopardised German prestige if it has been shown abroad with a bias against Germany; the Censorship Office can in this case make the granting of a licence dependent on the film being examined in the form in which it was shown in its country of origin.

8. The examination of a film by the Censorship Office must also decide whether the film is valuable from a political, artistic, educational or cultural point of view and, in the case of feature films, whether it is a film of any particular worth.

Upon application, the Censorship Office also has to decide whether the film is suitable to be used as an instructional film for teaching purposes.

9. Films in which the grounds for refusal of a licence only apply to a part of the material submitted can be licensed if the banned sections are cut out of the positives to be shown and handed over to the Censorship Office, together with the assurance that the banned sections will not be circulated. The licence can, however, be refused if the banned sections represent the major part of the film's content.

10. Films which have been refused a licence for unrestricted showing on account of point 7 can be given a licence for performance in front of special groups of people or with particular restrictions regulating the performances. The restricted nature of the performances must, however, be guaranteed in each case.

Paragraph 1 cannot be applied to films which have been refused a licence, because they endanger the vital interests of the State or public security, or because they offend against National Socialist or religious feeling.

11. Films which are not licensed for showing to children or young people under the age of eighteen years must not be performed in front of these persons. The Censorship Office decides *ex officio* on the granting of licences; if this is dependent on particular sections being cut out, then the permission of the applicant is required.

Besides the reasons stated in point 7, a licence to show a film to children or young people will also be refused if there is a danger of the film having a harmful effect on the moral, intellectual or physical development of young people or on their political education and the cultivation of a Germanic consciousness, or of over-stimulation of their imagination.

In special cases, the Censorship Office can restrict the licence of a film so that it may only be shown to young people over the age of fourteen years. Children under the age of six years may only be present at the showing of a film if the Reich Minister for Popular Enlightenment and Propaganda has given definite provision for this.

12. The Reich Minister for Popular Enlightenment and Propaganda can order the reconsideration by the Central Censorship Office of a film which has been licensed by the Censorship Office, and suspend further performances of the film until a decision has been made. If this reconsideration reveals the existence of grounds for rejecting the film under point 7, II para. 2, then the film's licence is to be revoked.

If the film, the reconsideration of which has been ordered according to para. 1, is not submitted for examination within the period laid down by the Central Censorship Office, then the licence can be withdrawn without further examination.

13. Included in the examination are the film pictures and the script, as well as any connecting passages and commentaries, spoken and written. With film operas and operettas, the singing and the dialogue are regarded as connecting passages. The examination of the title is carried out on the basis of the principles laid down in point 11, para.2. When the film is announced and in other forms of advertising, only the licensed title of the film may be used. When the film is being advertised, no reference may be made to previous prohibitions of the film.

Permission is required for any advertising pertaining to 'the performance of a film at, in or in front of the place of performance or at other places accessible to the public, or for advertising by means of the distribution of printed matter (pamphlets etc.). For advertising not yet approved by the Censorship Office and for advertising by individual cinema-owners permission can be granted by the local police authorities. It can only be refused under the regulations of point 7, para.2.

All the regulations relating to films and their examination are similarly applied to the advertising of films.

14. Films which deal with current events or the countryside, as well as short films, even if they are not in line with these regulations, can be given a licence for their district by the local police authorities, as long as there are no grounds for refusal under point 7, II para.2.

Foreign films which are obtained abroad and are shown exclusively on board German merchant ships can be licensed for this purpose by the offices designated by the Reich Government; on reaching home port, the films must be examined by the Censorship Office.

15. If a film's licence has been refused or revoked by the Censorship Office or by the Central Censorship Office, then the film can only be resubmitted in the revised form, which corresponds to the objections made in the original decision or revocation, or after the grounds for refusal or revocation have been omitted. When the film is resubmitted, the earlier decision must be declared.

The Censorship Office

16. The Censorship Office in Berlin is in charge of the licensing of films; its decisions are valid in the whole area of the Reich.
17. The permanently appointed chairman of the Censorship Office makes the actual decisions about licensing and evaluating films: with feature films he is assisted in these by four associate members.

Of the associate members one must come from the film industry, one from artists' groups and one from writers' groups.

The opinion of the associate member is established by the chairman. In cases of doubt, the chairman is required to call in experts for examination, especially those from the Reich Ministry for Popular Enlightenment and Propaganda.

18. The requisite number of associate members is suggested by the presidents of the individual chambers of the Reichskulturkammer (the Reich Board of Culture) and is appointed by the Reich Minister for Popular Enlightenment and Propaganda.

The associate members are required by the chairman on oath to make their judgements to the best of their knowledge without respect of persons.
They receive a fee fixed by the Reich Minister for Popular Enlightenment and Propaganda for their participation in the meetings of the censorship board and their travelling expenses.

19. If the film is refused a licence completely or in part or is not accepted on the grounds of point 8, then the applicant has the right of appeal against the decision (22), within two weeks from the date of the decision.

An appeal can also be made against refusal of recognition according to point 8, if the film has been licensed by the Censorship Office.

20. The final decision about an appeal is made by the Central Censorship Office, which is similarly staffed by a permanent chairman and

four associate members. The regulations of point 17, para.1 are here applied.

The decision of the film Censorship Office may then also be revised to the disadvantage of the applicant, if it is the latter who puts in the appeal.

21. With the exception of cases under point 14, a licence card is issued to the applicant.

On the occasion of film performances, these licence cards must be shown on demand to those officers of the public security service who have been entrusted by the relevant authorities with supervisory duties. The advertisements used for display or distribution must carry the licensing stamp.

22. If a film is rejected, the applicant must be given a document stating the reasons for this decision.
23. Fees are charged for the examination of films and advertisements, as well as the issuing of licence cards.

The applicant must pay in advance on presenting his application. The Reich Minister for Popular Enlightenment and Propaganda determines these compulsory fees.

Provisional and penal regulations

24. The Reich Minister for Popular Enlightenment and Propaganda is in charge of making the arrangements for the dissolution of the Munich Censorship Office.

Until the associate members have been appointed on the basis of point 18, para.1 of this law, the present associate members of the Censorship Office and of the Central Censorship Office can carry on in their present positions. The Central Censorship Office decides about applications for revocation which were made on the basis of the 'Cinema Law' of 12 May 1920, before the law came into effect, according to the previous regulations.

25. The penalty of up to one year's imprisonment and a fine, or one of these two penalties is imposed on:

   (a) whoever willingly shows or circulates in contravention of these regulations films or parts of films which have not been licensed by the competent authorities, or the showing of which has been suspended, or the licence of which has been revoked;
   (b) whoever willingly shows films to children or young people which are not licensed for showing to children or young people (11), or whoever willingly allows children or young people to see a preview of such films;
   (c) whoever willingly shows films which are licensed for showing to

special groups of persons, or which are licensed with other conditions, disregarding these particular regulations;

(d) whoever willingly allows children under the age of six years to attend cinema performances, without particular provision being made for this by the Reich Minister for Popular Enlightenment and Propaganda;

(e) whoever willingly uses or circulates for the purpose of public use an advertisement which has not been licensed;

(f) whoever willingly announces a film or the appropriate advertisement under a title other than that licensed by the Censorship Office;

(g) whoever willingly submits to the Censorship Office a film, the licence of which has already been refused or revoked, and knowingly suppresses this fact (point 15). If the offender acts negligently, then a fine is imposed.

26. A fine of up to RM 150 is imposed on:

(a) whoever does not present his licence card on demand to the official in charge of supervising cinema performances (point 21, para.2);

(b) whoever displays or distributes an advertisement, which has not been given a licence stamp (point 21, para.2).

27. A fine of up to RM 150 is imposed on:

(a) whoever willingly visits film shows which are only licensed for performances to special groups of persons, without belonging to these groups;

(b) whoever takes children or juveniles to cinema performances contrary to the regulations laid down or, if the child or juvenile is in his care or protection, gives permission for or tolerates the forbidden visit to the cinema.

The penalties imposed on juveniles are governed by the regulations of the law relating to the juvenile court.

28. In addition to these penalties, it can also be decided that in the cases of point 25, para.1 (a) and (c), the films or film extracts be confiscated, and that the plates and blocks used in the production of texts or advertisements be destroyed, even if the objects mentioned belong neither to the offender nor to an accomplice. If it is not possible to prosecute or sentence a particular person, then confiscation or destruction of the objects can be decided upon independently.

Moreover, in the case of point 25, para. 1, it can be pronounced in the judgement that the sentenced person be suspended for up to three months, or for repeated offences permanently banned from running a cinema business or being active in it. A person is considered to be guilty of repeated offences if he has already been convicted twice of an offence against point 25, para. 1, in the three years before committing the new offence, and if the second offence was committed after being found guilty in law on the first charge.

29. If during the conduct of cinema business a punishable offence according to point 25 is committed, then besides the offender himself the person owning the business and the person appointed by him to manage or supervise the business is:

    (a) liable to prosecution under point 25, para. (a), if the offence is committed with his knowledge and if he has intentionally done nothing to prevent the offence being committed;
    (b) liable to prosecution under point 25, para. (b), if he has been negligent in his choice or supervision of his subordinate, or in his own supervision of the business.

Point 28, para. 2 is correspondingly applied to business owners, managers or other supervisory personnel, who are sentenced on the basis of para. 1(a).

30. A prison sentence of up to one year and a fine, or one of these two penalties, is imposed on:

    (a) whoever runs a cinema business or is active in it or runs it through a person acting as a front, although his right to do so has been suspended under points 28, 29;
    (b) whoever runs a cinema business as the front man for another person, to whom such activities are forbidden under points 28, 29, knowing of this circumstance.

Final regulations

31. The Cinema Law of 12 May 1920 (RGBI.S. 953) – in the wording of the laws of 23 December 1922 (RGBI 1923 I S. 26) and of 31 March 1931 (RGBI I S. 127), as well as of the Third Decree of the Reich President to secure the economy of the finances and to combat political offences of 6 December 1931 (RGBI I S. 567) – no longer has effect.

32. The Reich Minister for Popular Enlightenment and Propaganda is empowered to issue decrees and general administrative regulations even of a supplementary nature, in order to enforce the law. Where the decrees and general administrative regulations affect the workings of the Entertainment Tax, the agreement of the Reich Finance Minister is required.

33. The law comes into effect on 1 March 1934.

Law to amend the Cinema Law of 13 December 1934[8]

Article 1.   The Cinema Law of 13 December 1934 is amended as follows:

1.   In point 1, the word 'must' is replaced by 'may'.
2.   The following wording is added to point 2:
     'If the Reich film adviser considers the draft of a film or the film script submitted to him worthy of encouragement, then he can at the request of the firm advise and assist them in the production of the script and film itself. The film is then bound to follow his directions.
3.   Point 3 is replaced by the following new regulations:
     The Reich film adviser keeps the film Censorship Office (points 16, 20) permanently informed of the result of the examinations undertaken by him. The Reich film adviser is entitled to take part in the examination of feature films.

Second law to amend the Cinema Law of 2 June 1935[9]

The 'Cinema Law' of 28 June 1935 is amended as follows:
Independent of the procedure of the Film Censorship Office and the Central Film Censorship Office, the Reich Minister for Popular Enlightenment and Propaganda can, even without ordering the re-examination of a film under point 12, para. 1 prohibit a licensed film for urgent reasons of the public good. The resubmission of a film prohibited in this way (point 15) is only permitted with the approval of the Reich Minister for Popular Enlightenment and Propaganda.

Article 2. This law also applies to prohibition made by the Reich Minister or at his instigation, before the law came into effect.

DOCUMENT 7

The debate about the precise role of the art critic did not suddenly erupt after the Nazi assumption of power. Right-wing groups had regarded the criticism of the arts with considerable suspicion and hostility throughout the Weimar Republic. Partly this was due to the fact that the dominant art critics of Weimar supported the Modernist movement and generally had impeccable left-wing or liberal–centre politics. For many Germans, however, art was perceived as a spiritual experience which was edifying in itself, and therefore to criticise art was a blasphemous act. Nazi ideology and aesthetics coincided with a deep disquiet within a rapidly modernising, but precariously 'enlightened', society. This protest against modernity is clearly outlined in Hitler's speech on the opening of the House of German Art (Document 8). Having established the Reich Chamber for Culture, the regime intended to assume complete responsibility for cultural life, including art criticism. It is surprising to discover that Goebbels' ministry did not start to formulate a specific policy regarding art criticism until 1935, when officials from the RMVP began to remind critics that their first responsibility was to the State and not to themselves. The banning of art criticism in 1936 was the result of a growing sense of frustration on the part of Goebbels that his warnings had gone unheeded. Critics apparently could not be persuaded that if a work of art had been officially approved by the Government, then it was not the role of the critics to criticise. The Government's somewhat perverse logic was rationalised by reference to the 'corrosive' effect of such criticism during the Weimar Republic. The legislation banned all art criticism by confining critics to write merely 'descriptive' reviews. In future all critics would need a special licence from the Reich Chamber of Culture and these would only be given to critics over the age of thirty. The ban on the thirty-year minimum age was revoked on 24 February 1937, provided a critic could show a record of National Socialist service. He would still require, however, his 'reporter's licence'.

Banning of art criticism, 27 November 1936[10]

In the context of the reconstruction of German cultural life, criticism of the arts is one of the most pressing but also one of the most difficult questions to solve. Since assuming power, I have given German critics four years to conform to National Socialist principles. The increasing number of complaints about criticism, both from the ranks of artists themselves and from other sections of the population, prompted me to summon the critics to a conference. At this conference I gave the German critics the opportunity to discuss in depth with the most prominent German artists the problem of criticism, at the end of which I expounded my own views on criticism in unambiguous terms. . . .

Since the year 1936 did not bring any satisfactory improvement in criticism, I finally forbid from today the continuation of criticism of the arts as hitherto practised.

Criticism of the arts as hitherto practised had been turned into art judgement in the days of Jewish cultural infiltration, and this was a complete distortion of the term 'criticism'. From today criticism of the arts will be replaced by commentary on the arts. The place of the critic will be taken by the arts editor. Articles on the arts will describe rather than evaluate. They will give the public the opportunity to make their judgement, encourage them to form an opinion about works of art on the basis of their own intellectual and emotional responses.

In taking such an incisive measure I base it on the point of view that only those who have a real understanding of the area they are criticising should criticise. Those who are themselves creatively gifted will be less occupied with criticising and will feel much more the urge towards their own creative achievement. I remember that the greatest critics of the past century – Lessing, Kleist, Tieck, Brentano, Fontane, Gustav Freytag and many others – had already achieved great creative works before they wrote reviews. The form which their involvement with art-reviewing took is a good example for our time. The great critics of the past wanted only to serve art. They were respectful of the achievements of others and did not set themselves up as infallible judges of someone else's work. This was the case up to the Jewish *literati* from Heinrich Heine to Kerr.

Future art reports require respect for artistic creation and achievement. They demand culture, tact, a proper attitude to and respect of artistic temperament. In the future the only ones able to discuss artistic works will be editors who undertake such tasks with honesty and in the spirit of National Socialism. Therefore we demand, as by right, that the art reviews should not be anonymous.

Therefore I order:

In the future, all art discussion must be signed fully by the writer. The office of the arts editor will need special authorisation in the professional register of the press, and this will depend on evidence of a really extensive background in the area of the particular art form with which the editor in question will be dealing. Since involvement with artistic works needs a certain maturity and experience of life, art editors must be at least thirty years old before they can be authorised to enter this branch of the German press.

DOCUMENT 8

As a 'failed' artist himself, Hitler held strong views about art. These views are nowhere more explicitly stated than in his speech of 18 July 1937, when he opened the House of German Art in Munich, which was intended to house only officially approved art. In his speech, Hitler compared his own views with those expressed by the modern artists whose works were being displayed simultaneously in another building under the title of 'Degenerate Art' and intended to demonstrate the extent to which the German nation had been corrupted by an international conspiracy of Jews and Bolsheviks. The alternative exhibition of 'Degenerate Art' was an extraordinary statement, even for the Nazis, of art that was to be abominated. Why, one might ask, did Hitler go to such lengths to convey his disgust for modern art? In his speech opening the rival exhibition, Hitler talked of modern art as being an expression of a world-view that had become 'adulterated' through the mixing of races and ideas. This had resulted in 'misformed cripples and cretins, women who inspire only disgust, men who are more like wild beasts'. Nazi racial theory underpins both Hitler's contempt for Modernist art and the type of idealised Nordic alternative that would embody the 'new human type'. Hitler's aesthetics were based on genetics. In his view, only the Aryans were capable of creating what he referred to as 'true' art. At stake was not merely German culture, but Germany itself: 'As in politics, so in German art-life, we are determined to make a clean sweep of empty phrases.' For Hitler, modern art spelt racial corruption – what he referred to as 'cultural Bolshevism'. Opening the House of German Art, Hitler spoke of art's duty to embody the 'experiences of the German people' and to 'express the essential character of the abiding people' as an 'eternal monument'. There is considerable irony in the fact that it has been estimated that some 20,000 visitors a day visited the exhibition of 'Degenerate Art' and it eventually toured thirteen venues in Germany and Austria and was seen by 3 million people.

Hitler's speech, at the opening of the House of German Art in Munich, 18 July 1937[11]

In the collapse of Germany after the war the economic decline was generally felt, the political decline was denied by many, the cultural decline was not even observed by the majority of the people. It was an age of phrases and catchwords: in the economic sphere the hard facts of misery and unemployment deprived these phrases of their force; in the political sphere such phrases as 'international solidarity' had more success and veiled from the German people the extent of the political collapse. But in the long run the failure of the parliamentary–democratic form of government, copied from the West – a West which, regardless of this democratic form, still continued to extort from Germany whatever there remained to extort – defeated the phrase-mongers. Far more lasting was the effect of these phrases in the cultural field, where they resulted in a complete confusion concerning the essential character of culture. Here the influence of the Jews was paramount, and through their control of the press they were able to intimidate those who desired to champion 'the normal sound intelligence and instinct of men'. Art was said to be 'an international experience', and thus all comprehension of its intimate association with a people was stifled; it was said that there was no such thing as the art of a people or, better, of a race: there was only the art of a certain period. Thus it was not Greeks who created the art of Greece, Romans the art of Rome, etc. – a particular period had found in each art its expression. Art is a 'time-conditioned phenomenon'. So today there is not a German or a French art, but a 'modern art'. This is to reduce art to the level of fashions in dress, with the motto 'Every year something fresh' – Impressionism, Futurism, Cubism, perhaps also Dadaism. These newly created art phrases would be comic if they were not tragic.

The result was uncertainty in judgements passed on art and the silencing of those who might otherwise have protested against this *Kulturbol-schewismus*, while the press continued to poison our sound appreciation of art. And just as in fashions one must wear 'modern' clothes whether they are beautiful or not, so the great masters of the past were decried. But true art is and remains eternal; it does not follow the law of the season's fashions; its effect is that of a revelation arising from the depths of the essential character of a people which successive generations can inherit. But those who do not create for eternity do not readily talk of eternities: they seek to dim the radiance of these giants who reach out of the past into the future in order that contemporaries may discover their own tiny flames. These facile daubers in art are but the products of a day: yesterday non-existent, today modern, tomorrow out of date. The Jewish discovery that art was just the affair of a period was for them a godsend: theirs could be the art of the present time. Theirs was a small art – small in form and substance – and at the same time intolerant of the masters of the past and the rivals of the present. There was a conspiracy of incapacity and mediocrity against better work of any age. The *nouveaux riches*, having no judgement of their own in art matters, accepted these artists at their own valuation. It was only an attraction that these works of art were difficult to understand and on that account very costly: no one wished to admit lack of comprehension or insufficient means! And if one does not oneself understand, probably one's neighbour will not either, and he will admire one's comprehension of obscurity.

For this 'modern art' National Socialism desires to substitute a 'German' art and an eternal art. This House of German Art is designed for the art of the German people – not for an international art. 'The people in the flux of phenomena' is the one constant point. It is this that is abiding and permanent, and therefore art as the expression of the essential character of the abiding people must be an eternal monument, itself abiding and permanent. There can be, therefore, no standard of yesterday and today, of modern or un-modern: there can be only the standard of 'valueless' or 'valuable', of 'eternal' or 'transitory'. And therefore in speaking of German art I shall see the standard for that art in the German people, in its character and life, in its feeling, its emotions and its development.

From the history of the development of our people we know that it is composed of a number of more-or-less distinct races which in the course of millennia, through the formative influence of a certain outstanding racial kernel, produced that mixture which we see before us in our people today. This force, which formed the people in time past and which still today continues that formative activity, lies in the same Aryan branch of mankind which we recognise as the support not only of our own civilisation but of the earlier civilisations of the ancient world.

The way in which our people was composed has produced the many-sidedness of our own cultural development, but as we look upon the final result of this process we cannot but wish for an art which may correspond to the increasing homogeneity of our racial composition, and thus present in itself the characteristics of unity and homogeneity. Many attempts have been made through the centuries to define what 'to be German' really means. I would not seek to give an explanation in the first instance. I would rather state a law – a law previously expressed by a great German: 'To be German is to be clear'; and that means that to be German is to be logical and true. It is this spirit that has always lived in our people, that has inspired painters, sculptors, architects, thinkers, poets, and above all our musicians. When on 6 June 1931 the Glass Palace was burned down, there perished with it an immortal treasure of German art. The artists were called Romantics, and yet they were but the finest representatives of that German search for the real and true character of our people, for an honest and decent expression of this law of life divined by our people. For it was not only their choice of subject that was decisive, but the clear and simple mode of rendering these sentiments. Many of their original works are lost, we possess only copies or reproductions; but the works of these masters are removed by a great gulf from the pitiable products of our modern so-called 'creative artists'. These masters felt themselves to be Germans, and consequently they created works which should be valued as long as there is a German people to appreciate them. But these modern works we would also preserve, as documents illustrating the depths of that decline into which the people have fallen. The exhibition of 'Degenerate Art' is intended as a useful lesson.

During the long years in which I planned the formation of a new Reich I gave much thought to the tasks which would await us in the cultural cleansing of the people's life: there was to be a cultural renascence as well as a political and economic reform. I was convinced that peoples which have been trodden underfoot by the whole world of their day have all the greater duty consciously to assert their own value before their oppressors, and there is no prouder proof of the highest rights of a people to its own life than immortal cultural achievements. I was therefore always determined that if fate should one day give us power I would discuss these matters with no one but would form my own decisions, for it is not given to all to have an understanding for tasks as great as these. Amongst the plans which floated before me in my mind both during the war and after was the idea of building a great new exhibition palace in Munich; and many years ago I thought of the place where the building now stands. In 1931 I feared that I should be anticipated and that the 'men of November' would erect an exhibition building. Plans indeed were produced for an edifice which might well have served for a railway station or a swimming-bath. But when we came to power in 1933 the plan had not been executed: the erection of the building was left to the Third Reich. And the building is so unique, so individual that it cannot be compared with anything else: it is a true monument for this city and – more than that – for German art. [Hitler here spoke in detail of the work of Professor Ludwig Troost and (after his death) of Professor Gall, both architects.] It represents a turningpoint, the first of the new buildings which will take their place amongst the immortal achievements of German artistic life.

But the House is not enough: it must house an exhibition, and if now I venture to speak of art I can claim a title to do so from the contribution which I myself have made to the restoration of German art. For our modern German State, which I with my associates have created, has alone brought into existence the conditions for a new and vigorous flowering of art. It is not Bolshevist art collectors or their henchmen who have laid the foundations, for we have provided vast sums for the encouragement of art and have set before art itself great new tasks. As in politics, so in German art-life, we are determined to make a clean sweep of empty phrases. Ability is the necessary qualification if an artist wishes his work to be exhibited here. People have attempted to recommend modern art by saying that it is the expression of a new age; but art does not create a new age, it is the general life of peoples which fashions itself anew and often looks for a new expression. . . . A new epoch is created not by *littérateurs* but by fighters, those who really fashion and lead peoples, and thus make history. . . . It is either impudent effrontery or an almost inconceivable stupidity to exhibit to people of today works which perhaps ten or twenty thousand years ago might have been made by a man of the Stone Age. They talk of primitive art, but they forget that it is not the function of art to regress from the development of a people: its sole function must be to symbolise that living development.

The new age of today is at work on a new human type. Men and women are to be healthier and stronger. There is a new feeling of life, a new joy in life. Never was humanity in its external appearance and in its frame of mind nearer to the ancient world than it is today. . . . [Hitler spoke of the Olympic Games and the proud vigour of youth.] This, my good prehistoric art stutterers, is the type of the new age, but what do you manufacture? Misformed cripples and cretins, women who inspire only disgust, men who are more like wild beasts, children who, were they alive, must be regarded as under God's curse. And let no one tell me that that is how these artists see things. From the pictures sent in for exhibition it is clear that the eye of some men portrays things otherwise than as they are, that there really are men who on principle feel meadows to be blue, the heavens green, clouds sulphur-yellow, or who, as perhaps they prefer to say, 'experience' them thus. I need not ask whether they really do see or feel things in this way, but in the name of the German people I have only to prevent these miserable unfortunates, who clearly suffer from defects of vision, from attempting with violence to persuade contemporaries by their chatter that these faults of observation are indeed realities or from presenting them as 'art'. There are only two possibilities here. If these 'artists' do really see things in this way and believe in what they represent, one has only to ask how the defect in vision arose and, if it is hereditary, the Minister for the Interior will have to see to it that so ghastly a defect of vision shall not be allowed to perpetuate itself. If they do *not* believe in the reality of such impressions but seek on other grounds to burden the nation with this humbug, then it is a matter for a criminal court. There is no place for such works in this building. The industry of architects and workmen has not been employed to house canvases daubed over in five hours, the painters being assured that the boldness of the pricing could not fail to produce its effect, that the canvas would be hailed as the most brilliant lightning creation of a genius. No, they can be left to cackle over each other's eggs!

The artist does not create for the artist. He creates for the people, and we will see to it that the people in future will be called in to judge his art. No one must say that the people has no understanding for a really valuable enrichment of its cultural life. Before the critics did justice to the genius of Richard Wagner, he had the people on his side, whereas the people has had nothing to do with so-called 'modern art'. The people has regarded this art as the outcome of an impudent and shameless arrogance or of a simply deplorable lack of skill. It has felt that this art stammer, these achievements which might have been produced by untalented children of eight or ten years old, could never be considered an expression of our own times or of the German future. When we know today that the development of millions of years, compressed into a few decades, repeats itself in every individual, then this art, we realise, is not 'modern'. It is, on the contrary, to the highest degree 'archaic', far older probably than the Stone Age. The people, in passing through these galleries, will recognise in me its own spokesman and counsellor. It will draw a sigh of relief and gladly express its agreement with this purification of art. And that is decisive: an art which cannot count on the readiest and most intimate agreement of the great mass of the people, an art which must rely upon the support of small cliques, is intolerable. Such an art only tries to confuse, instead of gladly reinforcing, the sure and healthy instinct of a people. The artist cannot stand aloof from his people. This exhibition is only a beginning, but the end of Germany's artistic stultification has begun. Now is the opportunity for youth to start its industrious apprenticeship, and when a sacred conscientiousness has at last come into its own, then I have no doubt that the Almighty, from the mass of these decent creators of art, will once more raise up individuals to the eternal starry heaven of the imperishable God-favoured artists of the great periods. We believe that especially today, when in so many spheres the highest individual achievements are being manifested, in art also the highest value of personality will once again assert itself.

DOCUMENT 9

Joseph Goebbels: Thirty Articles of War for the German people (26 September 1943)[12]

By the end of September 1943, the situation for Germany looked bleak indeed. Stalingrad represented a huge blow to German prestige and during September British planes alone had dropped 14,000 tons of bombs on German cities. On 3 September Allied troops had landed on the Italian mainland and on the same day the Badoglio Government had signed an armistice with them. The Propaganda Minister had persuaded a reluctant Hitler to broadcast to the German people on 10 September. The speech was largely confined to accusing Badoglio of treachery and praising Mussolini. But Goebbels was satisfied with the favourable feedback from the speech. Nevertheless, in his diary entries for September (see in particular, entries of 9 and 25 September) Goebbels indicates that he remains worried about the morale of the people and that these 'dos and don'ts' of the (eventual) 'Thirty Articles' were intended to guide them. His diary entry (see also entry for 25 September) reveals that it was intended as a sort of manifesto, to be issued as a pamphlet and circulated widely. Fanatical belief and an unbridled pride in the nation are the order of the day. Below is a synthesis of this document.

The keynote of the appeal is struck in **Article 1:** 'Everything may be possible in this war except one thing: that we should ever capitulate or bow to the force of the enemy. Those who spoke or even only thought of it were traitors and must be expelled from the fighting and working German community in utter disgrace'.

The defensive character of the war (*Verteidigungskrieg*) on the usual Nazi lines was stressed in **Article 3:** 'It has been imposed upon us by our enemies in order to cut off any national chances of living and developing. A lost war would mean that the present generation of Germans had gambled away the achievements of preceding generations. The people must trust the Government (even when silent) and must make every effort to integrate themselves and to let their deeds and thoughts be fed by the deepest sense of community from which the duties of the individual German in wartime derive'.

Article 11 refers to the impact of enemy propaganda: 'which attempts an old trick of political warfare to separate a people from its Government, in order to deprive it of its leadership and to make it defenceless.' The possible success of this trick would be the only means by which the enemy could overcome Germany. Those who fell prey to this ruse were branded blockheads or traitors and severe penalties were threatened against them. Other types denounced in more or less strong terms were the 'know-alls' ('*Sie sind zwar Besserwisser, aber keineswegs Besserkönner*' – **Article 12**), the thoughtless or careless talkers (**Article 13**), who often forgot that the enemy was listening, the war parasites who took no interest in the war effort (**Article 19**) and the amusement mob, who thought only of their creature comforts and lacked all historical sense (**Article 29**). Significantly, Goebbels also attacked 'the stupid phrase' that the leaders (*Leitung*) led a better life than the people. However heavy the material losses of some individuals might be, they could not be compared with the very heavy burden of responsibility carried by the leadership and involving never-ending worries (**Article 18**).

Goebbels justified his attacks on non-conformists at home with the need to be worthy of the soldiers at the front. Those who died at the front fulfilling their duties could 'demand that persons who sabotage or endanger the war at home should suffer death' (**Article 21**).

The sacrifices demanded are to be made for freedom. As was seen earlier, it was not individual freedom, but national freedom which Goebbels propagated with rationalisations of the existing situation such as 'It is better for a nation to come out of a war very poor but free than seemingly in full control of its property but "unfree"' (**Article 25**).

Goebbels used the argument of the better life to be enjoyed by future generations to justify sacrifices in war: 'If we have to renounce happiness for many years, at least our children and grandchildren will have a better life' (**Article 29**).

Finally, **Article 30** reminded the people of their duties to the Fatherland and Führer and the superiority of the 'chosen people': 'In everything you do and omit to do, you say and keep silent about, bear in mind that you are a German. Believe loyally and unshakeably in the Führer and in victory! Remember always that you are a child of the bravest and most industrious people on earth, a people that has to bear much adversity and suffering to reach its goal . . . in order to safeguard its freedom and its future' (**Article 30**).

DOCUMENT 10

Special report by the SD to the Party Chancellory: 'Basic issues concerning the mood and behaviour of the German people; trust in the leadership', 29 November 1943.[13]

The morale of the German people continued to deteriorate throughout the summer of 1943. The fall of Mussolini on 27 July 1943 had clearly shaken German public opinion. Although Goebbels had responded with his Thirty Articles of War, by November an important factor in the decline of popular morale was the growing contempt for much of its leadership. The following is taken from a special report from the SD to the Party Chancellory and is dated 23 November 1943. The report suggests that while faith in Hitler remained generally strong, the rest of the leadership was no longer trusted unconditionally. The report suggests a widening gulf between the 'ordinary' citizen and local Party leaders and it represents, a devastating critique of the failure of the Reich leadership to convince the population that sacrifices were being shared equally. This perception (whether real or imagined) represented a real challenge for Goebbels and Nazi propaganda in the final stage of the war.

The first serious shocks occurred with the reserves of the last two winters of the war in Russia. It was then that for the first time doubts emerged about whether the leadership was fully capable of grasping the enormous problems created by the war and mastering them. In the course of this year's developments the question had been raised more frequently. . . .

In such deliberations the population makes a clear *distinction between the Führer and other leading figures*. Whereas loss of trust in individual leading personalities or leading agencies occurs comparatively frequently, faith in the Führer is virtually unshaken. While it has certainly been subjected to various serious stresses, particularly after Stalingrad, recent months have revealed a strengthening of trust in the Führer. Recently it reached a high point with the *freeing of Mussolini and the Führer speech* on the night of 9 November. 'Here the German people believed that they were seeing the

Führer again in all his greatness.' . . . Many people see in the Führer the only guarantee of a successful conclusion of the war. The idea that anything could happen to the Führer is unthinkable.

Thus, while the Führer is the only person who is considered capable of mastering the present situation, the remaining leadership of the Reich is no longer trusted unconditionally. In particular, the failure of promises and prophecies to be fulfilled has seriously undermined trust in individual leaders as far as many compatriots are concerned.

Above all there is a marked loss of trust in the media. The attempt form time to time to disguise the true picture when the situation was serious or to play down ominous military developments, for example 'by portraying withdrawal as a success' or 'presenting territory which previously had been described as valuable as now being not so important at all' or 'thinking that periods of delay have to be filled with flannel-type reports about events in India or plutocractic excesses in England or America', have largely undermined trust in the press and radio which previously existed.

Thus in their desire for objectivity and openness and their dislike of attempts to portray things as better than they are the population has grad-ually begun to read between the lines and, in particular, increasingly to turn to the news from neutral and enemy states.

A further cause for mistrust in the leadership is the behaviour of individual local leading figures in the State and Party at lower and middle levels. Although the measures of the Reich Government are generally approved of, much of what they see being done by the executive organs of the State and Party gives compatriots cause for concern. For example the population note that barter and illicit trading keep spreading or that the 'total war' propagated by the leadership is not being fairly implemented (eg. in the case of the deployment of women, the question of housemaids, the allocation of housing and, above all, the granting of reserved worker status) and that some of the leading figures are not affected by the restric-tions which are imposed on everyone else. . . . This has led many to believe that the leadership does not always share in the nation's sacrifices. There are 'double standards' and they 'preach water but drink wine'. Poor behav-iour by individual persons in authority often damaged trust in the top leadership at the local level.

Workers' trust in the leadership of their plants, in the DAF (German Labour Front) and other organisations is often subject to particular strain. Many workers are once more beginning to *think in terms of classes* and talk of classes who would 'exploit' them.

As far as the Werhmacht is concerned, the population is convinced of the professional and personal qualities of the German military leadership . . . However, the excesses in the bases and to some extent in the home garrisons have been the subject of growing criticism. . . . Reference is made to the alleged growing gap between the officers and men among troops behind the front and at home. . . .

To sum up, the report reveals the following:

1. The population makes *a distinction between the Führer and the rest of the leadership* in its assessment of professional performance and personal behaviour.
2. The criticism of individual leading figures and of measures ordered by the leading agencies, which in some cases comes not from opponents or the usual complainers, but from wide circles of the population, indicates a certain reduction in trust in the leadership.
3. *Fairness and the equal distribution of the burdens of war will determine the degree of trust in the leadership.* The trust is undermined above all if measures are not applied equally or totally and when exceptions are made and when there are 'back doors' and when action is not taken irrespective of the person affected.

NOTES

INTRODUCTION

1 For a brief analysis of the *Historikerstreit* and the importance for a newly united Germany of understanding past history, see my postscript: 'Germany's Search for a Bearable Past'.

2 See D. Blackbourn and G. Eley, *The Peculiarities of German History* (Oxford, 1984). An excellent critique of the debate can be found in J. Kocka, 'German History before Hitler: The Debate about the German *Sonderweg*', *Journal of Contemporary History* 23 (1988), pp. 3–16.

3 The first statement of Hitler as a 'weak dictator' was made by Hans Mommsen in *Beamtentum im Dritten Reich* (Stuttgart, 1966), p. 98, note 26, where he stated that Hitler was 'in all questions which needed the adoption of a fundamental and definitive position, a weak dictator'. For a synthesis of the historiographical debate see J. Caplan, 'The Historiography of National Socialism', in M. Bently (ed.), *Companion to Historiography* (London, 1997), pp. 545–90. See also, T. Mason, 'Intention and Explanation: A Current Controversy about the Interpretation of National Socialism', in G. Hirschfeld and L. Kettenacker (eds), *Der 'Führerstaat': Mythos und Realität* (Stuttgart, 1981), pp. 23–42.

4 See I. Kershaw, *The Nazi Dictatorship: Problems and Perspectives of Interpretation* (London, 1985, 4th edn 2000); K. Hildebrand, *The Third Reich* (London, 1984); J. Hiden and J. Farquharson, *Explaining Hitler's Germany* (London, 1983); P. Ayçoberry, *The Nazi Question* (London, 1981).

5 My introductory remarks owe much to an excellent review of these issues by J. D. Noakes in *Times Literary Supplement*, July 1983, p. 689.

6 H. Arendt, *The Origins of Totalitarianism* (New York, 1951); C. J. Friedrich (ed.), *Totalitarianism* (Cambridge, Mass., 1954); C. Friedrich and Z. Brzezinski, *Totalitarian Dictatorship and Autocracy* (Cambridge, Mass., 1956).

7 K. D. Bracher, *Die Auflösung der Weimarer Republik* (Stuttgart, 1955), and, later, *The German Dictatorship* (Harmondsworth, 1973).

8 Cf. F. Meinecke, *Die deutsche Katastrophe* (Wiesbaden, 1946); G. Ritter *Europa und die deutsche Frage. Betrachtungen über die geschichtliche Eigenart des deutschen Staatsdenkens* (Munich, 1948).

9 The orthodox Marxist–Leninist approach, which analyses the Nazi State in terms of struggle within monopoly capitalism, can be found in the following standard East German texts: D. Eichholtz, *Geschichte deutscher Kriegswirtschaft* (East Berlin, 1969); and D. Eichholtz and W. Schumann (eds), *Anatomie des Krieges. Neue Dokumente über die Rolle des deutschen Monopolkapitals bei der Vorbereitung und Durchführung des Zweiten Weltkrieges* (East Berlin, 1969). See

also A. Dorpalen, *German History in Marxist Perspective: The East German Approach* (Detroit, Mich., 1985), especially ch. 8.

10 D. Schoenbaum, *Hitler's Social Revolution* (London, 1966), R. Dahrendorf, *Society and Democracy in Germany* (London, 1966).

11 M. Broszat, 'Resistenz und Widerstand. Eine Zwischenbilanz des Forschungs-projekte' in M. Broszat *et al.* (eds), *Bayern in der NS-Zeit IV. 12 Herrschaft und Gesellschaft im Konflikt*, Teil C (Munich, 1981), pp. 691–709.

12 By far the most impressive is the study of Bavaria under Hitler: see M. Broszat *et al.* (eds), *Bayern in der NS Zeit* (Oldenbourg and Vienna, 1977). Cf. similar regional studies: P. Sauer, *Württemberg in der Zeit des Nationalsozialismus* (Ulm, 1975); M. Domarous, *Nationalsozialismus, Krieg und Bevölkerung im Augsburg* (Munich, 1977), vol. 91. For sharp criticism of the limitations of *Alltagsgeschichte*, see H.-U. Wehler, 'Königsweg zu neuen Ufern oder Irrgarten der Illusionen? Die westdeutsche Alltagsgeschichte; Geschichte "von innen" und "von unten"', in F. J. Brüggemeier and J. Kocka (eds), *'Geschichte von unten – Geschichte von innen'. Kontroversen um die Alltagsgeschichte* (Fernuniversität Hagen, 1985), pp. 17–47.

13 For an excellent example of this approach, see D. Peukert, *Inside Nazi Germany: Conformity and Opposition in Everyday Life* (London, 1987).

14 Z. A. B. Zeman, *Nazi Propaganda* (Oxford, 1964; rev. edn 1973), p. 32.

15 M. Broszat, *German National Socialism* (Santa Barbara, Calif., 1966), p. 62.

16 W. Ruge, *Deutschland von 1917 bis 1933* (East Berlin, 1967), p. 354. Cf. also the work of Klaus Scheel, who stresses the extent to which the working class was manipulated by clever propaganda techniques: *Krieg über Ätherwellen. NS Rundfunk und Monopole 1933–45* (East Berlin, 1970).

17 R. Bessel. 'The Rise of the NSDAP and the Myth of Nazi Propaganda', *The Wiener Library Bulletin* 33, nos 51/52 (1980).

18 See Zeman, *Nazi Propaganda*; E. Bramsted, *Goebbels and National Socialist Propaganda 1925–1945* (East Lansing, Mich., 1965); Scheel, *Krieg über Ätherwellen*.

19 R. E. Herzstein, *The War that Hitler Won* (London, 1980).

20 See the various contributions in D. Welch (ed.), *Nazi Propaganda: The Power and the Limitations* (London, 1983), especially I. Kershaw, 'How Effective was Nazi Propaganda?' (pp. 180–205).

21 E. H. Carr, *The Twenty Years' Crisis, 1919–39* (New York, 1964), p. 132.

22 The SD documents are held in the Bundesarchiv Koblenz (hereafter BA) in the BA R58 series covering the Reich Security HQ (Reichssicherheitshauptamt) and comprise the following: Berichte zur innenpolitischen Lage (October–December 1939), Meldungen aus dem Reich (December 1939–June 1943), SD Berichte zu Inlandsfragen (June 1943–July 1944), and the parallel run of Meldungen wichtiger staatspolizeilicher Ereignisse (August 1941–November 1944). Selections have been published in H. Boberach (ed.), *Meldungen aus dem Reich* (Neuwied, 1965). For examples of morale and public opinion during the last stages of the war (April 1943–5), see the RMVP's own weekly 'activity reports', Tätigkeitsberichte, BA, R55/601.

23 *Deutschlands-Berichte der Sozialdemokratischen Partei Deutschlands (Sopade) 1934–1940*, 7 vols (Frankfurt-am-Main, 1980).

1 THE CONQUEST OF THE MASSES

1 For recent analyses of Weimar voting patterns and of who voted for the NSDAP, and why, see R. F. Hamilton, *Who Voted for Hitler?* (Princeton, NJ, 1982); and

T. Childers, *The Nazi Voter: The Social Foundations of Fascism in Germany 1919–1933* (London, 1983).

2 A. Huxley, 'Notes on Propaganda', *Harper's Magazine* 174 (December, 1936), p.39.

3 All quotations from *Mein Kampf* in this chapter are taken from the section on 'War Propaganda': *Mein Kampf*, introd. and trans. D. C. Watt (London, 1969), pp. 161–9. For a magnificent portrait of Hitler as a young man in Vienna see B. Hamann, *Hitler's Vienna. A Dictator's Apprenticeship* (Oxford, 1999).

4 Hitler, *Mein Kampf*, p. 196.

5 This is the contention of my work on German propaganda in the First World War, *Germany, Propaganda and Total War, 1914–1918* (London, 2000).

6 See H. Wanderscheck, *Weltkrieg and Propaganda* (Berlin, 1936), p. 5. Comparing British and German propaganda in the First World War, Hitler maintained that 'there [Britain], propaganda was regarded as a weapon of the first order, while in our country it was the last resort of the unemployed politicians and a haven for slackers' (*Mein Kampf*, p. 169).

7 ibid. p. 165.

8 ibid. p. 169.

9 E. K. Bramsted, *Goebbels and National Socialist Propaganda, 1925–45* (East Lansing, Mich., 1965), p. 454.

10 For a detailed analysis of *Der Angriff* see, R. Lemmons, *Goebbels and Der Angriff* (Kentucky, 1994).

11 See D. Welch, 'The Proletarian Cinema and the Weimar Republic', *Historical Journal of Film, Radio and Television*, Vol. 1, No. 1, (March, 1981), pp. 1–18.

12 Cf. Heinrich August Winkler, 'Vom Protest zur Panik. Der gewerbliche Mittelstand in der Weimarer Republik', in H. Mommsen, D. Petzina and B. Weisbrod (eds), *Industrielles System und politische Entwicklung in der Weimarer Republik* (Düsseldorf, 1974), pp. 778–91. See also Winkler, 'Mittelstandsbewegung oder Volkspartei? Zur sozialen Basis der NSDAP', in W. Schieder (ed.), *Faschismus als soziale Bewegung* (Hamburg, 1976), pp. 97–118.

13 See D. Welch, *The Hitler Conspiracies* (London, 2001), pp. 28–35.

14 J. W. Baird, *The Mythical World of Nazi War Propaganda 1925–45* (Minneapolis, Minn., 1974), p. 4.

2 GOEBBELS AS PROPAGANDIST

1 Quoted in W. A. Boelcke (ed.), *Kriegspropaganda 1939–1941. Geheime Ministerkonferenzen im Reichspropagandaministerium* (Stuttgart, 1966), p. 21.

2 *Völkischer Beobachter*, 23 March 1933.

3 Hitler, *Mein Kampf*, pp. 473–5.

4 Goebbels' address to the press of 15 March 1933, Bundesarchiv (BA) R43(Reichskanzlei)/II 1149, pp. 25–9. The speech is also reprinted in P. Meier-Benneckenstein (ed.), *Dokumente der deutschen Politik*, Bd. I (Berlin, 1939–40), pp. 289ff.

5 ibid., p. 27.

6 From a speech to the 1934 Nuremberg Party Rally, reprinted in *Der Kongress zu Nürnberg vom 5. bis 10. September 1934. Offizieller Bericht über den Verlauf des Reichsparteitages mit sämtlichen Reden* (Munich, 1934), p. 138.

7 G. Le Bon, *The Crowd. A Study of the Popular Mind* (New York, 1960), *passim*.

8 R. Semmler, *Goebbels – the Man Next to Hitler* (London, 1947), p. 75.

9 L. P. Lochner (ed.), *The Goebbels Diaries* (London, 1948), entry for 29 January 1942, p. 22. The most impressive and comprehensive work on Goebbels' diaries

is E. Fröhlich (ed.), *Die Tagebücher von Joseph Goebbels*, 4 vols (Munich, 1987). Wherever possible, however, I have tried to cite edited volumes that have appeared in English. See Bibliography and heading under 'Goebbels' for these sources.

10 BA R43/II 1149, pp. 27–8.

3 RESTRUCTURING THE MEANS OF COMMUNICATION

1 J. Goebbels, *Vom Kaiserhof zur Reichskanzlei* (Munich, 1935), entry of 22 January 1932.
2 Hitler made these points in his final address to the Nuremberg Party Congress of September 1935. The full speech is reproduced in N. H. Baynes (ed.), *The Speeches of Adolf Hitler*, 2 vols (Oxford, 1942), vol. 1, pp. 438–49.
3 Speech to representatives of the press, 15 March 1933; taken from Wolffs Telegraphisches Büro (WTB) press agency report of 16 March 1933, deposited Bundesarchiv, Koblenz.
4 L. P. Lochner (ed.), *The Goebbels Diaries* (London 1948), entry of 26 April 1942, p. 137.
5 Quoted in M. Balfour, *Propaganda in War* (London, 1979), p. 15.
6 Quoted in O. Kalbus, *Vom Werden deutscher Filmkunst*, Teil 2: *Der Tonfilm* (Altona and Bahrenfeld, 1935), p. 101.
7 Baynes (ed.), *The Speeches of Adolf Hitler*, vol. 1, pp. 584–92.
8 *Film-Kurier*, 13 May 1936.
9 *Völkischer Beobachter*, 29 November 1936. Also quoted in D. S. Hull, *Film in the Third Reich* (Berkeley and Los Angeles, 1969), p. 96. Hull uses the *New York Times* as his source.
10 Quoted in Lochner (ed.), *Goebbels Diaries*, p. xxvii. Lochner, who witnessed the scene, added that 'the few foreign correspondents who had taken the trouble to view this "symbolic act" were stunned. What had happened to the "Land of Thinkers and Poets"? they wondered.'
11 Cf. Bramsted, *Goebbels and National Socialist Propaganda*, p. 68.
12 E. Fröhlich, 'Die Kulturpolitische Presskonferenz des Reichspropaganda Ministeriums', *Vierteljahrshefte für Zeitgeschichte*, 22 April 1974, pp. 358–9; quoted in J. Noakes and G. Pridham (eds), *Nazism 1919–1945*, Vol. 2: *State, Economy and Society* (Exeter, 1984), p. 409.
13 For detailed accounts of broadcasting in the Third Reich, see A. Diller, *Rundfunkpolitik im Dritten Reich* (Gütersloh, 1964); H. Pohle, *Der Rundfunk als Instrument der Politik* (Hamburg, 1955); J. Hale, *Radio Power, Propaganda and International Broadcasting* (London, 1975) especially ch. 1, 'The Nazi Model', pp. 1–16.
14 H. Heiber (ed.), *Goebbels Reden*, 2 vols (Düsseldorf, 1971) vol. 1, pp. 82–107 for the full speech.
15 Quoted in Diller, *Rundfunkpolitik*, p. 89.
16 W. A. Boelcke (ed.), *Kriegspropaganda 1939–1941: Geheime Ministerkonferenzen im Reichspropagandaministerium* (Stuttgart, 1966), p. 78.
17 The Radio Chamber, which seems to have lost its way, was in fact dissolved in October 1939, when the outbreak of war provided a convenient excuse to disband it. Its duties were taken over by the Reichs-Rundfunk-Gesellschaft.
18 Quoted in Pohle, *Der Rundfunk*, p. 327, and Balfour, *Propaganda in War*, p. 20.
19 Quoted in M. Burleigh, *The Third Reich. A New History* (London, 2000), p. 206.
20 O. J. Hale, *The Captive Press in the Third Reich* (Princeton, NJ, 1964).

21 On 24 April 1935 the 'Anordnung zur Beseitigung der Skandalpresse' prohibited newspapers 'who maintain their character and sale by reporting events in an unsuitable way, so as to create sensation and to reflect on the press in general'.

22 The journalist was Fritz Sänger; quoted in J. Wulf (ed.), *Presse und Funk im Dritten Reich* (Gütersloh, 1964) p. 79.

23 In 1936 attempts were made to restore to the publishers some of the powers taken away from them by the *Schriftleitergesetz*, but it was quickly removed from the cabinet agenda when the extent of the opposition became clear.

24 It has been estimated that between mid-1934 and mid-1943 there were some 1,290 reported cases of newspapers and periodicals being reprimanded for carrying 'unwanted' topics. See K. Koszyk and M. Lindemann, *Geschichte der deutschen Press, 1914–1945* (Berlin, 1966–72).

25 For the full text of Hitler's speech, which was off the record, see 'Rede Hitlers vor der deutschen Presse', *Vierteljahrshefte für Zeitgeschichte*, vol. 6, no. 2, April 1958, pp. 175–91. For a first-hand account of Hitler's views on the press, see O. Dietrich, *12 Jahre mit Hitler* (Munich, 1955); English edition *The Hitler I Knew* (London, 1957).

26 The process is decribed in D. Orlow, *The History of the Nazi Party 1919–33* (London, 1971).

27 The number of cinemas had fallen from just over 5,000 in 1929 to 2,196 in 1932.

28 For further details of the organisation of the Nazi cinema, see D. Welch, *Propaganda and the German Cinema 1933–1945* (Oxford, 1983, revd edn, 2001), pp. 6–38.

29 Lochner (ed.), *The Goebbels Diaries*, entry for 22 January 1942, p. 5.

30 Goebbels' speech to the Reichsfilmkammer, 15 February 1941; quoted in Welch, *Propaganda and the German Cinema*, p. 45. For a detailed analysis of Nazi films, see ibid.; G. Albrecht, *Film im Dritten Reich* (Stuttgart, 1982); F. Courtade and P. Cadars, *Histoire du cinéma nazi* (Paris, 1972); E. Leiser, *Nazi Cinema* (London, 1974); R. Taylor, *Film Propaganda: Soviet Russia and Nazi Germany* (London, 1979); B. Drewniak, *Der deutsche Film 1938–1945. Ein Gesamtüberblick* (Düsseldorf, 1987); J. Wulf (ed.), *Theater und Film im Dritten Reich. Eine Dokumentation* (Gütersloh, 1964).

31 Speech to the Reich Film Chamber, 15 February 1941, quoted in Welch, *Propaganda and the German Cinema*, p. 45.

32 *Institut für Zeitgeschichte* (hereafter *If Z*), Munich, *Goebbels Tagebuch* (unpublished sections), entry for 15 May 1943.

33 *If Z*, *Goebbels Tagebuch*, entry for 1 March 1942.

34 F. Taylor (ed.), *The Goebbels Diaries, 1939–1941* (London, 1982), p. 419.

4 PROPAGANDA AND PUBLIC OPINION, 1933–9

1 Cf. Noakes and Pridham (eds), *Nazism*, p. 569; and M. Steinert, *Hitlers Krieg und die Deutschen. Stimmung und Haltung der deutschen Bevölkerung im Zweiten Weltkrieg* (Düsseldorf, 1970), pp. 43–4.

2 I have taken this phrase from Hiden and Farquharson, *Explaining Hitler's Germany*, p. 52. However, I arrive at different conclusions from these authors.

3 See I. Kershaw's excellent summary 'How Effective was Nazi Propaganda?', in Welch (ed.), *Nazi Propaganda*, pp. 180–205.

4 For an analysis of *völkisch* thought still unsuperseded, see G. Mosse, *The Crisis of German Ideology: Intellectual Origins of the Third Reich* (London, 1964). Cf. also J. Baird, *To Die for Germany: Heroes in the Nazi Pantheon* (Bloomington and Indianapolis, 1990).

5 For a discussion of these issues, see D. Welch, 'Goebbels, Götterdämmerung, and the Deutsche Wochenshauen', in S. Dolezel and K. Short (eds), *Hitler's Fall: The Newsreel Witness* (London, 1988), pp. 80–100.

6 Cf. Kershaw, 'How Effective', pp. 189–91.

7 The agreement which was signed on 27 November 1933 by Ley, Seldte (Ministry of Labour), Schmitt (Economics), and Hitler's representative for economic affairs, Keppler, can be found in Noakes and Pridham (eds), *Nazism*, pp. 338–9.

8 Quoted in Schoenbaum, *Hitler's Social Revolution*, p. 82.

9 According to Nazi figures, in 1938 the 'Strength through Joy' theatres were attended by 14 million, libraries numbered 5,260, sporting activities were attended by 22.5 million, and 10 million took advantage of State excursions; quoted in F. Neumann, *Behemoth: The Structure and Practice of National Socialism* (London, 1942), p. 426 n. 43.

10 G. Starcke, *Die Deutsche Arbeitsfront* (Berlin, 1940), p. 124; quoted in Noakes and Pridham (eds), *Nazism*, p. 350.

11 See T. W. Mason, *Arbeitsklasse und Volksgemeinschaft* (Opladen, 1975), *Sozialpolitik im Dritten Reich* (Opladen, 1977), translated in English (Berg, 1992), 'Labour in the Third Reich', *Past and Present* 33 (1966), pp. 112–41, and 'The Workers' Opposition in Nazi Germany', *History Workshop Journal* 11 (Spring, 1981), pp. 120–37. Cf. Kershaw's work on Bavaria, *Popular Opinion and Political Dissent: Bavaria 1933–1945* (Oxford, 1983).

12 *Deutschland-Berichte* 5 (February, 1938), p. 175.

13 *Sopade-Berichte* 6 (July, 1939), pp. 757–78.

14 ibid. (February, 1938), p. 172.

15 ibid. (April, 1939), p. 489. For students who cannot read German, a very useful source is Noakes and Pridham (eds), *Nazism*, who quote extensively from Sopade reports.

16 C. W. Guillebaud, *The Economic Recovery of Nazi Germany 1933–1938* (Cambridge, 1939). Cf. also Guillebaud, *The Social Policy of Nazi Germany* (Cambridge, 1941).

17 For a penetrating empirical study of the relationship between capitalism and fascism, see H. A. Turner, *German Big Business and the Rise of Hitler* (Oxford, 1985). An excellent account of the effects of the economic crisis on Nazi economic theory can be found in H. James, *The German Slump: Politics and Economics 1924–1936* (Oxford, 1986). On the 'primacy of politics' approach to the Nazi economy, see T. Mason, 'The Primacy of Politics – Politics and Economics in National Socialist Germany', in H. A. Turner (ed.), *Nazism and the Third Reich* (New York, 1972), pp. 175–200. More general surveys can be found in A. Milward, *The German Economy at War* (London, 1965); R. Overy, *The Nazi Economic Recovery 1932–38* (London, 1982); and A. Sohn-Rethel, *The Economy and Class Structure of German Fascism* (London, 1987).

18 *Völkischer Beobachter*, 15 September 1935.

19 For further details of the Nazis' control of teachers and schools, see R. Eilers, *Die nationalsozialistische Schulpolitik. Eine Studie zur Funktion der Erziehung im totalitären Staat* (Cologne, 1963); and W. Feiten, *Der nationalsozialistische Lehrbund. Entwicklung und Organisation* (Weinheim, 1981).

20 S. Roberts, *The House that Hitler Built* (London, 1937), p. 208. Cf. also A. Heck, *A Child of Hitler: Germany in the Days when God Wore a Swastika* (Colorado, 1985).

21 For a detailed account of the 'Edelweiss Pirates', see D. Peukert, *Die Edelweisspiraten: Protestbewegungen jugendlicher Arbeiter im Dritten Reich* (Cologne, 1980); for a brief discussion, see D. Peukert, 'Youth in the Third Reich', in R. Bessel (ed.), *Life in the Third Reich* (Oxford, 1987), pp. 25–40. See also A. Klönne, *Jugend im Dritten Reich. Die Hitler-Jugend und ihre Gegner* (Düsseldorf, 1982).

22 Cf. *Sopade-Berichte* 1 (1934), pp. 117–18; 2 (1935), pp. 1374–6; 5 (1938), p. 27.

23 After 1945, British educationalists undertook a critical assessment of the Weimar education system and came to the conclusion that, owing to the lack of reconstruction along democratic lines, a strong class structure remained along nineteenth-century lines. It recognised that the notion of *Volksgemeinschaft* had tried to pull down class barriers and that efforts had been made to curb extreme academic bias in favour of 'character-building'. Had it not been for the indoctrination of a perverse and unacceptable ideology (and for establishment of a new arrogant elite), the *principles* of the Nazi social revolution would have found some favour with British educational reformers. See D. Welch, 'Priming the Pump of German Democracy: "Reeducation" Policy in Germany after the Second World War', in I. Turner (ed.), *Reconstruction in Post-War Germany* (Oxford, 1989), pp. 215–39.

24 *Sopade-Berichte* 1 (June, 1934), p. 117.

25 One of the striking features to emerge from the oral history project directed by Lutz Niethammer on the experiences of the Ruhr workers was the stress on 'normality' and the manner in which even opponents of Nazism looked favourably on 'Strength through Joy' and the planned leisure activities as positive, compensatory features of the Nazi regime: See L. Niethammer (ed.), *'Die Jahre weiss man nicht, wo man die heute hinsetzen soll.' Faschismuserfahrungen im Ruhrgebiet* (Berlin, 1986).

26 *Sopade-Berichte* 3 (1936), pp. 683–4; *ibid* cf. 5 (1938), pp. 697–8.

27 Cf. *Sopade-Berichte* 3 (1936), pp. 157, 1249, 1389–92; ibid. 4 (1937), pp. 20–2; 5 (1938), pp. 394–5

28 Hitler, *Mein Kampf*, p. 357.

29 Quoted in Baird, *Mythical World*, p. 8.

30 Schoenbaum, *Hitler's Social Revolution*, p. 161. See also J. E. Farquharson, *The Plough and the Swastika: The NSDAP and Agriculture in Germany 1928–1945* (London, 1976).

31 Hans Günther, *Kleine Rassenkunde des deutschen Volkes* (Munich, 1933); quoted in J. Fest. *The Face of the Third Reich* (London, 1972), p. 154.

32 See J. Wulf (ed.), *Musik im Dritten Reich. Eine Dokumentation* (Gütersloh, 1963) and M. Meyer, 'The Nazi Musicologist as Myth Maker in the Third Reich', *Journal of Contemporary History* 10, no. 4 (1975). pp. 649–65.

33 H. Grebing, *Der Nationalsozialismus: Ursprung und Wesen* (Munich, 1959), p. 65; also quoted in R. Cecil, *Myth of the Master Race: A. Rosenberg and the Nazi Ideology* (London, 1974), p. 144. See also A. Bramwell, *Blood and Soil: Richard Walther Darré and Hitler's 'Green Party'* (Kensal, Bucks., 1985).

34 P. Brohmer, *Biologieunterricht und völkerische Erziehung* (Frankfurt, 1933), p. 72; quoted in G. Mosse, *Nazi Culture: Intellectual, Cultural and Social Life in the Third Reich* (London, 1966), p. 88.

35 I. Naab, *Ist Hitler ein Christ?* (Munich, 1931), p. 22; quoted in G. Lewy, *The Catholic Church and Nazi Germany* (London, 1964), p. 258.

36 For a more detailed discussion, see Lewy, *Catholic Church*, pp. 259–67. Cf. also E. Klee, *'Die SA Jesu Christi'. Die Kirche im Banne Hitlers* (Frankfurt-am-Main, 1989). For an analysis of the response of the Churches to the regime see Welch, *The Hitler Conspiracies*, pp. 98–119.

37 Quoted in N. H. Baynes (ed.), *The Speeches of Adolf Hitler* (Oxford, 1942), vol. I, p. 388. Recording a conversation with Hitler, Goebbels wrote in his diary: 'I put forward complaints about the Church. The Führer shares them completely, but does not believe that the Churches will try anything in the middle of a war. But he knows that he will have to get round to dealing with the conflict between Church and State . . . the technique must be to hold back for the present and

coolly strangle any attempts at impudence or interference in the affairs of the State' (Taylor (ed.), *Goebbels Diaries*, entry for 28 December 1939, p. 76).

38 *Sopade-Berichte* 1 (1934), p. 172.

39 Quoted in Noakes and Pridham (eds), *Nazism*, p. 587. For a wider analysis of the role of the Churches in the Third Reich, see J. Conway, *The Nazi Persecution of the Churches 1933–45* (London, 1968); E. C. Helmreich, *The German Churches under Hitler* (Detroit, Mich., 1979); C. King, *The Nazi State and the New Religions: Five Case Studies in Non-Conformity* (Lewiston, NY, 1982).

40 Quoted in G. Reitlinger, *The Final Solution* (London, 1953), pp. 125–6. The 'order' was initially an informal verbal command that had subsequently to be back-dated to 1 September 1939 – doubtless because of difficulties arising from this 'informal' arrangement.

41 Goebbels quoted in Lewy, *Catholic Church*, p. 265. Hitler quoted in H. Trevor-Roper (ed.), *Hitler's Table Talk, 1941–44* (Oxford, 1988), p. 555.

42 BA, R58/168, 15 January 1942. For a detailed analysis of *Ich klage an*, see D. Welch, *Propaganda and the German Cinema*, pp. 121–31.

43 The figures cited are for those gassed between 1939 and 1941 and are taken from Lewy, *The Catholic Church*, p. 264. See also K. Pätzold, 'Von der Vertreibung zum Genozid. Zu den Ursachen, Triebkräften und Bedingungen der anti-jüdischen Politik des faschistischen deutschen Imperialismus', in D. Eichholz and K. Grossweiler (eds), *Faschismusforschung. Positionen, Probleme, Polemik* (East Berlin, 1980), pp. 181–208. For the definitive treatment of the euthanasia issue, see E. Klee, *'Euthanasie' im NS-Staat. Die 'Vernichtung lebensunwerten Lebens'* (Frankfurt-am-Main, 1983); and E. Klee (ed.), *Dokumente zur 'Euthanasie'* (Frankfurt-am-Main, 1985). Cf. also H.-W. Schmuhl, *Rassenhygiene, National-sozialismus, Euthanasie* (Göttingen, 1987); B. Müller-Hill, *Murderous Science* (Oxford, 1988); J. Noakes, 'Social Outcasts in the Third Reich', in Bessel (ed.), *Life in the Third Reich*, pp. 83–96; M. Burleigh, 'Euthanasia and the Cinema in the Third Reich', *History Today* (February, 1990), pp. 11–16, and '"Euthanasia" in the Third Reich: Some Recent Literature', *The Society for the Social History of Medicine* 4 (1991), pp. 317–28.

44 For recent interpretations of public reactions to the Nazi anti-Semitic campaigns, see O. D. Kulka and A. Rodrigue, 'The German Population and the Jews in the Third Reich: Recent Publications and Trends in Research on German Society and the "Jewish Question"', *Yad Vashem Studies* 16 (1984), pp. 421–35; O. D. Kulka, 'Major Trends and Tendencies of German Historiography on National Socialism and the "Jewish Question" (1924–1984)', *Yearbook of the Leo Baeck Institute* 30 (1985), pp. 215–42; I. Kershaw, 'The Persecution of the Jews and German Popular Opinion in the Third Reich', *Yearbook of the Leo Baeck Institute*, 26 (1981), pp. 261–89; M. Richarz (ed.), *Jüdisches Leben in Deutschland. Selbstzeugnisse zur Sozialgeschichte 1918–45* (Stuttgart, 1982); K. Kweit and H. Eschwege, *Selbstbehauptung und Widerstand. Deutsche Juden im Kampf um Existenz und Menschenwürde 1933–45* (Hamburg, 1984); S. Gordon, *Hitler, Germans, and the 'Jewish Question'* (Princeton, NJ, 1984), ch. 6; H. Mommsen, 'The Realization of the Unthinkable: The "Final Solution of the Jewish Question" in the Third Reich', in G. Hirschfeld (ed.), *The Policies of Genocide* (London, 1986), pp. 97–144. A less detailed, but nevertheless concise, survey of current literature can be found in W. Carr, 'A Final Solution? Nazi Policy Towards the Jews', *History Today* 35 (November, 1985), pp. 30–6.

45 Cf. Kershaw, 'How Effective Was Nazi Propaganda?', pp. 193–4. For detailed reconsiderations of the question of popular attitudes towards the 'Jewish Question' and particularly the question of 'public indifference', see I. Kershaw, 'German Popular Opinion and the "Jewish Question", 1939–43: Some Further

Reflections', in A. Panchenfed (ed.), *Die Juden in Nationalsozialistichem Deutschland 1933–43/The Jews in Nazi Germany 1933–43* (London, 1986), and 'German Popular Opinion During the "Final Solution": Information, Comprehension, Reactions', in Y. Gelber (ed.), *Comprehending the Holocaust* (New York, 1987).

46 Hitler 1939: 512.

47 For general surveys and interpretations that chart the various stages leading to the 'Final Solution', see L. Dawidowicz, *The War against the Jews 1933–45* (Harmondsworth, 1977); C. Browning, *The Final Solution and the German Foreign Office* (New York, 1978); K. A. Schleunes, *The Twisted Road to Auschwitz: Nazi Policy toward the Jews, 1933–39* (Chicago and London, 1970); G. Hirschfeld (ed.), *The Policies of Genocide* (London, 1986); G. Aly, *'Final Solution'. Nazi Population Policy and the Murder of the European Jews* (London, 1999).

48 Cf. Gordon, *Hitler, Germans*, p. 171. The 'Eternal Jew', which had been touring the country, opened in Berlin on 12 November 1938, two days after *Kristallnacht*. It contained a special section entitled 'Jews in Berlin'.

49 *Sopade-Berichte* 2 (1935), pp. 1042–4. By January 1936 Sopade was reporting a widening gap between Gentiles and Jews because of a feeling that 'Jews were a different race': *Sopade-Berichte* 3 (1936), pp. 26–7.

50 Taylor (ed.), *Goebbels Diaries*, entry for 8 March 1941, p. 259. For a detailed analysis of *Jud Süss and Der ewige Jude*, see Welch, *German Cinema*, pp. 284–304.

51 For a more detailed analysis of anti-Semitic film propaganda, see D. Welch, '"Jews out!": Anti-Semitic Film Propaganda in Nazi Germany and the "Jewish Question"', *The British Journal of Holocaust Education* 1, no. 1 (Summer, 1992), pp. 55–73.

52 For an excellent summary of Hitler's personal role in the genesis of the 'Final Solution', see Kershaw, *Nazi Dictatorship*, ch. 5, pp. 82–106. See also the well-researched article by D. Bankier, 'Hitler and the Policy-Making Process in the Jewish Question', *Holocaust and Genocide Studies* 3 (1988), pp. 1–20.

53 Taylor (ed.), *Goebbels Diaries*, entry for 17 October 1939, p. 23. Goebbels was reviewing the film from the early rushes, before it had been edited.

54 See M. Broszat's devastating critique of D. Irving's *Hitler's War* (London, 1977), in 'Hitler und die Genesis der "Endlösung". Aus Anlass der Thesen von David Irving', *Vierteljahrshefte für Zeitgeschichte* 26 (1977), pp. 735–75, English translation: 'Hitler and the Genesis of the "Final Solution": An Assessment of David Irving's Theses', in H. W. Koch (ed.), *Aspects of the Third Reich* (London, 1985), pp. 390–429. For a different interpretation of Hitler's role in the 'Final Solution', see G. Fleming, *Hitler and the Final Solution* (Oxford, 1986). These are precisely the questions that I attempt to answer in *Hitler. Profile of a Dictator* (London, 2001), see chapter 5. See also the interesting compilation of essays in I. Davies (ed.), *Teaching the Holocaust. Educational Dimensions, Principles and Practice* (London, 2000).

55 BA R58/157, 20 January 1941. Cf. Boberach, *Meldungen*, pp. 220–5; and M. Steinert, *Hitlers Krieg*, p. 243.

56 The poignant quotation from Kershaw can be found in *Popular Opinion*, p. 277.

57 The phrase was first used by Hans Mommsen in his outstanding essay, 'The Realisation of the Unthinkable'.

58 Neumann, *Behemoth*, pp. 382–9. Cf. also Bankier, 'Hitler and the Policy-Making Process'.

59 E. R. Huber; quoted in Noakes and Pridham (eds), *Nazism*, p. 199; and D. M. Phillips, *Hitler and the Rise of the Nazis* (London, 1975), p. 26.

60 Noakes and Pridham (eds.), *Nazism*, pp. 199–200.

61 R. Semmler, *Goebbels, the Man Next to Hitler*, entry of 12 December 1941, pp. 56–7.

62 Cf. I. Kershaw, *Der Hitler-Mythos. Volksmeinung und Propaganda im Dritten Reich* (Stuttgart, 1980), English translation *The 'Hitler Myth': Image and Reality in the Third Reich* (Oxford, 1987), and, more briefly, 'The Führer Image and Political Integration: The Popular Conception of Hitler in Bavaria during the Third Reich' in G. Hirschfeld and L. Kettenacker (eds), *Der Führerstaat: Mythos und Realität* (Stuttgart, 1981), pp. 133–163, also 'The Hitler Myth', *History Today* 35 (November, 1985), pp. 23–9, and, more recently, *Hitler* (London, 1991). Finally, Kershaw has now published his two volume definitive 'biography' of Hitler; *Hitler 1896–1936: Hubris* (London, 1998) and *Hitler 1936–1945: Nemesis* (London, 2000).
63 Kershaw, *Hubris*, p. 535.
64 *Das schwarze Korps*, 19 June 1935, p. 12, quoted in Adams, *Arts of the Third Reich*, p. 171.
65 *Sopade-Berichte* 1 (1934), pp. 471–2; 3 (1936), pp. 1249–51; 6 (1939), pp. 450–1.
66 See Boberach, *Meldungen*, pp. 202–6. Cf. also Steinert, *Hitlers Krieg*, pp. 263–73.
67 Cf. SD report for 21 July 1944, 'Erste stimmungsmässige Auswirkungen des Anschlags auf den Führer'; quoted in Baird, *Mythical World*, p. 232. The report makes clear that even in areas which did not support Hitler there was considerable relief at his escape, which many put down to divine intervention.
68 For a detailed analysis of *Triumph des Willens*, see Welch, *Propaganda*, pp. 147–59.
69 J. Goebbels, *Der Kampf um Berlin. Der Anfang* (Munich, 1932), p. 18.
70 Wilhelm Treue (ed.), 'Rede Hitlers vor der deutschen Presse (10 November 1938)', *Vierteljahrshefte für Zeitgeschichte* 6 (April, 1958), pp. 175–91; Baird, *Mythical World*, p. 23. Cf. also W. Wette, 'Ideologien, Propaganda und Innenpolitik als Voraussetzungen der Kriegspolitik des Dritten Reiches' in W. Deist *et al.* (eds), *Das deutsche Reich und der Zweite Weltkrieg* (Stuttgart, 1979).

5 PROPAGANDA AT WAR, 1939–45

1 H. Trevor-Roper, (ed.), *The Goebbels Diaries. The Last Days* (London, 1978), entry for 30 March 1945, p. 277 and p. 282.
2 For a more detailed analysis of the organisation and content of Nazi newsreels, see D. Welch 'Nazi Wartime Newsreel Propaganda', in K. Short (ed.), *Film and Radio Propaganda in World War II* (London, 1983), pp. 201–19, and 'Goebbels, Götterdämmerung, and the Deutsche Wochenschauen', in K. Short and S. Dolezel (eds), *Hitler's Fall: The Newsreel Witness* (London, 1988), pp. 80–99.
3 Taylor (ed.), *The Goebbels Diaries*, entry for 14 November 1940, p. 172.
4 BA R58/151, 20 June 1940.
5 Boberach, *Meldungen*, p. 77.
6 Quoted in Baird, *To Die for Germany*, p. 206.
7 ibid., p. 207.
8 The poem was entitled, 'Der Führer in Compiègne'.
9 Boberach, *Meldungen*, pp. 153, 102.
10 Hitler referred to the 'Jewish–Bolshevik' motif for the last time on 15 April 1945, in his final appeal to his troops and the German people. See the final section on 'Retreat into Mythology and Promises of Retaliation' for a brief analysis of this speech.
11 Quoted in Baird, *Mythical World*, p. 152. Hitler had been concerned about German public opinion and had received assurances from Goebbels that the concealment of the invasion has been successful and that a massive propaganda campaign consisting of 30 million leaflets had been preparerd by the RMVP to justify the war in the East. See diary entries for 12, 14, 16, 19 and 22 June 1940.

NOTES

12 See R. Semmler, *Goebbels: The Man Next to Hitler* (London, 1947), pp. 47–9. Semmler was one of Goebbels' aids in the RMVP, and this work is a 'diary' of his time there.

13 BA, R58/205, 24 July 1941.

14 Boelcke, *Wollt Ihr den totalen Krieg?*, pp. 195–6.

15 See Bramsted, *Goebbels and National Socialist Propaganda*, p. 250.

16 Kershaw, *Hitler Mythos*, pp. 176–7. Hitler's Reichstag speech of the 30 January 1942 was intended to commemorate the ninth anniversary of his take-over of power. On 23 December 1941, having issued a decree imposing the death penalty on anyone misappropriating articles of clothing for the Winter Help collection, Hitler referred to the collection in his speech: 'Behind this front there is now a homeland worthy of it. . . . I made an appeal to the German people. I want now to express my thanks. This appeal was also a vote. The others speak of democracy; this was true democracy! . . . Anyone who enriches himself on the proceeds will die. . . . I shall represent the interests of the soldiers here and I know that the whole of the German nation stands behind me on this.' Quoted in Noakes, *Nazism*, vol. 4, pp. 484–5.

17 Lochner (ed.), *Goebbels Diaries*, p. 61.

18 The Nazis also produced a short documentary film entitled *Das Sowjetparadies* to coincide with the exhibition. For a brief analysis of the film, see Welch, *Propaganda and the German Cinema*, p. 250. Cf. also the short documentary film *Europa bekämpft dem Bolshevismus* (1942), which was also produced by the film section of the RMVP.

19 The article of 27 December 1942 is reproduced in Goebbels, *Der steile Aufstieg*, pp. 95–102. It is also discussed in an interesting chapter on the 'Myth of death in World War II' in Baird, *To Die for Germany*, pp. 202–42.

20 Boberach, *Meldungen*, p. 421.

21 Semmler, *Goebbels*, entry for 29 January 1943, p. 68.

22 For a discussion of this and other Nazi newsreels during the first two years of the war, see Welch, 'Nazi Wartime Newsreel Propaganda', pp. 201–19.

23 A. Speer, *Inside the Third Reich* (London, 1971), p. 354. Goebbels recorded his own verdict on the response to his 'total war' speech in his diary for 20 February 1943: 'I received the type of reception I had worked for . . . in an hour of idiocy . . . if I'd told them to throw themselves out of the third-storey windows, they'd have done it.'

24 For Goebbels' account of his discussion with Hitler regarding 'total war' and the Führer's endorsement of his anti-Bolshevik propaganda, see Lochner (ed.), *Goebbels Diaries*, entry for 9 March 1943, p. 216. Goebbels continued to press for a more ruthless mobilisation of Germany's resources for total war and eventually Hitler appointed him Reich Plenipotentiary for Total War Mobilisation on 25 July 1944. This was partly in recognition of Goebbels' crucial role in foiling the attempted coup by the 20 July plotters.

25 Boberach, *Meldungen*, p. 387.

26 For more detailed analysis of the mobilisation of women for war work, see D. Winkler, *Frauenarbeit im Dritten Reich* (Hamburg, 1977); see also L. J. Rupp, *Mobilising Women for War: German and American Propaganda 1939–45* (Princeton, NJ, 1978).

27 For a discussion of workers' morale, see S. Salter, 'Structures of Consensus and Coercion: Workers' Morale and the Maintenance of Work Discipline, 1939–45', in Welch (ed.), *Nazi Propaganda*, pp. 88–116.

28 ibid., p. 95.

29 W. A. Boelcke (ed.), *'Wollt Ihr den totalen Krieg?' Die geheimen Goebbels-Konferenzen 1939–1943* (Stuttgart, 1967) pp. 440–41.

30 Lochner (ed.), *Goebbels Diaries*, entry for 14 April 1943, p. 253.
31 ibid., p. 270. Cf. the entry for 28 April 1943: 'The commentators marvel at the extraordinary cleverness with which we have been able to convert the Katyn incident into a highly political question. There is grave apprehension in London about this success of German propaganda. . . . There is talk of total victory by Goebbels! . . . One can call it a triumph of German propaganda. Throughout this whole war we have seldom been able to register such a success.'
32 Noakes, *Nazism*, vol. 4, p. 497.
33 H. Rumpf, *The Bombing of Germany* (London, 1963); see also N. Frankland, *The Bombing Offensive against Germany* (London, 1965).
34 M. Steinert, *Hitlers Krieg und die deutsche Stimmung und Haltung der deutschen Bevölkerung im Zweiten Weltkrieg* (Dusseldorf, 1970).
35 BA, R58/144; See also Baird, *To Die for Germany*, p. 238.
36 For an interesting and balanced analysis of Allied bombing and Goebbels' attempts to offset its effects, see G. Kirwin, 'Allied Bombing and Nazi Domestic Propaganda', *European History Quarterly* 15, no. 3 (July, 1985), pp. 341–62.
37 E. Fröhlich (ed.), *Die Tagebücher von Joseph Goebbels, II: Diktate 1941–45* (Munich, 1993), pp. 593–5 – for the full conversation between Hitler and Goebbels.
38 Kershaw, *Nemesis*, p. 556.
39 Noakes, *Nazism*, vol. 4, pp. 458–9.
40 For a comprehensive account of Goebbels' public references to the miracle weapons, see Bramsted, *Goebbels and National Socialist Propaganda*, pp. 316–25.
41 Steinert, *Hitlers Krieg*, p. 570.
42 BA, R58/191, 27 December 1943.
43 W. von Oven, *Mit Goebbels bis zum Ende*, 2 vols (Buenos Aires, 1949–50), vol. 2, p. 27.
44 For a detailed analysis of *Der grosse König*, see Welch, *Propaganda and the German Cinema*, pp. 174–83.
45 Boelcke, *Wollt Ihr den totalen Krieg?*, p. 333.
46 H. Trevor-Roper (ed.), *The Goebbels Diaries: The Last Days* (London, 1978), entry for 9 March 1945, p. 91.
47 Trevor-Roper (ed.), *Goebbels Diaries*, entry for 12 March 1945, p. 112; see also entry for 4 April 1945, when Goebbels actually cites bread riots in Berlin (p. 315). For examples of morale and public opinion during the last stages of the war (April 1943 to 1945), see the weekly 'activity reports' (*Tätigkeitsberichte*) BA R55/601.
48 V. Harlan, *Im Schatten meiner Filme. Selbstbiographie* (Gütersloh, 1966), p. 263.
49 J. Fest, *The Face of the Third Reich* (London, 1972), p. 151.
50 Semmler, *Goebbels*, entry for 17 April 1945, p. 194.
51 Activity reports of 21 February 1945; quoted in Baird, *Mythical World*, p. 243. Baird also outlines Goebbels' promotion of Werwolf tactics during the last months of the war (pp. 245–53).
52 CF. H. Krausnick *et al.*, *The Anatomy of the SS State* (London, 1968).

CONCLUSION

1 Herzstein, *The War that Hitler Won*, pp. 24–5, 414–15.
2 These remarks owe much to an excellent review of the literature on the subject by J. D. Noakes, *Times Literary Supplement*, 1 July, 1983, p. 689.
3 F. Stern, *Dreams and Delusion: The Drama of German History* (London, 1987), p. 135.

224

4   BA R43/II, 114, Goebbels' speech of 15 March 1933 to representatives of the press.
5   Quoted in Heiber, *Goebbels Reden*, vol. 1, p. 85. Strangely enough, the notion of Germans becoming 'Swiss-like' is precisely the term applied to 'bourgeois' West Germany by Luigi Barzini in his work *The Impossible Europeans* (London, 1983).

POSTSCRIPT

1   On the basis of a report from a commission of twelve historians, presented to them in June 1987, the German parliament approved the budget for the museum and the first stone was laid in 1987. For a wide-ranging account including some trenchant observations, see B. Heuser, 'Museums, Identity and Warring Historians – Observations on History in Germany', *The Historical Journal* 33, no. 2 (1990), pp. 417–40.
2   See the excellent synthesis of this debate in Kershaw, *Nazi Dictatorship*, ch. 9, pp. 168–91.
3   E. Nolte, *Der Faschismus in seiner Epoch* (Munich, 1963), English translation *The Three Faces of Fascism* (London, 1965).
4   Cf. the works of Hannah Arendt and of Carl Friedrich, which argued that there were no real differences between the millions of victims of the GPU or the NKVD (People's Commissariat for International Affairs) and the millions of victims of the SS and the Gestapo. See Introduction, note 5. Jürgen Kocka, on the other hand, believes that Germany should only be compared with Western civilisations, rather than with the regimes of Pol Pot or Idi Amin: see J. Kocka, 'German History before Hitler: The Debate about the German *Sonderweg*', *Journal of Contemporary History* 23, no. 1 (1988), p 11.
5   E. Nolte, *Der europäische Bürgerkrieg 1917–1945. Nationalsozialismus und Bolschevismus* (Berlin, 1987), English translation *European Civil War 1917–45* (London, 1988).
6   From the wealth of material that now exists, see H. V. Wehler, *Entsorgung der deutschen Vergangenheit? Ein polemischer Essay zum 'Historikerstreit'* (Munich, 1988); C. Maier, *The Unmasterable Past: History, Holocaust, and German National Identity* (Cambridge, Mass., 1988); R. J. Evans, *Out of the Shadow of Nazism* (London, 1990). For an interesting symposium, referred to as the Wheatland Conference and attended by many of the protagonists in the debate (sadly without Nolte and Hillgruber), see G. Thomas (ed.), *The Unresolved Past: A Debate in German History* (London, 1990).
7   D. Irving, *Hitler's War* (London, 1977).
8   I am indebted to James Sheehan, who made this point at a meeting of the American Historical Association (Cincinnati) in December 1988. The following point was made by Hans Mommsen in his contribution to the Wheatland Conference: 'Under the circumstances everybody knew or could have known that the battle being fought was one about the search for a new paradigm to replace the critical one which focuses on the question of why German history led to 1933': Thomas (ed.), *The Unresolved Past*, p. 31.
9   H. Schmidt, *Die Zeit*, 25 January 1991. Schmidt made this point in the wider context of the Gulf War, and what he claimed was a moral conflict between Germany's commitment to the 'Palestinians' right of self-determination . . . and our duty to uphold the murderous and inextinguishable memory of Auschwitz'. Interviewed by *Die Tageszeitung* in February 1991, the author Günter Grass argued that the German Government should resign over its behaviour in the Gulf War, accusing it of 'failing to recognise the lessons

of Auschwitz' by selling arms to Iraq. For Germany, even contemporary involvement in international affairs cannot be divorced from its past. The interview is reprinted in *The Guardian*, 1 March 1991.

10 Hauser, 'Museums', p. 420.

11 *Der Spiegel*, 21 (1966), pp. 48–77.

12 For the full article see, H.-U. Wehler, 'The Goldhagen Controversy: Agonizing Problems, Scholarly Failure and the Political Dimension', *German History*, Vol. 15, No. 1 (1997), pp. 80–91. For a highly critical analysis of Goldhagen's work see N. Finkelstein and R. Bettina Birn, *A Nation on Trial. The Goldhagen Thesis and Historical Truth* (New York, 1998).

13 Cf. Welch, *Modern European History 1871–2000. A Documentary Reader* (London, 1999), pp. 11–13; Welch, *German Propaganda and Total War 1914–18*, pp. 200–1.

14 R. Gellately, *Backing Hitler. Consent and Coercion in Nazi Germany* (Oxford, 2001). The book was also launched in a rather sensationalist manner – no doubt to capitalise on the current interest for all things Nazi. *The Guardian* in a detailed piece to launch the book carried the headline: 'Germans Knew of Holocaust Horror'. As an example of 'evidence' to support this claim is the poster reproducing part of Hitler's 30 January 1939 'prophecy' speech to the Reichstag that can be found in Plate 18. *Guardian*, 17 February 2001, p. 13.

15 C. Browning, *Ordinary Men: Reserve Police Battalion 101 and the Final Solution in Poland* (New York, 1992).

16 Kershaw provides a characteristically perceptive analysis of the 'Goldhagen phenomenon' in the fourth edition of *The Nazi Dictatorship*, pp. 251–62.

17 Mr Justice Gray, Transcript of Trial. Judgement to be Handed Down, 11 April 2000. See in particular paragraphs 7.6–7.8., pp. 164–6.

18 For two very different but fascinating accounts of the 'Irving trial' see, R.J. Evans, *Lying About Hitler. History, Holocaust and the David Irving Trial* (New York, 2001) and D.D. Guttenplan, *The Holocaust on Trial. History, Justice and the David Irving Libel Case* (London, 2001).

19 For a classic example of 'advocacy' history, see Michael Burleigh's *The Third Reich. A New History* (London, 2000), an immense work combining perceptive analysis and animated rage.

20 Kershaw, *Nazi Dictatorship*, p. 270. I am immensely grateful to Professor Richard Evans for sharing his views on the Goldhagen phenomenon when he talked to students at the University of Kent at Canterbury in 1999. Needless to say, I remain responsible for the comments made in this postscript.

SELECTED DOCUMENTS

1 Translated from the WTB (Wolffs Telegraphische Büro) press agency report of 16 March 1933, deposited in Bundesarchiv, R43(Reichskanzlei)/II 1149, pp. 25–9.

2 The speech is reproduced in full in H. Heiber (ed.), *Goebbels Reden*, 2 vols (Düsseldorf, 1971), vol. I, pp. 82–107.

3 The speech is reproduced in C. Belling, *Der Film in Staat und Partei* (Berlin, 1936), pp. 27–31.

4 RGBl I (1933), p. 661.

5 See Document 6.

6 RGBl I (1933), p. 713.

7 RGBl I (1934), p. 59.

8 RGBl I (1934), p. 1236.

9 RGBl I (1935), p. 1235.

10 J. Wulf (ed.) *Die bildenden Künste im Dritten Reich. Eine Dokumentation* (Gütersloh, 1963) pp. 119–20.

11 The translation is based on Baynes (ed.), *The Speeches of Adolf Hitler*, pp. 589–92.

12 'Die 30 Kreigsartikel für das deutsche Volk', *Das Reich*, 26 September 1943, pp. 464–74.

13 H. Boberach (ed.), *Meldungen aus dem Reich. Die geheimen Lageberichte des Sicherheitsdienstes der SS 1938–1945*, Vol. 15 (Herrsching, 1984), pp. 6064–5. See also, Noakes, *Nazism*, Vol. 4, pp. 550–1.

BIBLIOGRAPHY

GENERAL HISTORIOGRAPHICAL SURVEYS

Ayçoberry, P., *The Nazi Question* (London, 1981)

Burleigh, M. (ed.), *Confronting the Nazi Past: New Debates on Modern German History* (London, 1996)

—— *The Third Reich. A New History* (London, 2000)

Crew, D. F. (ed.), *Nazism and German Society, 1933–1945* (London, 1994)

Frei, N., *National Socialist Rule in Germany. The Führer State 1933–45* (London, 1993)

Hiden, J. and Farquharson, J., *Explaining Hitler's Germany. Historians and the Third Reich* (London, 1984)

Kershaw, I., *The Nazi Dictatorship. Problems and Perspectives of Interpretation* (London, 1985, 4th edn 2000)

Noakes, J., *Nazism. The German Home Front in World War II*, vol. 4 (Exeter, 1998)

Noakes, J. and Pridham, G. (eds), *Nazism, 1919–1945. A Documentary Reader*, vols 1–4 (Exeter, 1983–8)

Sax, B. and Kuntz, D. (eds), *Inside Hitler's Germany: A Documentary History of Life in the Third Reich* (Lexington, Mass., 1992)

THE RISE OF THE NSDAP

Allen, W. S., *The Nazi Seizure of Power: The Experience of a Single German Town, 1930–35* (Chicago, 1965)

Bessel, R., *Political Violence and the Rise of Nazism* (New Haven, Conn., and London, 1984)

Bohnke, W., *Die NSDAP im Ruhrgebiet 1920–33* (Bonn and Bad Godesberg, 1974)

Broszat, M., *Hitler and the Collapse of Weimar Germany* (Leamington Spa, 1987)

Childers, T., 'The Social Bases of the National Socialist Vote', *Journal of Contemporary History* 11 (1976), pp. 17–42

—— *The Nazi Voter* (Chapel Hill, NC, 1983)

Childers, T. (ed.), *The Formation of the Nazi Constituency 1919–1933* (London and Sydney, 1986)

Fischer, C., 'The SA of the NSDAP: Social Background and Ideology of the Rank and File in the Early 1930s', *Journal of Contemporary History* 17 (1982), pp. 651–70

Franz-Willing, G., *Ursprung der Hitlerbewegung 1919–22* (Oldendorf, 1974)

Hamilton, R. F., *Who Voted for Hitler?* (Princeton, NJ, 1982)

Kater, M., *The Nazi Party: A Social Profile of Members and Leaders 1919–1945* (Oxford, 1983)

Kehr, H., and Langmaid, J., *The Nazi Era 1919–1945* (London, 1982)

BIBLIOGRAPHY

Milatz, A., *Wähler und Wählen in der Weimarer Republik* (Bonn and Bad Godesberg, 1965)

Mühlberger, D., *Hitler's Followers: Studies in the Sociology of the Nazi Movement* (London, 1991)

Noakes, J., *The Nazi Party in Lower Saxony 1921–33* (Oxford, 1971)

Noakes, J., and Pridham, G. (eds), *Nazism 1919–1945: A Documentary Reader*, 4 vols (Exeter, 1983–8)

Orlow, D., *The History of the Nazi Party 1919–33* (London, 1971)

Pridham, G., *Hitler's Rise to Power: The Nazi Movement in Bavaria 1923–33* (London, 1973)

Schoenbaum, D., *Die braune Revolution* (Munich, 1980)

Stachura, P. D., *Gregor Strasser and the Rise of Nazism* (London, 1983)

Steinbach, P. (ed.), *Participation als Mittel der politischen Modernisierung* (Stuttgart, 1981)

HITLER

Baynes, N. H. (ed.), *The Speeches of Adolf Hitler*, 2 vols (Oxford, 1942)

Binion, R., *Hitler among the Germans* (New York, 1976)

Bracher, K. D., *The German Dictatorship: The Origins, Structure and Consequences of National Socialism* (London, 1973)

Broszat, M., *Der Staat Hitlers* (Munich, 1969), translated as *The Hitler State: The Foundation and Development of the Internal Structure of the Third Reich* (London, 1981)

Bullock, A., *Hitler: A Study in Tyranny* (London, 1962)

—— *Parallel Lives: Hitler and Stalin* (London, 1991)

Carr, W., *Hitler: A Study in Personality and Politics* (London, 1978)

Dietrich, O., *12 Jahre mit Hitler* (Munich, 1955), translated as *The Hitler I Knew* (London, 1957)

Domarus, M. (ed.), *Hitler. Reden und Proklamationen 1932–45*, 4 vols (Munich, 1965)

—— (ed.), *Hitler's Proclamations and Speeches* (London, 1990)

Fest, J., *Hitler* (Frankfurt-am-Main, 1973), English translation (London, 1974)

—— *The Face of the Third Reich* (London, 1974)

Geary, R., *Hitler and Nazism* (London, 1993)

Gordon, H. J., *Hitler and the Beer Hall Putsch* (Princeton, NJ, 1972)

Haffner, S., *The Meaning of Hitler* (London, 1979)

Hamann, B., *Hitler's Vienna. A Dictator's Apprenticeship* (Oxford, 1999)

Hanfstaengel, E., *Hitler: The Missing Years* (London, 1957)

Hauner, M. 'Did Hitler Want a World Dominion?', *Journal of Contemporary History* 13, no.1 (January, 1978), pp. 15–32

Hesse, F., *Hitler and the English* (London, 1954)

Hildebrand, K., *The Foreign Policy of the Third Reich* (London, 1973)

—— *Das Dritte Reich* (Munich, 1979)

Hirschfeld, G., and Kettenacker, L. (eds), *The 'Führer-State': Myth and Reality* (Stuttgart, 1981)

Hitler, A., *Mein Kampf* (Munich, 1937; London, 1939)

—— *Mein Kampf*, introd. D. C. Watt (London, 1969)

—— *Hitler's Table Talk 1941–44*, introd. and with a new preface by H. R. Trevor-Roper (London, 1973)

Hoffmann, H., *Hitler was my Friend* (London, 1955)

Housden, M., *Hitler. Study of a Revolutionary?* (London, 2000)

Jackel, E., *Hitler in History* (Hanover and London, 1984)

—— *Hitler's 'Weltanschauung': A Blueprint for Power* (Middletown, Conn., and London, 1972)

James, J., and Barnes, P. P., *Hitler's 'Mein Kampf' in Britain and America* (Cambridge, 1980)

Kershaw, I., *Der Hitler-Mythos. Volksmeinung und Propaganda im Dritten Reich* (Stuttgart, 1980)

—— *The 'Hitler Myth': Image and Reality in the Third Reich* (Oxford, 1987)

—— *Hitler* (London, 1991)

—— '"Working Towards the Führer". Reflections on the Nature of the Hitler Dictatorship', *Contemporary European History 2*, no.2 (1993), pp. 103–18

—— *Hitler 1896–1936: Hubris* (London, 1998)

—— *Hitler 1936–1945: Nemesis* (London, 2000).

Kershaw, I. and Lewin, M. (eds), *Stalinism and Nazism: Dictatorships in Comparison* (Cambridge, 1997)

Lukacs, J., *The Hitler of History* (New York, 1998).

Neumann, F., *Behemoth: The Structure and Practice of National Socialism* (London, 1942)

Peterson, E. N., *The Limits of Hitler's Power* (Princeton, NJ, 1969)

Picker, H. H., *Hitlers Tischgespräche im Führerhauptquartier 1941–2* (Stuttgart, 1976)

Rauschning, H., *Hitler Speaks* (London, 1940)

Rebentisch, D., *Führerstaat und Verwaltung im Zweiten Weltkrieg* (Stuttgart, 1989)

Stern, J. P., *Hitler: The Führer and the People* (London, 1975)

Stokes, G., *Hitler and the Quest for World Domination: Nazi Ideology and Foreign Policy in the 1920s* (Leamington Spa, 1987)

Stone, N., *Hitler* (London, 1980)

Toland, J., *Adolf Hitler* (New York, 1976)

Trevor-Roper, H. R., *The Last Days of Hitler* (London, 1962)

Waite, R., *The Psychopathic God: Adolf Hitler* (New York, 1977)

Weinstein, F., *The Dynamics of Nazism: Leadership, Ideology and the Holocaust* (London, 1980)

Welch, D., *Hitler: Profile of a Dictator* (London, 2001)

GOEBBELS

Boelcke, W. A. (ed.), *'Wollt Ihr den totalen Krieg?' Die geheimen Goebbels-Konferenzen 1939–1943* (Stuttgart, 1967)

Le Bon, G., *The Crowd. A Study of the Popular Mind* (New York, 1960)

Ebermayer, E., and Roos, H., *Gefährtin des Teufels. Leben und Tod der Magda Goebbels* (Hamburg, 1952)

Fröhlich, E. (ed.), *Die Tagebücher von Joseph Goebbels: Sämtliche Fragmente*, 4 vols (Munich, 1987)

—— (ed.), *Die Tagebücher von Joseph Goebbels, II: Diktate 1941–45* (Munich, 1993)

Goebbels, J., *Michael. Ein deutsches Schicksal in Tagebuchblättern* (Munich, 1929)

—— *Das eherne Herz. Reden und Aufsätze aus den Jahren 1941–2* (Munich, 1943)

—— *Vom Kaiserhof zur Reichskanzlei. Eine historische Darstellung in Tagebuchblättern* (Munich, 1934)

—— *Der Kampf um Berlin. Der Anfang* (Munich, 1932)

—— *Die Zeit ohne Beispiel. Reden und Aufsätze aus den Jahren 1939–41* (Munich, 1943)

Heiber, H. (ed.), *The Early Goebbels Diaries. The Journal of Joseph Goebbels from 1925–6* (London, 1962)

—— (ed.), *Goebbels Reden*, 2 vols (Düsseldorf, 1971)

BIBLIOGRAPHY

—— *Goebbels* (London, 1973)
Höver, U. B., *Josef Goebbels: Ein nationaler Sozialist* (Bonn, 1992)
Lemmons, R., *Goebbels and 'Der Angriff'* (Kentucky, 1992)
Lochner, L. P. (ed.), *The Goebbels Diaries* (London, 1948)
Manvell, R., and Fraenkel, H., *Dr Goebbels* (London, 1960)
Martin, H. L., *Unser Mann bei Goebbels* (Neckargemund, 1973)
Meisner, O., *Magda Goebbels* (London, 1979)
Moltmann, G., 'Goebbels Rede zum totalen Krieg', *Vierteljahrshefte für Zeitgeschichte* 12 (January, 1964), pp. 13–43
Oven, W. von, *Mit Goebbels bis zum Ende*, 2 vols (Buenos Aires, 1949–50)
Reimann, V. *Dr Joseph Goebbels* (Vienna, 1973), translated as *The Man who Created Hitler* (London, 1977)
Reiss, C., *Joseph Goebbels: A Biography* (London, 1949)
Reuth, R. G. (ed.), *Goebbels. Tagebücher* (Munich, 1992)
—— *Goebbels* (London, 1994)
Semmler, R., *Goebbels: The Man Next to Hitler* (London, 1947)
Stephan, W., *Joseph Goebbels. Damon einer Diktatur* (Stuttgart, 1949)
Taylor, F. (ed.), *The Goebbels Diaries 1939–41* (London, 1982)
Taylor, R., 'Goebbels and the Function of Propaganda', in D. Welch (ed.), *Nazi Propaganda: The Power and the Limitations* (London, 1983)
Trevor-Roper, H. R. (ed.), *The Goebbels Diaries: The Last Days* (London, 1978)
Wykes, A., *Goebbels* (New York, 1973)

ART AND CULTURE

Adam, P., *The Arts of the Third Reich* (London, 1992)
Barron, S., *Degenerate Art: The Fate of the Avante-Garde in Nazi Germany* (New York, 1991)
Bischoff, R. F., *Nazi Conquest through German Culture* (Cambridge, Mass., 1942)
Bosmajian, H. A., 'The Role of the Political Poster in Hitler's Rise to Power', *Print* (May, 1966), pp. 28–31
Brenner, H., *Die Kunstpolitik des Nationalsozialismus* (Hamburg, 1963)
Causton, B., 'Art in Germany under the Nazis', *London Studio* 12 (November, 1936), pp. 235–46
Cuomo, G. R. (ed.), *National Socialist Cultural Policy* (New York, 1995)
Darkal, V., 'Adventures in Art under Hitler', *Horizon* 9 (March, 1944), pp. 192–204
Dulffer, J., Thies, J., and Henke, J. (eds), *Hitlers Städte Baupolitik im Dritten Reich* (Cologne and Vienna, 1978)
Hinz, B., *Art in the Third Reich* (Oxford, 1980)
Kater, M., *Different Drummers. Jazz in the Culture of Nazi Germany* (Oxford, 1992)
Larsson, L. O., *Die Neugestaltung der Reichshauptstadt* (Stockholm and Stuttgart, 1978)
Lehmann-Haupt, H., *Art under Dictatorship* (London, 1954)
Levi, E., *Music in the Third Reich* (London, 1994)
Mosse, G., *Nazi Culture: Intellectual, Cultural and Social Life in the Third Reich* (London, 1966)
Reichel, P., *Der schöne Schein des Dritten Reiches. Faszination und Gewalt des Faschismus* (Munich and Vienna, 1992)
Schmidt, M., *Albert Speer. Das Ende eines Mythos* (Bern and Munich, 1982)
Schnell, R. (ed.), *Kunst und Kultur im deutschen Faschismus* (Stuttgart, 1978)
Schonberger, A., *Die neue Reichskanzlei von Albert Speer* (Berlin, 1981)
Schroeder, R., *Modern Art in the Third Reich* (Offenburg, 1952)
Speer, A., *Inside the Third Reich* (London, 1971)

—— *Architektur Arbeiten 1933–42* (Frankfurt-am-Main, Berlin and Vienna, 1978)

Steinweis, A., *Art, Ideology, and Economics in Nazi Germany: The Reich Chambers of Music, Theater and Visual Arts* (North Carolina, 1993)

Taylor, B., and van der Will, W. (eds), *The Nazification of Art: Art, Design, Music, Architecture and Film in the Third Reich* (Winchester, 1990)

Taylor, R., *The Word in Stone: The Role of Architecture in the National Socialist Ideology* (Berkeley and Los Angeles, 1974)

Thies, J., *Architekt der Weltherrschaft. Die 'Endziele' Hitlers* (Düsseldorf, 1976)

—— 'Hitler's European Building Programme', *Journal of Contemporary History* 13 (1978), pp. 413–31

Wulf, J. (ed.), *Die bildenden Künste im Dritten Reich. Eine Dokumentation* (Gütersloh, 1963)

FILM

Albrecht, G., *Nationalsozialistische Filmpolitik. Eine soziologische Untersuchung über die Spielfilme des Dritten Reichs* (Stuttgart, 1969)

—— *Film im Dritten Reich* (Stuttgart, 1982)

Barkhausen, H., 'Die NSDAP als Filmproduzentin. Mit Kurzübersicht: Filme der NSDAP 1927–45', in G. Moltmann and K. F. Reimers (eds), *Zeitgeschichte im Film- und Tondokument* (Göttingen, 1970), pp. 145–76

Bauer, A., *Deutscher Spielfilm-Almanach 1929–50* (Berlin, 1950)

Becker, W., *Film und Herrschaft* (Berlin, 1973)

Belling, C., *Der Film in Staat und Partei* (Berlin, 1936)

Blobner, H., and Holba, H., 'Jackboot Cinema: Political Propaganda in the Third Reich', *Film and Filming* 8, no.3 (December, 1962), pp.14–18

Bredow, W. von, and Zeruk, R. (eds), *Film und Gesellschaft in Deutschland. Dokumente und Materialien* (Hamburg, 1975)

Courtade, F., and Cadars, R., *Histoire du cinéma nazi* (Paris, 1972)

Eckert, G., 'Filmintendenz und Tendenzfilm', *Wille und Macht, Führerorgan der nationalsozialistischen Jugend* 4 (November, 1938), pp. 19–25

Fox, J., *Filming Women in the Third Reich* (Oxford, 2000)

Frauen und Film. Faschismus (special issue) nos 44/45 (October, 1988)

Harlan, V., *Im Schatten meiner Filme. Selbstbiographie* (Gütersloh, 1966), translated as *Souvenirs, ou Le Cinéma allemand selon Goebbels* (Paris, 1974)

Hoffman, H., *The Triumph of Propaganda. Film and National Socialism, 1933–1945* (Oxford, 1995)

Hollstein, D., *Antisemitische Filmpropaganda. Die Darstellung des Juden im national- sozialistischen Spielfilme* (Munich, 1971)

Hull, D. S., *Film in the Third Reich* (Berkeley and Los Angeles, 1969)

Kalbus, O., *Vom Werden deutscher Filmkunst. Teil 2: Der Tonfilm* (Altona and Bahrenfeld, 1935)

Kracauer, S., *From Caligari to Hitler: A Psychological History of the German Film* (Princeton, NJ, 1947; repr. 1973)

Kreigk, O., *Der deutsche Film im Spiegel der Ufa. 25 Jahre Kampf und Vollendung* (Berlin, 1943)

Kurowski, U. (ed.), *Deutsche Spielfilme 1933–45. Materialien*, 5 vols (Munich, 1981)

Leiser, E., *Nazi Cinema* (London, 1974)

Lowry, S., *Pathos und Politik: Ideologie in Spielfilmen des Nationalsozialismus* (Tübingen, 1991)

Phillips, M. S., 'The Nazi Control of the German Film Industry', *Journal of European Studies* (March, 1971), pp. 37–68

—— 'The German Film Industry and the New Order', in P. D. Stachura (ed.), *The Shaping of the Nazi State* (London, 1978), pp. 257–81

Rabenalt, A. M., *Film im Zwielicht* (Hildesheim and New York, 1978)

—— *Joseph Goebbels und der 'Grossdeutsche' Film* (Munich and West Berlin, 1985)

Rentschler, E., *The Ministry of Illusions. Nazi Cinema and its Afterlife* (Cambridge, Mass., 1996)

Riefenstahl, L., *Hinter den Kulissen des Reichsparteitagfilms* (Munich, 1935)

Spiker, J., *Film und Kapital* (Berlin, 1975)

Taylor, R., *Film Propaganda: Soviet Russia and Nazi Germany* (London, 1979)

Traubner, R., 'The Sound and the Führer', *Film Comment* 14, no.4 (July/August, 1978), pp. 17–23

Weinberg, D., 'Approaches to the Study of Film in the Third Reich: A Critical Appraisal', *Journal of Contemporary History* 19, no. 1 (January, 1984), pp.105–26

Welch, D., 'The Proletarian Cinema and the Weimar Republic', *Historical Journal of Film, Radio and Television* 1, no. 1(1981), pp. 3–18

—— *Propaganda and the German Cinema 1933–45* (Oxford, 1983, revised edn London, 2001)

—— 'Nazi Wartime Newsreel Propaganda', in K. Short (ed.), *Film and Radio Propaganda in World War II: A Global Perspective* (London, 1983), pp. 201–19

—— 'Goebbels, Götterdämmerung, and the Deutsche Wochenschauen', in K. Short and S. Dolezel (eds), *Hitler's Fall: The Newsreel Witness* (London, 1988)

—— 'Nazi Film Policy: Control, Ideology and Propaganda', in G. Cuomo (ed.), *National Socialist Cultural Policy* (New York, 1994)

Wulf, J. (ed.), *Theater und Film im Dritten Reich. Eine Dokumentation* (Gütersloh, 1964)

PRESS AND RADIO

Abel, K. D., *Die Presselenkung im NS-Staat* (Munich, 1968)

Diller A., *Rundfunkspolitik im Dritten Reich* (Gütersloh, 1964)

Doherty, M., *Nazi Wireless Propaganda* (Edinburgh, 2000).

Eksteins, M., *The Limits of Reason: The German Democratic Press and the Collapse of Weimar Democracy* (Oxford, 1975)

Frei, N., and Schmitz, J., *Journalismus im Dritten Reich* (Cologne, 1989)

Gombrich, E. H., *Myth and Reality in German Wartime Broadcasts* (London, 1970)

Hagemann, W., *Publizistik im Dritten Reich. Ein Beitrag zur Methodik der Massenführung* (Hamburg, 1948)

Hale, O. J., *The Captive Press in the Third Reich* (Princeton, NJ, 1964)

Heyde, L., *Presse, Rundfunk und Film im Dienste der Volksführung* (Dresden, 1943)

Koszyk, K., *Geschichte der deutschen Presse, 1914–45* (Berlin, 1966–72)

Kris, E., and Speyer, H., *German Radio Propaganda: Report on Home Broadcasts during the War* (London, 1944)

Lacey, K.E.R., *Bridging the Divide: Women, Radio and the Regeneration of the Public and Private Spheres in Germany, 1923–1945* (Ph.D Thesis, University of Liverpool, 1993)

Longerich, P., *Propagandisten im Kreig. Die Presseabteilung des Auswärtigen Amtes unter Ribbentrop* (Munich, 1987)

Pohle, H., *Der Rundfunk als Instrument der Politik* (Hamburg, 1955)

Scheel, K., *Krieg über Ätherwellen. NS-Rundfunk und Monopole 1933–45* (Berlin, 1970)

Wulf, J. (ed.), *Presse und Funk im Dritten Reich* (Gütersloh, 1964)

YOUTH AND EDUCATION

Aley, P., *Jugendliteratur im Dritten Reich* (Gütersloh, 1967)
Becker, H., *German Youth: Bound or Free?* (London, 1946)
Belling, C., and Schutze, A., *Der Film in der Hitlerjugend* (Berlin, 1937)
Brandenburg, H. C., *Die Geschichte der Hitlerjugend* (Cologne, 1968)
Ebeling, H., *The German Youth Movement* (London, 1945)
Eilers, R., *Die nationalsozialistische Schulpolitik* (Cologne, 1963)
Hagen, L., *Follow my Leader* (London, 1951)
Hellfeld, M. von, *Bündische Jugend und Hitlerjugend. Zur Geschichte von Anpassung und Widerstand 1930–39* (Cologne, 1987)
Kamenetsky, C., *Children's Literature in Hitler's Germany* (Athens, Ga, and London, 1984)
Klönne, A., *Hitlerjugend. Die Jugend und ihre Organisation im Dritten Reich* (Hanover, 1960)
—— *Jugend in Dritten Reich. Die Hitler-Jugend und ihre Gegner* (Düsseldorf, 1982)
Koch, H. W., *The Hitler Youth: Origins and Development 1922–45* (London, 1975)
Kuhn, H. *et al.*, *Die deutsche Universität im Dritten Reich* (Munich, 1966)
Laqueur, W., *Young Germany: A History of the German Youth Movement* (New York and London, 1962)
Loewenberg, P., 'The Psychological Origins of the Nazi Youth Cohort', *American Historical Review* 76, no. 5 (December, 1971), pp. 1457–502
McKee, I., *Tomorrow the World* (London, 1960)
Peukert, D., 'Youth in the Third Reich', in R. Bessel (ed.), *Life in the Third Reich* (Oxford, 1987), pp. 25–40
Sander, A. U., *Jugend und Film* (Berlin, 1944)
Schirach, B. von, *Die Hitlerjugend. Idee und Gestalt* (Berlin, 1934)
Schmidt, A., *Jugend im Reich* (Berlin, 1942)
Stachura, P. D., 'The Ideology of the Hitler Youth in the *Kampfzeit*', *Journal of Contemporary History* 8 (1973), pp. 155–67
—— *Nazi Youth in the Weimar Republic* (Santa Barbara, Calif., 1975)
—— *The German Youth Movement 1900–45* (London, 1981)
Steinberg, M. S., *Sabres and Brown Shirts: The German Student's Path to National Socialism 1918–31* (London, 1977)
Stephenson, J., 'Girls' Higher Education in Germany in the 1930s', *Journal of Contemporary History* 10, no.1 (1975), pp. 41–69
Walker, L. D., *Hitler Youth and Catholic Youth 1933–36* (Washington DC, 1971)

WOMEN

Evans, R. J., *The Feminist Movement in Germany 1894–1933* (London, 1976)
Gersdoff, U. von, *Frauen im Kriegsdienst 1914–45* (Stuttgart, 1969)
Kirkpatrick, C., *Women in Nazi Germany* (London, 1939)
Koonz, C., 'Mothers in the Fatherland: Women in Nazi Germany', in R. Bridenthal and C. Koonz (eds), *Becoming Visible. Women in European History* (Boston, Mass., 1977) pp. 445–73
—— *Mothers in the Fatherland: Women, the Family, and Nazi Germany* (New York, 1987)
Liggerhaus, R., *Frauen unterm Nationalsozialismus* (Wüppertal, 1984)
McIntyre, J., 'Women and the Professions in Germany 1930–40', in A. and E. Mattias (eds), *German Democracy and the Triumph of Hitler* (London, 1971) pp. 175–213
Mason, T. W., 'Women in Germany, 1925–40: Family, Welfare and Work', *History Workshop Journal* (Spring/Autumn, 1976), pp. 74–113, 5–32

Pine, L., *Nazi Family Policy, 1933–1945* (Oxford, 1997)
Rupp, L. J., *Mobilising Women for War: German and American Propaganda 1939–45* (Princeton, NJ, 1978)
Scholtz-Klink, G., *Die Frau im Dritten Reich* (Tübingen, 1978)
Schwertfeger, R., *Women of Theresienstadt: Memoirs and Poems from a Concentration Camp* (Oxford, 1988)
Stephenson, J., *Women in Nazi Society* (London, 1975)
—— '"Reichsbund der Kinderreichen": The League of Large Families in the Population Policy of Nazi Germany', *European Studies Review* (July, 1979), pp. 350–75
—— *The Nazi Organisation of Women* (London, 1981)
—— 'Middle-Class Women and National Socialist "Service"', *History* 67, no. 219 (1982), pp. 32–44
Winkler, D., *Frauenarbeit im "Dritten Reich"* (Hamburg, 1977)

LABOUR AND THE ECONOMY

Barkai, A., *Nazi Economics: Ideology, Theory and Policy* (New Haven, Conn., and Oxford, 1990)
Bessel, R., and Jamin, M., 'Nazis, Workers and the Uses of Quantitative Evidence', *Social History* 4, no.1 (1979), pp. 112–14
Broszat, M., Fröhlich, E., and Wiesemann, F. (eds), *Bayern in der NS-Zeit. Soziale Lage und politisches Verhalten der Bevölkerung im Spiegel vertraulicher Berichte* (Munich and Vienna, 1977)
Broszat, M. *et al.* (eds), *Bayern in der NS-Zeit. III/IV: Herrschaft und Gesellschaft im Konflikt Teil B/C* (Munich and Vienna, 1981)
Carroll, B. A., *Design for Total War: Arms and Economics in the Third Reich* (The Hague, 1968)
Corni, G., *Hitler and the Peasants: Agrarian Policy of the Third Reich, 1930–1939* (New York/Oxford, 1990)
Farquharson, J. E., *The Plough and the Swastika: The NSDAP and Agriculture in Germany 1928–45* (London, 1976)
Fischer, W., *Deutsche Wirtschaftspolitik 1918–45* (Opladen, 1968)
Gillingham, J. R., *Industry and Politics in the Third Reich* (London, 1985)
Hayes, P., *Industry and Ideology: IG Farben in the Nazi Era* (Cambridge, 1987)
Kele, M. H., *Nazis and Workers: National Socialist Appeals to German Labor 1919–33* (Chapel Hill, NC, 1972)
Kitchen, M., *Nazi Germany at War* (New York, 1995).
Mason, T. W. 'Labour in the Third Reich', *Past and Present* 33 (April, 1966), pp. 112–41
—— *Arbeiterklasse und Volksgemeinschaft. Dokumente und Materialien zur deutschen Arbeiterpolitik 1936–39* (Opladen, 1975)
—— *Sozialpolitik im Dritten Reich. Arbeiterklasse und Volksgemeinschaft* (Opladen, 1977)
—— *Social Policy in the Third Reich. The Working Class and the 'National Community', 1918–39*, ed. J. Caplan (Oxford, 1992)
—— 'The Workers' Opposition in Nazi Germany', *History Workshop Journal* 11 (Spring, 1981), pp. 120–37
Milward, A. S., *The German Economy at War* (London, 1965)
Overy, R.J., *The Nazi Economic Recovery 1932–1938* (London, 1982)
—— 'Germany, "Domestic Crisis", and War in 1939', *Past and Present* 116 (1987), pp. 138–68

—— *War and Economy in the Third Reich* (Oxford, 1994)

Petzina, D., 'Soziale Lage der deutschen Arbeiter und Probleme des Arbeitseinsatzes während des zweiten Weltkrieges', in W. Dlugoborski (ed.), *Zweiter Weltkrieg und sozialer Wandel* (Göttingen, 1981), pp. 65–86

Petzina, D., Abelshauser, W., and Faust, A. (eds), *Sozialgeschichtliches Arbeitsbuch III. Materialien zur Statistik des deutschen Reiches 1914–45* (Munich, 1978)

Peukert D., *Die KPD im Widerstand Verfolgung und Untergrundarbeit an Rhein und Ruhr 1933 bis 1945* (Wüppertal, 1980)

Reulecke, J. (ed.), *Arbeiterbewegung an Rhein und Ruhr* (Wüppertal, 1974)

Schoenbaum, D., *Hitler's Social Revolution: Class and Status in Nazi Germany* (London, 1967)

Schweitzer, A., *Big Business in the Third Reich* (London, 1964)

Silverman, D., *Hitler's Economy in the Third Reich* (London, 1998)

Smelser, R., *Robert Ley: Hitler's Labour Front Leader* (Oxford, 1988)

Sohn-Rethels, A., *The Economy and Class Structure of German Fascism* (London, 1987)

Welch, D., 'Manufacturing a Consensus: Nazi Propaganda and the Building of a "National Community" (*Volksgemeinschaft*)', *Contemporary European History* 2, no. 1 (1993), pp. 1–15

Zandtmoyer, L. von, *The Kraft durch Freude Movement in Nazi Germany 1933–39* (East Lansing, Mich., 1977)

RACIAL POLICY, EUTHANASIA AND THE 'JEWISH QUESTION'

Aly, G., 'Final Solution'. *Nazi Population Policy and the Murder of the European Jews* (London, 1999)

Bankier, D., 'Hitler and the Policy-Making Process on the Jewish Question', *Holocaust and Genocide Studies* 3 (1988), pp. 1–20

—— *The Germans and the Final Solution: Public Opinion Under Nazism* (Oxford, 1992)

Bartov, O., *The Eastern Front 1941–45: German Troops and the Barbarisation of Warfare* (London, 1985)

Bauer, Y., *The Holocaust in Historical Perspective* (London, 1978)

BenGershom, E., *David: A Testimony of a Holocaust Survivor* (Oxford, 1988)

Breitman, R., *The Architect of Genocide. Himmler and the Final Solution* (London, 1991)

Browning, C., *Fateful Months* (New York, 1985)

—— *The Path to Genocide. Essays on Launching the Final Solution* (Cambridge, 1992)

—— *Ordinary Men. Reserve Police Battalion 101 and the Final Solution in Poland* (New York, 1992)

Burleigh, M., *Germany Turns Eastward: A Study of 'Ostforschung' in the Third Reich* (Cambridge, 1988)

—— 'Surveys of Developments in the Social History of Medicine, III: "Euthanasia" in the Third Reich: Some Recent Literature', *The Society for the Social History of Medicine* 4 (1991), pp. 317–28

—— *Death and Deliverance: 'Euthanasia' in Germany 1900–1945* (Cambridge, 1994)

Burleigh, M., and Wippemann, W., *The Racial State: Germany 1933–1945* (Cambridge, 1992)

Burrin, P., *Hitler and the Jews. The Genesis of the Holocaust* (London, 1993)

Dawidowicz, L., *The War Against the Jews, 1933–45* (Harmondsworth, 1977)

Engel, D., *The Holocaust. The Third Reich and the Jews* (London, 1999)

Evans, R. J., *Lying about Hitler. History, Holocaust and the David Irving Trial* (New York, 2001)

Evans, R. T., *In Hitler's Shadow* (New York and London, 1989)

BIBLIOGRAPHY

Finkelstein, N. and Bettina Birn, R. *A Nation on Trial. The Goldhagen Thesis and Historical Truth* (New York, 1998)

Fleming, G., *Hitler and the Final Solution* (Oxford, 1986)

Friedländer, H., *The Origins of Nazi Genocide: From Euthanasia to the Final Solution* (Chapel Hill, NC/London, 1995)

Friedländer, S., *Nazi Germany and the Jews. The Years of Persecution, 1933–39* (London, 1997)

Ganssmüller, C., *Die Erbgesundheitspolitik des Dritten Reiches. Planung, Durchführung und Durchsetzung* (Cologne and Vienna, 1987)

Gellately, R., *The Gestapo and German Society. Enforcing Racial Policy, 1933–1945* (Oxford, 1990)

Gerlach, C., 'The Wannsee Conference, the Fate of German Jews, and Hitler's Decision in Principle to Exterminate All European Jews', *Journal of Modern History* 70 (1998), pp. 759–812

Goldhagen, D., *Hitler's Willing Executioners* (New York, 1996)

Gordon, S., *Hitler, Germans and the 'Jewish Question'* (Princeton, NJ, 1984)

Guttenplan, D. D., *The Holocaust on Trial. History, Justice and the David Irving Libel Case* (London, 2001)

Hilberg, R., *The Destruction of European Jews* (New York, 1973)

Hirschfeld, G. (ed.), *The Policies of Genocide* (London, 1986)

Kater, M., *Doctors under Hitler* (London/Chapel Hill, NC, 1989)

King, C., *The Nazi State and the New Religions: Five Case Studies in Non-Conformity* (New York and Toronto, 1982)

Klee, E., *'Euthanasie' im NS-Staat. Die 'Vernichtung lebensunwerten Lebens'* (Frankfurt-am-Main, 1983)

—— (ed.), *Dokumente zur 'Euthanasie'* (Frankfurt-am-Main, 1985)

Krausnick, H. et al., *The Anatomy of the SS State* (London, 1968)

Maier, C., *The Unmasterable Past: History, Holocaust, and German National Identity* (Cambridge, Mass., 1988)

Marrus, M., *The Holocaust in History* (London, 1988)

Mayer, A., *Why did the Heavens not Darken? The Final Solution in History* (New York, 1989)

Mommsen, H., *From Weimar to Auschwitz* (London, 1990)

Müller-Hill, B., *Murderous Science: Elimination by Scientific Selection of Jews, Gypsies, and Others: Germany 1933–45* (Oxford, 1988)

Nowak, K., *'Euthanasie' und Sterilisation im 'Dritten Reich'* (Göttingen, 1984)

Pehle, W. (ed.), *November 1918: From 'Kristallnacht' to Genocide* (Oxford, 1991)

Proctor, R. N., *Racial Hygiene: Medicine under the Nazis* (Cambridge, Mass., 1988)

Reitlinger, G., *The Final Solution* (London, 1971)

Schleunes, K. A., *The Twisted Road to Auschwitz: Nazi Policy Towards the Jews, 1933–39* (Chicago and London, 1970)

Schmuhl, H.-W., *Rassenhygiene, Nationalsozialismus, Euthanasie* (Göttingen, 1987)

Silfen, P. H., *The 'Völkisch' Ideology and the Roots of Nazism* (New York, 1973)

Thomas, G. (ed.), *The Unresolved Past: A Debate in German History*, introd. R. Dahrendorf (London, 1990)

Weindling, P., *Health, Race and German Politics* (Cambridge, 1989)

Welch, D., '"Jews Out!": Anti-Semitic Film Propaganda in Nazi Germany and the "Jewish Question"', *The British Journal of Holocaust Education* I, no.1 (Summer, 1992), pp. 55–73

CONSENSUS, COERCION, PROPAGANDA AND RESISTANCE

Albrecht, D., *Katholische Kirche im Dritten Reich* (Mainz, 1976)

—— (ed.), *Widerstand und Exil 1933–45* (New York and Frankfurt, 1986)

Aretz, J., *Katholische Arbeiterbewegung und Nationalsozialismus* (Mainz, 1978)

Baird, J. W., *The Mythical World of Nazi Propaganda 1939–45* (Minneapolis, Minn., 1974)

—— *To Die For Germany: Heroes in the Nazi Pantheon* (Indianapolis, Ind., 1990)

Balfour, M., *Propaganda in War 1939–45: Organisations, Policies and Publics in Britain and Germany* (London, 1979)

—— *Withstanding Hitler* (London, 1988)

Bessel, R. (ed.), *Life in the Third Reich* (Oxford, 1987)

Boberach, H., *Meldungen aus dem Reich. Auswahl geheimen Lageberichten des Sicherheitsdienstes der SS 1939–44* (Berlin and Neuwied, 1965)

Boelcke, W. A., *Kriegspropaganda 1939–41. Geheime Ministerkonferenzen im Reichs-Propagandaministerium* (Stuttgart, 1966)

—— '*Wollt Ihr den totalen Krieg? Die geheimen Goebbels-Konferenzen 1939–43* (Stuttgart, 1967), translated as *The Secret Conferences of Dr Goebbels 1939–43* (London, 1970)

Bramsted, E. K., *Goebbels and National Socialist Propaganda 1925–45* (East Lansing, Mich., 1965)

Broszat, M., *German National Socialism* (Santa Barbara, Calif., 1966)

Bull, H. (ed.), *The Challenge of the Third Reich* (Oxford, 1986)

Burden, H. T., *The Nuremberg Rallies 1932–39* (London, 1967)

Cecil, R., *Myth of the Master Race: A. Rosenberg and the Nazi Ideology* (London, 1974)

Conway, J. S., *The Nazi Persecution of the Churches 1933–45* (London, 1968)

Delmar, S., *Black Boomerang* (New York, 1962)

Driencourt, J., *La Propagande, nouvelle force politique* (Paris, 1950)

Ellul, J., *Propaganda: The Formation of Men's Attitudes* (New York, 1973)

Farago, L. (ed.), *German Psychological Warfare: Survey and Bibliography* (New York, 1941; repr. 1972)

Fraser, L., *Propaganda* (London, 1957)

Gellately, R., *Backing Hitler. Consent and Coercion in Nazi Germany* (Oxford, 2001)

George, A., *Propaganda Analysis: A Study of Inferences Made from Nazi Propaganda in World War II* (Evanston, Ill., 1959)

Glaser, H., *The Cultural Roots of National Socialism* (London, 1978)

Grami, H. *et al.*, *The German Resistance to Hitler* (London, 1970)

Grünberger, R., *A Social History of the Third Reich* (London, 1974)

Hadamovsky, E., *Propaganda und nationale Macht. Die Organisation der öffentlichen Meinung für die nationale Politik* (Oldenbourg, 1933)

Hagemann, W., *Vom Mythos der Masse* (Heidelberg, 1987)

Helmrich, E. C., *The German Churches under Hitler* (Detroit, Mich., 1979)

Herma, H., 'Goebbels' Conception of Propaganda', *Social Research* 10, no. 2 (May, 1943), pp. 200–18

Herzstein, R. E., *The War that Hitler Won: The Most Infamous Propaganda Campaign in History* (London, 1979)

Hoffmann, P., *German Resistance to Hitler* (Cambridge, Mass., 1988)

—— *Stauffenberg: A Family History, 1905–1944* (Cambridge, 1996)

Housden, M., *Resistance and Conformity in the Third Reich* (London, 1997)

Kershaw, I., 'The Persecution of the Jews and German Popular Opinion in the Third Reich', *Year Book of the Leo Baeck Institute* 26 (1981), pp. 261–89

—— *Popular Opinion and Political Dissent in the Third Reich* (London, 1983)

—— 'How Effective was Nazi Propaganda?' in D. Welch (ed.), *Nazi Propaganda: The Power and the Limitations* (London, 1983), pp.180–205

BIBLIOGRAPHY

Kettenacker, L. (ed.), *Das andere Deutschland im zweiten Weltkreig* (Stuttgart, 1977)

Kirwin, G., 'Waiting for Retaliation: A Study in Nazi Propaganda Behaviour and German Civilian Morale', *Journal of Contemporary History* 16 (July, 1981), pp. 565–83

Kloss, E., *Redens des Führers. Politik und Propaganda Adolf Hitlers 1922–45* (Munich, 1967)

Koch, H. W. (ed.), *Aspects of the Third Reich* (London, 1985)

Large, D. C. (ed.), *Contending with Hitler. Varieties of German Resistance in the Third Reich* (Cambridge, Mass., 1991)

Lerner, D. (ed.), *Propaganda in War and Crisis* (New York, 1951)

Lewy, G., *The Catholic Church and Nazi Germany* (London, 1964)

Löwenthal, R., and von zur Mühlen (eds), *Widerstand und Verweigerung in Deutschland 1933 bis 1945* (Bonn, 1982)

Mammach, K., *Widerstand 1933 – Geschichte der deutschen Antifaschisten, Widerstandsbewegung im Inland und in der Emigration* (Cologne, 1984)

Mann, R., *Protest und Kontrolle im Dritten Reich* (Frankfurt-am-Main/New York, 1987)

Marks, S., 'Black Watch on the Rhine: A Study in Propaganda, Prejudice, and Prurience', *European Studies Review* 13 (July, 1983), pp. 297–334

Merkl, P., *Political Violence under the Swastika* (Princeton, NJ, 1975)

Merson, A., *Communist Resistance in Nazi Germany* (London, 1987)

Mosse, G., *The Crisis of German Ideology: Intellectual Origins of the Third Reich* (London, 1964)

Muller, G. W., *Das Reichsministerium für Völksaufklärung und Propaganda* (Berlin, 1940)

Munzenberg, W., *Propaganda als Waffe* (Paris, 1937)

Neumann, F., *Behemoth: The Structure and Practice of National Socialism* (London, 1942)

Nicosia, F., and Stokes, L. (eds), *Germans against Nazism: Noncompliance, Opposition and Resistance in the Third Reich* (Oxford, 1990)

Nolte, E., 'A Past That Will Not Pass Away (A Speech It was Possible to Write, But Not to Present)', *Yad Vashem Studies* 19 (1988), pp. 65–73

Paterna, E. *et al.*, *Deutschland 1933–39* (Berlin, 1969)

Peukert, D., *Inside Nazi Germany: Conformity and Opposition in Everyday Life* (London, 1987)

Qualter, T., *Propaganda and Psychological Warfare* (New York, 1962)

Ritter, G., *The German Resistance: Carl Goerdeler's Struggle against Tyranny* (New York, 1959)

Scheel, K., 'Faschistische Kulturpropaganda im Zweiten Weltkreig. Ihr Einsatz zur Irreführung des deutschen Volkes während der ersten Kriegsjahre (1939–41)', *Jahrbuch für Volkskunde und Kulturgeschichte* 21 (Berlin, 1979)

Schmädeke, J., and Steinbach, P. (eds), *Der Widerstand gegen Nationalsozialismus* (Munich, 1985)

Scholl, I., *Students against Tyranny. The Resistance of the White Rose, Munich 1942–43* (Middletown, Conn., 1983)

Shirer, W., *Berlin Diary 1934–41* (London, 1972)

Sington, D., and Weidenfeld, A., *The Goebbels Experiment: A Study of the Nazi Propaganda Machine* (London, 1942)

Speer, A., *Inside the Third Reich* (London, 1971)

Speier, H., 'Nazi Propaganda and its Decline', *Social Research* 10, no. 3 (September, 1943), pp. 358–77

Stachura, P. (ed.), *The Nazi Machtergreifung 1933* (London, 1983)

Stern, F., *The Politics of Cultural Despair: A Study in the Rise of the Germanic Ideology* (Berkeley, Calif., 1961)

Wedel, H. von, *Die Propagandatruppen der deutschen Wehrmacht* (Neckargemund, 1962)

Welch, D. (ed.), *Nazi Propaganda: The Power and the Limitations* (London, 1983)

—— 'Propaganda and Indoctrination in the Third Reich: Success or Failure?', *European History Quarterly* 17 (October, 1987), pp. 403–22

—— *Modern European History, 1871–2000: A Documentary Reader* (London, 1999)

—— *Germany, Propaganda and Total War, 1914–1918* (London, 2000)

—— *The Hitler Conspiracies* (London, 2001)

Wykes, A., *The Nuremberg Rallies* (New York, 1970)

Zeman, Z. A. B., *Nazi Propaganda* (Oxford, 1973)

—— *Selling the War: Art and Propaganda in World War II* (London, 1978)

INDEX